CHAPTERS IN THE HISTORY

OF ABBEVILLE COUNTY

THE "BANNER COUNTY"

OF SOUTH CAROLINA

BY

LOWRY WARE

HERITAGE BOOKS
2016

HERITAGE BOOKS

AN IMPRINT OF HERITAGE BOOKS, INC.

Books, CDs, and more—Worldwide

For our listing of thousands of titles see our website
at
www.HeritageBooks.com

Published 2016 by
HERITAGE BOOKS, INC.
Publishing Division
5810 Ruatan Street
Berwyn Heights, Md. 20740

International Standard Book Numbers
Paperbound: 978-0-7884-5723-4
Clothbound: 978-0-7884-6450-8

Preface

In the 1980's I began planning to write a standard narrative history of Abbeville County, but I soon found that the disastrous Court House fire of 1873 had wiped out many of the public records prior to that time and a large portion of the ante-bellum newspaper files had also been lost. Therefore I decided to deal primarily with the town of Abbeville, and in 1992 that idea led to *Old Abbeville: Scenes of a Town Where Old Time Things Are Not Forgotten.*

In the two decades since, I have collected material which covers the county's history in the 19th century up to modern times. I had particular interest in the slavery experience in this county and in race relations. I was very interested in W. Christie Benet's account of the Jeff David case; in the *New York Times* coverage of the Brooks' Dinner in Ninety Six, in October 1856; in Mrs. Colhoun, John C. Calhoun's mother-in-law, and the story of her two nephews, James Edward Boisseau and Wentworth Boisseau; in Harold Lawrence's poems "Hominy Pot" and "Trouble at the Primary" in his *Southland* collection; and two articles which I had written on "Abbeville Lynchings" and "Abbeville Newspapers & Special Emphasis upon Three Publishers/Editors."

Most of the very lengthy index deals with the Federal census records.

Lowry Ware
April 10, 2012

CONTENTS

W. C. Benet and the Jeff David Case

David L. Wardlaw by tradition was the first white child born in Old Abbeville, and he became one of the most prominent figures of the county in the middle of the nineteenth century. The oldest of his five daughters, Susan, was born in 1828, and in 1851, she married Samuel McGowan, the Laurens native who became the most prominent public citizen in Abbeville by the middle and later years of the century. Her daughter, also named Susan, married W. C. (William Christie) Benet , a Scottish born lawyer who achieved public prominence comparable to his father-in-law and Judge Wardlaw earlier.

In 1925, W. C. (William Christie) Benet wrote the Greenwood (S. C.) *Index-Journal* in answer to what he said was a question often asked of him. "How did it happen that you, a young Scotchman, after landing in New York in 1868, came to South Carolina and settled in Abbeville County in the little village of Cokesbury?" This is how it happened:

At the beginning of the session in 1866 at the University of Edinburgh, I was sitting in my place in the Logic classroom just before the lecture began. A side-door near me opened and in came two young men. Their long black frocked coats and broad brimmed black hats show they were strangers "Yankees," said I to myself, using the term there applied to all Americans. I invited them to a seat beside me. At the close of the lecture we walked together and talked a little while in the quadrangle. They thanked me for my kindness; told me that they had just landed from America; one was from South Carolina, the other from Mississippi, that they desired to enter the university, but did not know what steps to take to matriculate. I gave them the desired information; and then the younger one (whose name was William Vance, and who came from Cokesbury, South Carolina) told me that about twenty young men from the Southern states had come to attend the university; adding that if I could spare the time to go with them to Montagu Street and give the other Southerners the same help, they would be very grateful. Of course I went and met the young strangers. There were nine from South Carolina, three from New Orleans, two from Louisville, the rest from Virginia, North Carolina, Mississippi and Alabama. This accidental introduction ripened into a close and pleasant friendship with these fine young Southern gentlemen. They called themselves the "Rebel Gang," and did me the honor to elect me a member. I may say here that, in common with the most of my countrymen, I had been very much of a Southern sympathizer during the Civil War, influenced to some extent, no doubt, by the fact that the relations existing between the North and South bore a historical resemblance to those that for centuries had existed between England and Scotland.

W. C. Benet and the Jeff David Case

When I finished my course at the University in 1868, I determined to visit the Southern states, and sailed from Glasgow on the 12th of August, several of the "Rebel Gang" having accompanied me to Glasgow to wish me bon voyage, and to give me letters of introduction to their families and friends in the South. Of the three sons of Major Kincaid Vance of Cokesbury, Wistar, Sam, and William, the second, Sam W. Vance, so well known afterwards in public life in South Carolina, had returned home at the end of the first session in very bad health. He had recovered, however, and when I arrived at the Hodges Depot, he was there to welcome me to his home in Cokesbury.

Benet stayed in Cokesbury and became the principal of the male academy. The Vance family there had a long time connection with General Samuel McGowan. McGowan and J. Kincaid Vance had left Laurens at the same time to attend high school in Greenwood and the South Carolina College. Benet studied law in Abbeville and when he married Susan McGowan, he moved into the McGowan household.

Perhaps the most famous of Benet's early cases was featured in **Old Abbeville** in "The Benedict Homicide, 1884", where John C. Ferguson was tried four times until in 1886 he was freed on the basis of insanity.

Three decades later, Ferguson met the same fate as his victim, Arthur Benedict, had in 1884. The Abbeville *Press and Banner*, Dec. 22, 1915 reported that *John C. Ferguson, formerly of this county, but who has resided in Atlanta in recent years, was shot and killed at Barnett, Ga., Sunday morning His remains were brought to Abbeville for interment.*

Mr. Ferguson was a son of the late A. J. Ferguson, a prosperous farmer of this county, and a brother of Andrew J. Ferguson, James and Joseph Ferguson, prosperous farmers of the county.

He married first Miss Brooks, .daughter of Wm. H. Brooks, a prominent citizen of the county. After her death he married a Miss Hubert of Georgia.

Thirty-one years ago this Christmas Eve, Ferguson shot and killed Arthur M. Benedict. He was tried several times for the offense and finally acquitted on the ground of insanity.

The following account of his death is taken from the *Atlanta Georgian*. *News came to Atlanta Monday that H. N. Maxey, a Barnett (Ga.) merchant, shot and instantly killed J. C. Ferguson, an Atlanta real estate agent, Sunday morning at 2 o'clock at Walnut Grove, seven miles south of Loganville, Ga..*

Ferguson and Maxey were said to have quarreled over an old debt owed to Ferguson. As they sat in the home of A. Embry, Ferguson remarked, according to a dispatch to the *Georgian*, that he had not been treated right, and Maxey pulled. out a pistol and shot him through the heart.

W. C. Benet and the Jeff David Case

Maxey then went to a telephone at John Smith's home, called Sheriff Gibson at Monroe and gave himself up.

Ferguson was connected with the W. L. Cline Mazxie then Realty Company at Room No. 322, Healty Building. He lived at Barnett and was accustomed to go there for the weekends. W. L. Cline failed to hear from him Monday and began a search.

Mr. Cline said that Ferguson had been writing Maxey asking for a settlement of the debt, and that last week Ferguson's lawyer also. A letter came to Ferguson saying that Maxey was prepared to make a payment, so Ferguson left for Loganville, telling his employer that he would then go to Barnett and be back in the office on Monday.

Maxey formerly ran a mercantile business at Walnut Grove, and recently sold out to Embry & Crow, and it is said Ferguson put through the deal. Debtor and Creditor are said to have met accidentally, and sitting around Embry's fire, the subject of the debt and the business changes came up.

Ferguson is survived by his invalid wife, who resides at Barnett; a daughter in Atlanta who is said to be a trained nurse, and several brothers in Abbeville, S. C., whence he came.

Maxey has a wife and eight children.

The *Associate Reformed Presbyterian*, March 4, 1886, noted that "Mr. Benet will deliver an address before the Medical College of Georgia this week on 'Insanity As a Legal Defense.' He doubtless has an inexhaustive supply of knowledge on this subject." The Abbeville *Press and Banner*, June 15, 1892, reported that Benet used insanity as a defense in the McIntosh case in a speech of over 3 hours. Nevertheless McIntosh was sent to prison.

In the July 6, 1892 issue of the *Press and Banner*, Hugh Wilson commented that Benet's speech on Sale Day was "perhaps the most inflammatory that he has ever delivered and seemed to us to have for its purpose the incitement of bad feeling between our fellow citizens. Wilson thought "it not well received by either the side [the Tillmanites] whose battles he has so recently assumed or those [the Conservatives]with whom he was so long associated." On December 6, 1893, the *Press and Banner* reported that the Tillman forces in the legislature had failed to re-elect Samuel McGowan [a Conservative] to the State Supreme Court, but had replaced him with another Abbevillian, Lieut. Gov. Frank B. Gary, a Tillman man. At the same time W. C. Benet was elected to a Circuit Court post.

Whatever he might have thought about Benet's political realignment, Hugh Wilson paid generous tribute to Benet for his persistence in the Jeff David case. In July, 1889, he wrote that for Benet "the very weakness of the poor ignorant and penniless creatures in defending themselves against the great State

W. C. Benet and the Jeff David Case

of South Carolina not only awakens his deepest sympathies, but calls for the exercises of the great power of a fearless and independent lawyer. Last year Benet received the largest vote ever made in this county, despite the fact that he has saved more negroes from the gallows than any lawyer in the state."

In 1915, Benet wrote the following account of the Jeff David case for his grandson, Sam, and it was published in *True Detective Magazine* in February,1944:

Secret in a Lonely Cabin
by Judge W. C. Benet

My Dear Sam:

You ask me for "a full history" of the Jeff David case. Do you know how long ago it is since the Franklin murders of which the old negro was accused? Christmas Eve in 1877. That is a long time ago. And sitting here in the heart of the Blue Ridge Mountains [Cashiers,N. C.] I have to depend entirely upon my memory. Fortunately I am blessed with a good one; and besides, the Jeff David case was marked by so many unusual and exciting incidents that it is not strange I should still have a vivid recollection of them. My life as a lawyer and judge made me familiar with some remarkable murder trials, but the Jeff David case transcends them all in thrilling interest. Indeed in that regard I have read nothing in the annals of crime which can surpass it. So, here goes: I will a tale unfold that will justify the saying that truth is stranger than fiction.

The scene of the double murder of old George Franklin and his elderly sister, Miss Drusilla, was at Indigo Springs in Abbeville County, South Carolina, at a point in the public road leading from Abbeville to Laurens, about sixteen miles from the Court House, and some four miles from the town of Greenwood. Half a mile of so beyond the Springs was a hamlet called Simms Cross Roads. Let me draw a map or chart in pencil, to show you the main points in the locality of the murder. Even a rough drawing, hastily made, will give you a clearer idea than any words of description. How well I remember the rural scene, every house and hut, and fence and field, road and path, wood and spring, from the famous Persimmon Sapling stump, to the conspicuous tall pine behind the Franklin home.

The Indigo Springs that give their name to the place are in a sudden bend in the highway, in a grove of oaks. The Franklin house stood about fifty yards from the road at the top of a slope, on the east side of the road just beyond the springs. It was a primitive log cabin, divided into two rooms by a thin partition, with one small window in front and another still smaller in the back. There was

- 4 -

only one door, and a big unhewn stone served for a doorstep. There was no porch. On a corresponding slope on the opposite side of the public road, 180 yards from the Franklin house, was the cabin of the old negro, Jeff David. The nearest white neighbor was fully a quarter of a mile to the west.

George and Drusilla Franklin were brother and sister, both over seventy years of age, old bachelor and old maid, living together in this humble and solitary abode. They owned a small farm, the laborers being Jeff David and his family. They were well known to be very miserly in their habits, making and selling good crops of cotton, and spending nothing beyond their negro servants' wages. It was not known where they kept their money; they certainly did not deal with any bank, and it was generally supposed that miser-like, they hid their money in or about the house.

On that Christmas morning, Captain Frank Fuller and another farmer, the two nearest white neighbors, were alarmed by old Jeff David coming in haste and telling them that old Marse George was lying dead and all bloody in his doorway, and that Miss Drusilla wouldn't answer when called. Jeff told them that his young son, a lad about ten or twelve years old, had gone as usual to make a fire and carry water to the Franklin house. There was a very heavy fog that morning, and the negro boy was half-way up the path to the door before he saw the bloody head of old George Franklin lying on the doorstep. He fled in terror and shouted for his father to come. Old Jeff said he then went across to the Franklin yard, and saw Marse George lying dead; that he called aloud several times for Miss Drusilla, but no answer came. He had not gone into the house; he said he was scared to do so until white folks came. Jeff went to alarm the neighborhood, and in a short while several white men went along with Captain Fuller into the Franklin house.

There they found the corpse of old George on the floor with his gray head clotted with blood, resting on the stone doorstep. The dead body of Drusilla was found in the bedroom, face down across her bed, the feet touching the floor. Dr. Waddell, from Simms Cross Roads, one of the first to view the scene, saw that their skulls had been broken by several blows with a blunt instrument. An unfinished meal on the table indicated that they had been killed at suppertime the night before. There were signs everywhere in the cabin that the murderer had made a thorough search for the money of his victims. Boxes and trunks had been broken open, drawers and cupboard searched, and pockets of George Franklin had been turned inside out.

Jeff David was immediately sent to Greenwood to give the alarm and notify the magistrate who would act as coroner. After a while he returned, accompanied by the coroner and a numerous company of excited citizens. As

Jeff David Case

the tidings of the atrocious double murder spread throughout the neighboring towns and villages, the numbers who came to the Franklin house increased every hour, until by midday there had assembled a large crowd, all eager to discover the murderer. After a while, suspicion began to point to old Jeff David. And so satisfied were many of the men that he and the members of his family were guilty of murder that Jeff, his wife Mary, his son and son-in-law were arrested and taken to the county jail in Abbeville.

On the first Monday in February, 1878, just five weeks afterwards, Judge Thomas J. Mackey opened the Court of General Sessions, and Jeff David and his three fellow prisoners were tried for the murder of the Franklins. When arraigned and charged with the crime it was seen that they had no counsel, and Judge Mackey then assigned me to their defense. I knew nothing about the case except what I had read in the newspapers; but while I took charge of the case with great reluctance and a deep sense of the responsibility, I determined to do the best I could for the poor negroes. There was not a single witness to put up on their behalf. In a private examination of the prisoners all the evidence I could elicit from them was simply that they knew nothing about the murder, that they were all at home in the cabins opposite the Franklin cabin the whole evening, and that they were innocent and did not know who had killed their old master and mistress.

The trial came on; an intelligent jury was empanelled; and on the evidence adduced by the State they found a verdict of guilty against Jeff David, but not guilty as to his wife and son and son-in-law. The proof of guilt seemed clear and sufficient. The three leading witnesses were Gideon O'Neill, nephew and neighbor of the Franklins; Captain James N. King, and Thomas Arnold.

O'Neill, a man of excellent character and unusual intelligence, testified that he found in Jeff David's pocket a new knife, bought just three days before the murder; that the large blade plainly showed the stain of persimmon. It had been proved that the poor old victims had been brained by a persimmon club which was in evidence with bloodstains and gray hairs still upon it. O'Neill's testimony was damning. Cross-examination could not shake it. He was positive the stain on Jeff's knife blade was persimmon, "a sort of yellowish stain," he said , "unlike that made by any other tree."

Captain King and Tom Arnold testified to finding Jeff David's footprints on a path leading from his cabin to the place where the persimmon club had been cut, and from that place to the Franklin house. Many other minor details were given in evidence, chiefly by King and Arnold, all tending to establish the theory of Jeff's guilt; but the evidence as to the stain on the knife blade, and as to the footprints of Jeff David, was the weightiest.

Jeff David Case

Before sentence of death was pronounced, I made a motion for a new trial. I had drawn out of Gid O'Neill by cross-examination, very good evidence as to Jeff's good character and long and faithful service, and evident friendliness between him and his old Marse George and Miss Drusilla. And I laid great stress on the fact that there was not a particle of testimony that Jeff had any money, while it was plain that the murder had been committed for the sake of robbery; and it had been shown that there must have been about ten or eleven thousand dollars in the Franklin cabin--that about five thousand dollars only were found there after the murder--that the murderer must have carried off five or six thousand dollars.

These facts, of course, furnished me good grounds for arguing for a new trial. I reminded the Court, too, that the prisoners had come to trial in their paucity and ignorance without counsel; that I, knowing nothing of the facts of the case, had been appointed by the Court to defend them; and that I felt sure if time were allowed me, I should find testimony favorable to the negro. But Judge Mackey refused the motion and passed sentence of death on Jeff David. At the time it seemed to me that all had been done that should have been done. The Judge's charge to the jury and his rulings during the trial had been entirely unobjectionable, and furnished no ground for appeal to the Supreme Court. Although I found it hard to believe that old Jeff could have done the horrible deed--his countenance, his expression, his manner, his talks with me, all pleaded in his behalf and seemed to assert his innocence--still I could not blame the jury for their verdict of guilty, nor the Judge for refusing to grant a new trial.

Two days afterwards, while walking through the corridor on the ground floor of the Court House, Captain King met me with a sheet of paper in his hand. He stopped me and said, "Squire, here's a paper I would like for you to sign."

"What is it?" I asked.

"It's a petition to Governor Hampton to pay the reward for the conviction of Jeff David to Tom Arnold and me."

"A reward, did you say?"

"Oh, yes; in fact, there's two rewards. Governor Hampton offered $250, and Gid O'Neill and the other Franklins offered $500."

"Seven hundred and fifty dollars reward, eh!"

"Yes, Squire, and the Judge has signed the petition, and Colonel Cothran, the solicitor, and every member of the jury. And although you defended old Jeff, I hope you won't object to sign it, too."

Then I said very seriously and as calmly as I could.

-7-

Jeff David Case

"Captain, this is all news to me about the rewards. Now mark what I say; I will not sign your petition. If I had known about the rewards, Jeff David would not have been convicted. And I now tell you he will not be hanged, and you and Tom Arnold will not get the money you have worked for so hard."

King was a giant of a man, six feet, three or four in height and of colossal build. But I knew him to be lacking in physical courage though much of a braggart. I also knew his reputation for untruthfulness; and, indeed, he had been proved to have testified falsely in a certain case. Tom Arnold, too, was not a man of good character; but I had not any reason during the trial to suppose that he and King were giving false testimony against a poor negro on trial for his life. But seven hundred and fifty dollars! That sum to be gained by swearing falsely against an old negro. I felt on the instant that King and Arnold were the men to do it, and that they had done it.

As soon as Court adjourned I went down to Indigo Springs. Surely a kind Providence directed me to stay with my good friend, Captain Frank Fuller at Coronaca. He lived about half a mile from the Franklin cabin. Almost the first thing he said was:

"Old Jeff David may be guilty but I don't think he is. I wasn't at the trial but I've heard a good deal about it. I hate to think of his being hanged on that evidence. All that testimony of Jim King's and Tom Arnold's about Jeff's tracks--there's not one word of truth in it. How could there be? It was near eleven o'clock when they came from Greenwood with the Coroner, and crowds of men and boys had covered all the roads and paths and banks of sand with footprints hours before King and Arnold came. It was impossible for them or any man then to find or identify Jeff's tracks or any man's tracks. Bob Nickles and I looked for tracks long before the crowd gathered. We came along that path and crossed the ditch at that sand bank where King and Arnold swear they found Jeff's tracks and made him put his foot into them to see if they fitted, and there was not a footprint on that sand; and Jeff had then been sent to Greenwood for the coroner. Those two witnesses saw a great deal that no one else saw."

This to me was a statement of vital importance, voluntarily made by a man of integrity and truth. Captain Frank Fuller, a one-armed Confederate veteran, was a most excellent man, modestly but sincerely pious in heart, speech and behavior. When I told him that my errand was to make a thorough investigation of all the circumstances surrounding the murder, and to examine those who first came to the Franklin cabin, he said he would do all he could do to help me. I asked what he thought about Gideon O'Neill's evidence about persimmon stain on Jeff's knife blade.

"Gid O'Neill," said Fuller, "is a good man, an honest man. He believes *what he testifies is true. But he is very bull-headed in his opinions. Once he makes up his mind, you can't change him. That persimmon stain, well it may be so; Gid believes it, but I doubt it. I don't think a man should be hanged on such testimony. You know Bob Nickles, how full of mischief he is; you ought to hear how he kids Gid about that 'simmon stain.' I'll send for Bob Nickles to meet us in the morning at the Franklin cabin. He knows more than I do about tracks and other things he saw on the day after the murder. He was among the first to be there, and he made a thorough search inside the cabin and all around it long before the crowd gathered."*

Before going to bed that night I asked Captain Fuller about the money of the Franklins, how much he thought was carried off by the murderer, and where the rest of the money was found. He said:

"Well, counting up the value of the cotton crops they had made since the war, and allowing for their necessary expenses in running the farm, they spent money on nothing else, they were misers--there must have been ten or eleven thousand dollars in that house; hidden in all sorts of queer places. We found money in match boxes, in old broken dishes, in an old coffee-pot and it was plain that the murderer had made a very thorough search for money in trunks and boxes and drawers--even in old George Franklin's pockets. Trunks that had been locked had been forced open; and strange to say an unlocked little trunk under Miss Drusilla's bed had not been touched by the murderer, and in it we found several rolls of greenbacks, amounting to near $4,000.

"It was old Jeff David that told us about that money in the little trunk. Didn't Captain King tell that at the trial? What! No? Why, sir, on the way back from Greenwood with the Coroner and the crowd, King asked Jeff if the murderer had got all the Franklins' money. Jeff said he didn't know; he hadn't been in the cabin; but if the man that killed them didn't get the money that was in a little 'haar'-covered trunk under Miss Drusilla's bed' they would find money there. Jeff said that he had sold the Franklins' cotton in Greenwood on Friday, just three days before, and when he handed the money to Miss Drusilla, she pulled out the little 'haar-covered trunk' and put the money into a big roll of money. And sure enough, it was just as old Jeff had told Jim King; there was the little hair-covered trunk, and in it were several rolls of greenbacks. And you tell me Jim King said nothing about that at the trial? He ought to have told that. That doesn't look as if Jeff was after the money."

Next morning Captain Fuller and I left his home to go to the Franklin cabin where we were to meet Bob Nickles. At a point in the highway about 200 yards from the house, Fuller stopped and pointed to a little bank of sand in the dry bed of the roadside ditch--but let him do the talking:

Jeff David Case

"There's the bank of sand," said he, "where Jim King and Tom Arnold swore they found the plain tracks of Jeff David. You see that is where the footpath from Jeff's cabin joins the big road. I suppose more than a hundred men and boys had crossed the ditch and stepped on that little sand patch that morning before King and Arnold came from Greenwood. The tracks they swore they measured and identified were supposed to have been made by Jeff David the night before, while on his way to that grove across the road where the persimmon club was cut. And yet those two men testified they found Jeff's footprints there. As I told you last night, me and Bob Nickles had come along that path and crossed the ditch looking for tracks hours before the crowd gathered and there wasn't a track either of white man or negro then on that patch of sand. Now let us go and see the stump of the persimmon sapling where the murderer cut the club with which he killed the Franklins."

Fuller led the way across the road into the woods for about twenty or twenty-five yards. He stopped at a place where there were several young persimmon saplings of various sizes. He took hold of a stout sapling with his right hand--his only hand, for he had lost his left arm in battle. The top part of the sapling had been cut off just at the height of his shoulder. Looking at me very seriously and speaking as solemnly as if he were on his oath, Captain Fuller then said:

"There is no doubt that the persimmon club with which old George Franklin and old Miss Drusilla were murdered was cut from this sapling. The size of the club, and the knife marks on it and on this stump show that; and then there were on that old wood-wad there the plain tracks of man going from here towards the Franklin house. If the crowd had known as much as I do about the cutting of that club, they might have arrested me and tried me for the murder. There is no doubt in my mind that the club was cut by a one-armed man just about my height. He had no left hand to help him, for I can tell by the knife marks it was cut by the right hand. Let me show you; when a man tries to cut a young sapling like this he is obliged to have something to keep the sapling stiff and steady and not to bend and give way. You, for instance, would grab the sapling with your left hand to hold against the force of your right hand. But how could I cut it? How could any one-armed man cut it? He can only cut it at his shoulder or at his knee. The shoulder or the knee can press against the force of the cutting, not as well as a hand, but he can cut more than half-way through without danger of cutting himself, then he can break it and twist it into ribbons and then run his knife easily through the ribbons. He can use the knife better and cut deeper at the shoulder than at the knee. And that is just what happened *here. Look at this: the one-armed man that cut this, cut it at his shoulder until it was about two-thirds cut through; then, turning his back, he broke it over his shoulder and pulled it hither and yon until the uncut part was in ribbons. Don't you see the knife marks and the ribbons?*

"Now look at those two saplings over there, leaning over halfway to the ground. The man that cut this at his shoulder had tried first to cut those at his knee." They were just a few steps off, and Fuller and I went and examined them. He then continued, "You see he had cut just at the height of my knee until the sapling was about half cut through. You can't cut deeper at the knee. Then he tried to break it on his knee, but the roots loosened and sprung up and he had to quit. Then he tried this second one at his knee; but again, you see, the roots didn't hold when he wanted to break it; and he failed again, and left those two saplings half-cut and leaning over showing their roots, just as you see. And then, using his shoulder, he succeeded at last in cutting that other sapling and getting the club. There is no doubt that the persimmon club we found in the yard near the cabin, with blood and gray hairs on it, was cut off that sapling, and cut by a one-armed man--the third he had tried."*

As I listened to Frank Fuller while he made this convincing statement, I was astounded. It looked as if Providence was working for poor Jeff David. For here was strong confirmation of a suspicion already in my mind that the murderer of the Franklins was a young white man of that neighborhood, a one-armed man.

Of this suspicion I had given no hint to Fuller; nor did I ask him whom he suspected; and yet I believed we were both thinking of the same man.

Who was that man?

In this narrative I shall call him Martin but that is not his name. This young man, with an armless left sleeve, like Frank Fuller, lived at the Simms cross-roads, running a little country store. He had a wife and several young children. His wife and he were well-connected. Just two weeks before the Franklin murder, Martin and his cousin, a young man like himself, fell out about some business matters; the ill-feeling brought on a fight in which both drew and used pistols, and Martin had the misfortune to kill his cousin. Aided by his friends he evaded arrest; indeed, it was thought at the time that hardly any effort to arrest him was made. He fled the State just about the time of the Franklin murders.

In a talk with Jeff David in jail after his conviction, I had asked him if he had any idea who it was that had murdered his old master and mistress. Jeff said he had not, he couldn't think of any man white or black. I had asked him if he had seen or heard any one, stranger or neighbor, white or black, at the Franklin cabin near the time of the murder. He then recalled that on the

Jeff David Case

Saturday evening late, Mr. Martin and Marse George had high words about paying an account. Marse George owed a negro blacksmith for blacksmith and farm work, and the blacksmith owed Mr. Martin at his store; and had given him a paper to get the money from Marse George; but he wouldn't pay the money to Mr. Martin; he would settle with the blacksmith himself. At that Mr. Martin got sort o' mad and cursed, and went away on his horse. It was then "dusky dark" on Saturday night.

This statement of Jeff's had set me to thinking: Here was a young man with his cousin's blood on his hands, hiding from the law; in great need of money to get safely away from South Carolina, this I had learned from other sources. I had learned also that he had gone on horseback to Greenville, some seventy miles, had taken the train there the second morning after the Franklin murder; but that a letter from him had been received, dated in Greenville the day of the murders, which was plainly meant to mislead, for he could not have reached Greenville on that day even if he had started on the night Jeff saw and heard him with old George Franklin. Add to all this Frank Fuller's startling statement about the cutting of the club by a one-armed man. Does it surprise you that my suspicion grew stronger and stronger that Martin was the murderer of the Franklins?

But let us rejoin Frank Fuller and go with him to meet Bob Nickles at the Franklin cabin. We found him waiting for us there. Very soon I learned from what he said that he agreed with Fuller in his opinions about Jeff David, and the verdict, and the witnesses. He ridiculed the testimony of King and Arnold, and told how he kidded Gideon O'Neill about his "simmon stain." He and Fuller had been the first to arrive at the cabin and search for tracks, and for any other clue that might indicate who had murdered two helpless old victims. In the hard-beaten front yard, while no tracks were visible, they found two half-burnt sperm candles. There were no such candles in the cabin--the old couple were too miserly to buy such--they used only home-made tallow-dips; one such tallow-dip had burned to the socket in a tin candle stick on the supper table. I afterwards learned there were sperm candles in Martin's store. The candles had not been mentioned at the trial.

A few feet from the candles was found the persimmon club, still bloody, and with gray hairs sticking to the heavy end. It makes me always think of the line describing the parricidal knife in Tam O'Shanter--"the gray hairs still stack to the heft."

- 12 -

Jeff David Case

It was an ugly bludgeon, about 18 inches long, 2 1/2 to 3 inches thick at the one end and about 1 1/2 at the other.

Following the direction indicated by the candles and the club, they found distinct tracks leading toward a pig-pen, and into the pen. There were two pig-pens, and the tracks were plain in both, as there were no hogs in them. The murderer in his flight had blundered into one pen, then into the other. The tracks led toward a ploughed field behind the cabin, and here in the soft earth it was plainly seen there were two sets of footprints, one set very large, the other rather small, evidently the footprints of a negro and a white man. The tracks led straight across the field, and the length of the footsteps showed that the two men had been running. They led as straight as a bee-line to a very tall dead pine on the edge of the woods just outside the fence. Here was found evidence that a horse had been hitched, and it was plain that the man with the small foot here mounted the horse, the man with the large foot walking beside him for some distance in the direction of Greenwood until they parted at a fork in the road where the man on the horse turned to the right, riding toward Cokesbury (the direction Martin would take in riding to Greenville).

Coming back to the tall pine tree, search was made for tracks leading to the cabin; for it was reasonable to suppose that the horse had been hitched there before the murderers went to the house. The tree was conspicuously tall and had evidently been chosen as the rendezvous. The ingoing tracks were soon found--the same large and small footprints. They led from the tree to the rail fence on the upper side of the field. There was clear moonlight on Christmas Eve, the night of the murder, and the two men in approaching the cabin from behind had sulked in the shadow of the tall sassafras and pokeberry bushes that filled the fence corners, so as not to be seen, for it was still early and they must have seen the light in the back window. The out-going steps had been made by men running in haste--the in-going steps were much shorter, and irregular, as of men walking and occasionally halting. Close to the cabin, the large footprints led to the back window as if the negro had gone there and looked in. No doubt he saw old George Franklin and his aged sister sitting quietly and unsuspectingly at their frugal meal.

It must be remembered that all this evidence of the double set of tracks behind the house furnished by Fuller and Nickles, was new to me. It had not been referred to at the trial. These two intelligent men, the first to examine the house and the surroundings, had not been summoned as witnesses. The State's solicitor had relied almost entirely on the track testimony of King and Arnold. I could not help noticing that while Fuller and Nickles ridiculed the King and Arnold testimony and again and again declared their belief in Jeff

Jeff David Case

David's innocence, at the same time they never mentioned the name of Martin; and yet I felt sure he was in their minds all the time. I respected their desire not to commit themselves; for Martin had been their neighbor, and he and his wife had many respectable connections and kindred in the neighborhood and therefore I, too, did not mention Martin's name.

Along with Dr. Waddell they had thoroughly examined the cabin inside, before others came. They were sure from the signs they saw of the search for money, that the murderer or murderers must have spent at least twenty or thirty minutes in that search.

They gave me a pathetic account of what they found on the little supper table--the bits of cornbread and sausage on the plates, the half-emptied cups of coffee, the small tin candlestick with the tallow-tip burned to the socket.

Dr. Waddell examined minutely the wounds on the two corpses. On the top of George Franklin's head was the mark of a heavy blow sufficient to stun and fell an man, and on the back of his head lower down, repeated blows had broke the skull and crushed it inwards.

On the old woman's left temple a severe blow had made a gash that had bled profusely. She had evidently lain on the floor beside her chair for some time after that blow was struck; there was a little pool of blood on the floor, in which were some gray hairs, and there were marks that satisfied the doctor that poor old Drusilla's head had lain there and had moved backwards and forwards in the blood. It would seem that, struck down and rendered unconscious for a while, the bleeding had cleared her brain and restored her senses, and that she then rose and tottered into the bedroom, where the robbing murderers were, and was then cruelly struck on the back of the head and killed. Her body was found half lying on the bed, face down, and her feet on the floor.

Had the appearance of the old woman in the bedroom startled the murderers in their work of robbery? When she recovered consciousness and saw the bright light of the two sperm candles in the bedroom where her treasure was hid, had her instincts roused her to go there to guard her money? Had she then recognized Martin, her young neighbor, well known to her? Did she call his name? Did he then feel that murder had to be done to keep his robbery a secret in that lonely cabin? Had his first purpose been, not to murder, but to stun and rob, to render unconscious and then obtain their money which he needed so much? Who knows?

The blow on the old man's head and that on his old sister's left temple fitted that theory. They were sufficient to have caused unconsciousness, but not to kill. And they were such as could have been easily and quickly struck with the club when the burglar suddenly opened the door. George Franklin's back was right at the door; and Drusilla was facing him at the end of the little yard-long table. It was probably the work of an instant for the big negro with his club to strike down the two old victims--I say the negro, for, of course, the white man, Martin, would not risk being recognized by his old neighbors.

Then began the search for money. The sperm candles were lighted; trunks were opened; boxes burst open; drawers were drawn out and ransacked. They started out to make a careful and thorough search and this showed coolness and deliberation. The burglars even searched in the pockets of the old man as he lay there on the floor at the open door. They must have thought he was still alive; they would hardly have turned inside out the pockets of a murdered corpse. They were in no hurry, it was night, they were in the secluded cabin-- and the two aged inmates were lying on the floor unconscious; the burglary was making the burglars rich; they were discovering thousands of dollars; Martin knew there must be at least ten thousand dollars in the misers' hoard; they must get it all.

Something brought their search to a sudden stop. The looting was unfinished. The robbers who had been looking for money so coolly and deliberately fled from the cabin in a frenzy of haste, carrying the bloody club for some distance, and even the candles in their hands; blundering into one pig pen then into another; and then running full speed away from the house through the telltale ploughed field to the tall pine tree, not seeking to hide by the rail fence now, but seeking only to get away from the cabin of the murders, as far as they could.

Don't you see my theory of the murder? Martin and the negro--his hired helper--went there to rob; and they had to commit murder to conceal their crime of burglary. Poor old Drusilla Franklin, her senses recovered, raised her head from the pool of blood, arose from the floor, staggered toward the bedroom, blood dropping on the floor as she went; the apparition of the old woman, her gray hair dabbled in blood and blood trickling down her aged cheeks, what a startling spectacle for Martin! She knows him. She calls his name. And burglary ends in a hurried and horrible murder of the two old people.

The finding of the bloody club in the yard, thrown away by the murderers in their flight, shows that it had just then been used to crush the skull of the two victims. If the murder had been committed when they first entered the cabin there would have been no further use for the club, and it would not have been in the hand of either murderer when they fled. So there you have my theory of the Franklin murders. It is far more than a theory, it was and still is my undoubting belief. And public opinion after a while agreed with me

- 15 -

Jeff David Case

When I returned to Abbeville next day, I made very full and careful written memoranda of all I had seen and heard at Indigo Springs. And then began my real fight for the life and liberty of old Jeff David--and a long and hard fight it was. He was lying in the county jail under sentence of death. The day set for his execution on the scaffold was only three weeks off. The first thing to be done was to get a respite from Governor Hampton postponing the day of execution beyond the next term of the Court, so that I might move for a new trial on after-discovered evidence.

The motion for a new trial could not be made before a Judge who had not presided at the first trial unless the State Solicitor would agree to a written statement of the testimony then taken. There was no stenographic report, for at that time there were no Court stenographers in South Carolina. I had taken very full notes of the testimony at the trial; and there were also in the record the brief notes taken by Judge Mackey in his very large half-inch tall handwriting.

With those notes combined I was able to make a sufficiently full and perfectly fair statement of the testimony, so that the Judge hearing the motion could see what the verdict of guilty was based on, and compare that testimony with the newly discovered evidence. But Solicitor Cothran, who had prosecuted old Jeff at his trial, would not agree. He had always been, and he continued always to be, hostile to me personally. He insisted that the motion could be made only before the Judge who had tried the case. And he knew that under our system of rotation Judge Mackey would not be back in our Circuit for almost three years.

My only hope now was in Governor Hampton and most gratefully do I recall his kindness and consideration and the deep personal interest he took in Jeff David. Nor can I forget the invaluable help given me by Major Wade Manning, his private secretary. He was an intimate friend of mine, and he gave me information of vital importance more than once during my long fight for Jeff.

A second respite for a considerable period was granted by the Governor. Meanwhile Governor Hampton advised the employment of a detective to get on the trail of the murderers. As one of them seemed to be a negro, he suggested the employment of a negro detective who had already done some clever work for him; and he added it would give him pleasure to pay the detective's expenses out of the Governor's contingent fund. To this, of course, I agreed; but I begged the Governor not to give the negro detective any of the information which my papers furnished, to let him blaze out his own trail.

That detective--I never liked him; nor did I think he was fit for detective

Jeff David Case

work among country negroes, field hands and laborers; for he was a town-bred man; and if he had the smartness he had also the faults of that class. But he went to work, under various disguises, in the neighborhood of Indigo Springs and in Laurens County. On information and suspicion furnished by a Laurens planter named Sullivan, a man of eccentric habits and low associates, yet of university education, the negro detective got on the trail of an Irishman, named McNulty, that is the name or near it. With some strange evidence about his tobacco pipe said to have been found in the Franklin house, and some other suspicious circumstances, Sullivan and the detective prevailed on Solicitor Cothran to have the Irishman arrested. He was indicted and tried for the murder of the Franklins and acquitted in short order.

The granting of the second respite by Governor Hampton had been harshly criticized, and even denounced in some of the newspapers. It was declared that the Governor was being "bamboozled" by Jeff David's lawyer; that the public was sick of the law's delay; that the "black fiend" ought to be hanged, there was no doubt that he was guilty; one paper saying that somebody had to be hanged, "if they had to begin with Jeff's lawyer." Acting on reliable information of a plot to attack the jail, the Sheriff had Jeff David removed to Columbia and placed in the penitentiary for safe keeping.

Public opinion was very bitter and hostile to the old negro prisoner, especially in the country around Indigo Springs and in the neighboring towns. It even took the form of a petition to the Governor, couched in strong and truculent language, protesting against the delay in the execution of Jeff David, and urgently requesting that no further respite be granted. This blood-thirsty petition was signed by many. Private Secretary Manning kindly sent me a copy, adding that it was a foolish mistake to expect that such a petition could affect Governor Hampton.

Even Judge Mackey had busied himself against Jeff David. His home was in Columbia and he had assured the Governor that there could be no doubt of the negro's guilt. He was certain that if placed on the scaffold "the black fiend" would confess his guilt; and he strongly advised that Jeff should be subjected to that terrible test.

Accordingly, when I applied for a third respite, Governor Hampton told me of Judge Mackey's suggestion. Who but Mackey would have thought of such a cruel test? The Governor asked if I would accept a respite on condition that it be kept a profound secret, and that Jeff David be placed on the scaffold on the day set for the execution as if he were really then to be hanged. What could I do but consent? The fatal Friday was two weeks off. As the day drew near the

Jeff David Case

newspapers noticed the fact that no respite had been granted and commended the Governor's course.

Two days before the day of execution the Governor's respite came to me, having been sent not in the mail but by a trustworthy private messenger, who did not know the contents of the official envelope. I put the important paper in my safe. The existence of such a paper was known only to the Governor, his private secretary and myself. To prevent suspicion I refused to go to the jail when the poor old man prayed and begged that I should come. All the ghastly preparations for the execution were made.

On Friday morning I sent for the Sheriff--I had sacredly kept the secret, but I believed that the Sheriff should be informed at the last moment, so as to prevent any fatal mistake. I also sent for Dr. Robertson of Due West who had been requested by the Sheriff to be present at the execution. Having heard and read that men doomed to death had sometimes, because of heart failure or collapse of some kind, died on the scaffold before the headsman's axe or the hangman's rope had touched their necks, I told the physician of the secret respite and asked him to watch Jeff David very closely. Both he and the Sheriff were sworn by me on their Masonic oath not to divulge the secret. Another physician, Dr. Wenck of Ninety-Six, had requested permission to attend, but he was not informed of the respite.

At the hour appointed for the execution, poor old Jeff was conducted by the Sheriff and his deputies from his prison cell to a barn-like building in the jail yard. A negro preacher named Jefferson walked beside him, a man of good repute among both white and black. Inside the building were the twelve or more citizens whom the Sheriff had summoned according to law to be witnesses of the execution. There was the scaffold, with the gibbet and noosed rope, the simple but ghastly apparatus for a hanging.

Jeff David mounted the few steps and was placed standing on the scaffold, the rope dangling over his head. The negro preacher offered up a prayer for the condemned man--a most fervent, heartfelt prayer, simple, solemn and impressive. He then said to the prisoner, "Brother, you are now about to die and appear before Almighty God. It would be a fearful thing to come before His presence with a lie upon your lips. Tell me now the truth. Do not let your latest breath be a lie. Did you take the life of old George Franklin and old Miss Drusilla? Are you guilty of the murders?"

There stood Jeff David, his ankles tied together, his hands tied behind his back, the rope hanging over his head, the Sheriff at his side with the black cap in his hand, the deputies as their post ready to make the drop do its deadly work.

Jeff David Case

With tears running down his cheeks, the old negro, erect as an Indian, raised his eyes and looking upward said: "I know that I am going to die right now. I hope I'm going to see Jesus. If I get thar I hope I'll meet my ole Marse George and Miss Drusilla, my good ole mistis: they know it wa'n't me tha killed them."

The Sheriff then read the sentence of death passed by the Court. The black cap was drawn over Jeff David's head and face. The noose was placed round his neck. It was now my turn to take my part in the terrible ordeal. I said, "Stop, Mr. Sheriff, go no further: Jeff David will not be hanged today. Here in my hand is a respite granted by Governor Hampton until the 15th of next January." The Sheriff read the respite: ordered the jailer to take the prisoner back to his cell; and the spectators left the building, all of them amazed and some disappointed. The tragic ordeal was ended, the cruel test advised by Judge Mackey had been tried: the "black fiend"--Mackey's expression-- had not confessed his guilt.

"A ghastly farce, very well performed."

" A hollow mockery."

"The old nigger played his part well. Of course he knew about the respite."

"You can't fool the public."

These and such as these were the expressions of public opinion in the press and on the lips of the people. This was not surprising to me; and I had prepared to meet it. Dr. Robertson and Dr. Wenck made a joint affidavit that Jeff's pulse had weakened and slowed down to forty-two when the black cap was drawn over his face; that it suddenly changed and quickened till it went over 100, when the announcement was made that he was not to be hanged. This sworn statement by two reputable physicians clearly proved that Jeff knew nothing of the respite. He could not control the beating of his pulse.

Even as it was, it had been a fearful ordeal for Jeff. When he re-entered the jail, reaction set in, and he was threatened with a complete collapse. Strong stimulants had to be given, and some hours passed before he recovered.

God forgive me for having consented to subject the old negro to a test so horrible and cruel. But Governor Hampton had yielded to the persistence of Judge Mackey, and I could not refuse the respite because of its hard conditions. I will not attempt to describe my feelings while standing close to Jeff on the scaffold. It is enough to say that if I did wrong in permitting him to be so cruelly treated, I paid the penalty by my sufferings that day.

Threats of lynching were made and the prisoner was taken to the State Penitentiary for safekeeping.

Shortly after this, Governor Hampton was elected to the office of United

Jeff David Case

States Senator, and by operation of law, Lieutenant Governor Simpson succeeded him as Governor.

This boded no good for Jeff. Hampton had been friendly to the negro from the first, and did what he thought right in spite of public opinion. He was a man of generous nature, big heart, and strong common sense, and his long experience as owner of many hundreds of slaves before the war made him take a deep, kindly, personal interest in old Jeff. Governor Simpson was of a different type; he was a good man, of high character, as were all the men of the numerous Simpson family. I knew them all intimately. They were rigid Presbyterians; Simpson had been a prominent lawyer, and he was soon promoted to the office of Chief Justice of the Supreme Court.

The 15th of January was drawing near when the third respite would expire. I went again to Columbia and asked for another respite. It was easily seen that Governor Simpson was unfriendly. Although I had been on the most pleasant terms with him and his family, and with his brothers and other kindred, on learning my errand he assumed a cold and stiff and stern manner, made no effort to conceal his impatience while I read my petition and accompanying papers; unlike his usual suave style he spoke curtly and brusquely. Finally he said, and showed temper while he said it, "It is still four weeks before the 15th of January. If you do not bring me evidence to satisfy me that Jeff David is innocent, he will be hanged on that day." Simpson's angry manner made me too, lose my temper, and I replied, with some heat, "Governor, you know well enough I cannot satisfy you of Jeff's innocence before that day, but I will tell you he will not be hanged on the 15th of January."

With that we parted, both somewhat ashamed, no doubt, at having allowed our angry passions to rise. The Governor's hostile attitude was plain, and it perplexed me. The fact that Solicitor Cothran was perhaps his most intimate friend surely couldn't account for it. My faithful friend, Wade Manning, threw some light on it. He told me that the Governor's sister-in-law from Atlanta had been on a visit to the Executive Mansion; that she was bitter against Jeff David and was sure he was guilty of the Franklin murders; that he was a negro of very bad character, in fact, a dangerous man: she had known him in his boyhood and youth when he belonged to her father, Skinner Smith, who sold him to George Franklin; that the Governor should grant no more respites, should let him be hanged as he ought to be.

My hope was still in Hampton. He was then in Washington attending to his duties as Senator. I wrote to him, informing him of Simpson's ultimatum and impossible condition, and earnestly desiring him to intercede. At the Christmas recess he came home to Columbia. Before going to his house he drove straight

Jeff David Case

to Governor Simpson's office, and said-- "Simps"--addressing him by a familiar appellation-- "Simps, old Jeff David is my nigger, I doubt very much if he is guilty. Mr. Benet has satisfied me he ought to have a new trial. He is not asking for a pardon, but he must get a respite until Judge Mackey can hear the motion. Now, my dear Governor, I ask you to grant that respite." And granted it was, thanks to Senator Wade Hampton. The respite was drawn so as to include the time of the Abbeville Court when Judge Mackey would next preside there. That Court came on in November, 1880, nearly three years after the trial at which Jeff was convicted and sentenced to death.

This narrative, my dear Sam, is lengthening out far beyond the limits you counted on, I fear. But the fight for Jeff David's life and liberty was long-continued and marked by many strange vicissitudes. You asked me to give you "full details," but I must condense, and be as brief as I can, although I could with more ease make the story much longer.

When Judge Mackey opened that Court so long wished for and patiently waited for, I felt that I was thoroughly prepared to move for a new trial on after-discovered evidence. Fuller, Nickles, Dr. Waddell and other important witnesses had made strong affidavits setting forth the facts I have narrated. I strongly felt that on the showing I would make, Jeff would be entitled to a new trial. Public opinion was still strongly against him; the press still was hostile and demanding his execution.

Besides, I knew that the Judge had himself done much to rouse feeling against old Jeff by telling the story of the atrocious Franklin murders wherever he went all over the State, as he held Court in county after county. And he must have told it well. Judge Mackey was a wonderful raconteur. The stage lost in him a natural tragedian. He was an actor while sitting on the Bench. His deep-tone voice, his sallow complexion, his coal-black hair, which he wore very long, his unusually large and expressive eyes, reminding me of the eyes of Edwin Booth, his tout ensemble (excuse the French) was that of a tragic actor. And it was his delight to recount tales of blood and horror.

How often to spell-bound listeners he had spoken of Jeff David as "that black fiend" who had murdered the Franklins and of whose guilt there was not the shadow of a doubt. Still, in spite of all that, I had confidence in the merit of my motion for a new trial. The public, the press and the Judge were all unaware of the evidence embraced in the affidavits; but I knew how great was the weight of that evidence, and so, strong in the strength of my cause, I made the motion for a new trial.

It was not a time for long argument. I read the affidavits slowly, carefully, emphasizing the more striking parts, and pointing out how they flatly

Jeff David Case

contradicted the testimony upon which Jeff David had been convicted. Judge Mackey's manner was very encouraging. He listened most attentively: I saw he was deeply impressed. The State Solicitor resisted the motion in his most cynical style, pooh-poohing the affidavits and trying to belittle their force: he would not waste the time of the Court in an argument against a motion that was entirely without merit; and he asked the Court to refuse the motion and let the law take its course; it had been delayed and tampered with too long.

The Judge then announced his decision. Thirty-five years have passed since then, but I can still hear the sepulchral tones of his voice as he said, very slowly and with deliberation: "The Court"--(he seldom made use of the first person pronoun while on the Bench, but rolled "the Court" like a sweet morsel under his tongue)- "The Court has heard the motion for a new trial in this case on after-discovered evidence. The affidavits submitted by the learned counsel comply with all the requirements of the rules of evidence. The evidence contained in them is clearly after-discovered and could not have been with due diligence discovered and adduced at the trial three years ago; for it is not forgotten that the learned counsel was assigned by the Court to the defense of the poor prisoners charged with the murder of George and Drusilla Franklin. The learned counsel, therefore, had then neither the time nor the opportunity to obtain the evidence now submitted. The wisdom of the Court in selecting him for the defense has been amply proved by the learning, ability and untiring zeal with which the learned counsel has conducted and still conducts that defense, without fee or reward or hope of reward.

"The Court has been profoundly impressed by the weight of the evidence embraced in the affidavits; and has little doubt that had the evidence been submitted to the jury at the trial, the verdict should have been a verdict of not guilty.

"But nearly three years have elapsed since that trial and conviction and with sincere regret the Court deems that it has not now the power to order a new trial. Mr. Solicitor, you will prepare the order refusing the motion for a new trial."

I had been standing while the Judge was rendering his decision. When he announced his refusal of the motion I suddenly sat down, dumfounded. One's mind acts rapidly at a crisis. I rose and said, "May it please your Honor, will you permit me to draw the order and to embody your grounds of refusal? This request I make for the purpose of appeal to the Supreme Court." The Judge then said, "It affords the Court great pleasure to grant your very reasonable request."

The Judge signed the order I prepared, and I gave notice of appeal. This made it necessary to obtain another respite, which was granted by interim

Jeff David Case

Governor Jeter. Governor Simpson had been made Chief Justice, and Jeter, president of the Senate, was by operation of law, acting as Governor.

Another respite! Is there no end to the law's delays? Is Justice to be always trifled with, and the gallows cheated?

Again public opinion showed its hostility; but Jeff was safe in the State Penitentiary, and I quietly prepared my brief and argument for the Supreme Court. At its next session the appeal was argued; and that Court at once decided that Judge Mackey had committed error of law in holding that he had not the power to grant a new trial so long after the first trial. So my appeal was sustained, the Court holding there was no time limit in such a case; and they ordered the case back, for the Circuit Court to hear the motion for a new trial.

The case was now, in my opinion, greatly simplified; and at the next term of the Court in Abbeville, I renewed my motion. Judge Hudson was presiding, an excellent Judge. After reading the order of refusal passed by Judge Mackey, and the decision of the Supreme Court reversing that order, Judge Hudson at once granted a new trial to Jeff David.

The trial could not be heard until the next term of the Court, in November, 1881. Again a respite had to be obtained, this time from Governor Hagood.

While making ready for the second trial I re-visited Indigo Springs. I took with me Mr. McCord, a county surveyor, who made an accurate survey of the locality immediately surrounding the Franklin house. A large plat or chart was prepared of the area embraced in the evidence, from the persimmon stump to the tall pine tree, showing the fields and woods, the paths, the rail-fences and pig-pens, and the Franklin house in the center, with Jeff David's cabin on the other side of the public road. A ground plan of the Franklin house was also prepare

As the time for the second trial drew near, public interest and displeasure were plainly increased. In my own county and town there were very few who were friendly to Jeff David; nearly all believed firmly in his guilt. Among my brethren at the Bar that was the prevailing sentiment. Not one brother lawyer gave me a word of encouragement, or wished me success.

Indeed, one member of our Bar did the unprofessional thing of volunteering into the case to assist the Solicitor in the prosecution, alleging that he had been employed in the case. Solicitor Orr, a new official, asked me who had employed him, for he had not and didn't desire his assistance. Had he been employed by the Franklin heirs? Mr. Gideon O'Neill, the administrator, assured me they had not employed any counsel. The lawyer referred to is now dead, so I shall neither name him nor say any more about his conduct than this, that in his argument to the jury he made a bitter attack on me; and that in reply I unsparingly exposed him to the jury as a blood-thirsty meddler, who had

Jeff David Case

thrust himself into the case, that the State had not employed him, and denounced without mercy a volunteer prosecutor.

When, some weeks before Court, the county papers published the list of jurors, I was very glad to see that of the thirty-six petit jurors at least twenty were men whom I knew to be men of integrity and intelligence, who could be trusted to do their sworn duty, just the sort of jury I desired. By the exercise of the prisoner's right to object, I felt sure I should be able to select a just and fair jury.

An incident occurred the week before Court that is well worthy to be remembered. On the public square one day I was stopped by Andrew Wardlaw, then a merchant and afterwards president of the National Bank, a good friend of mine and a man of the highest character. He said, "Benet, I see I am on the jury list and I was just thinking that as we are good friends you might not object to have me on your Jeff David jury. But I want to warn you, I heard the evidence at the first trial, and I was convinced then and believe still that Jeff is guilty. I think it right to tell you this."

I replied, "Major"--(you remember Andrew Wardlaw; he was a major in your grandfather's brigade)-- "Major, it is very good of you to tell me; but I shall not be afraid to place Jeff David's fate in the hands of twelve men just like you, even though they may at present believe as you do that he is guilty. You may be sure if your name is drawn I will not object to you. The evidence will compel you to change your mind."

At this term of the Court, Judge Fraser presided, a man of modest and retiring demeanor, but a learned and upright Judge. On the day set for the new trial the close-packed throng in the Courthouse showed the intense interest and excitement of the public. Fortune favored me in the selection of a jury. The prisoner's right to object was exercised only four times, and a jury was sworn which for intelligence and excellence of character could not be surpassed.

All but one of the twelve men were over forty years of age; there were merchants and other businessmen, and planters, and farmers, every one of them a man of good reputation for honesty, integrity and truthfulness. When the panel was filled, my old friend, Mr. Burt, the Nestor of our Bar, said to me, "You must think Jeff David is not guilty. You are a bold man to select a jury like that."

The jury retired to choose a foreman. In a few minutes they returned to the jury box, and the foreman they had chosen was Andrew Wardlaw!

The trial proceeded. As at the first trial the leading witnesses for the prosecution were Captain Jim King, Tom Arnold and Mr. Gideon O'Neill. King had weakened considerably; his direct testimony was not nearly so strong as at

- 24 -

the former trial; and in cross-examination he was forced to admit that Jeff David had told him about the big roll of money in the "haar-covered trunk." When asked why he had not told this at the first trial, he gave the answer always given by witnesses who suppress and withhold evidence favorable to the other side--his answer was, "I forgot it; and I reckon I wasn't asked about it."

King was compelled to admit also that he and Arnold and some other men had taken Jeff apart from the crowd before he was arrested, had put a rope round his neck, had told him to tell all about the murder or they would hang him right there; that poor Jeff had protested his innocence; that then throwing the rope over the branch of a tree they hanged the old negro there until he was nearly strangled. King did not play the bold witness part at this trial. As he passed me when he left the witness stand, he said, "Thank you, Squire; you let me off light."

Arnold, a weak tool of King's, followed King's example. His testimony was not of much value. Neither he nor King was positive or clear as to Jeff's tracks.

Then came Gideon O'Neill, a very different type of man, both as to intelligence and truthfulness. His well-remembered testimony about the persimmon stain of Jeff David's knife blade he repeated with the same clearness and positive certainty. He had to be carefully handled. His terrible testimony, fatal to the prisoner if believed, had to be successfully contradicted. The ordinary methods of cross-examination would, I knew, only make him more emphatic and more convincing in his statements. But I was prepared to use a different method. I said:

"Mr. O'Neill, I know you well and respect you for your excellent character. The jury, most of them, are acquainted with you and know you to be a man of truth and honesty. You know that the testimony you have given, if believed in by them, will have a damning effect on Jeff David. Do you solemnly swear that you cannot be mistaken about the stain on Jeff's knife-blade? Are you positively certain it was persimmon stain?"

Without hesitation he replied, "Mr. Benet, I expected you to question me very close and try to make out I might be mistaken; but since the last trial I have made experiments several times cutting saplings of different kinds and examining the stain on the knife, and I can tell the persimmon stain every time. There is no other tree that makes a stain like it. Now I don't pretend to know or identify the stains made by different trees, like the hickory, or oak, or ash, or elm, or pine and so on. Their stains are pretty much the same but none is like the persimmon. I can tell it every time. I cut some saplings just last week, just *to make sure; and there was the same yellowish stain of the persimmon."*

O'Neill's words visibly affected the jury. The profound silence in the court room showed that the crowd of listeners knew this was a crisis in the trial. A small cardboard box was then handed to the witness.

But let me tell you what was in that box. Through an Abbeville merchant I had procured twelve new knives of the same size and make as Jeff's. Just four days before the trial I had employed a trustworthy young man, George Shillito, to go to the woods and cut a sapling with each one of the dozen knives, the twelve saplings to be of twelve different kinds of trees. He was instructed to make a written memorandum of the kind of sapling cut by each separate knife, numbering them from 1 to 12, and marking the knives on the back-edge of the blade with corresponding file marks. Among the saplings thus cut was to be one persimmon. Shillito was put on his Masonic oath to keep all the proceedings secret, and not even to let me know what saplings the respective knives had cut. He carried out my instructions faithfully and well.

That was the box I handed up to Mr. O'Neill. He was requested to examine the big blade of each knife, and if he found stain on it, to tell the jury what tree it had cut. Truthful man though he was, O'Neill was evidently disturbed and taken aback by this kind of cross-examination. It is so much easier to answer a question than to make an actual experiment. He hesitated and then said, "You know, Mr. Benet, I told you I didn't pretend to recognize tree stains of every kind?"

"Quite so, Mr. O'Neill; but you asserted most positively that you never make a mistake about the stain of a persimmon. Just do the best you can, now. Tell the jury what each knife cut, if you can; and tell them also the number of file-marks you see on the back of each big blade."

It was a gloomy November day, rather dark in the court room, and I asked the Judge to allow the witness to take the box of knives to a window-sill where the light was better. It was a trying ordeal for O'Neill; and I must confess it was a most anxious time for me.

All I knew from Shillito was that one knife had cut a persimmon, but that knife's number I did not know--indeed I had refused to be informed, lest my manner should betray me. But I could not help thinking, "What if O'Neill should recognize that persimmon stain?" My anxiety was soon relieved, however; the third or fourth knife he examined chanced to be Number 6. The usual queries were put:

"Do you see any stain on that blade?"

"I do, a slight stain."

"Would you swear that is persimmon stain?"

Jeff David Case

"No sir; not at all like persimmon stain."

When O'Neill put down Number 6, Shillito whispered in my ear: "That's the knife that cut persimmon--Number 6!" I could hardly hide the feelings of joy and gratitude which then thrilled me. The danger was over; and I knew that by this rather daring experiment O'Neill's testimony against Jeff David had been successfully disposed of. O'Neill's manner, too, had changed on the witness stand. His answer was no longer given with his customary positive assurance, but in a hesitating, shaky and uncertain manner. In not a single instance did he pretend to recognize the stain, but only said it was not persimmon.

Other witnesses for the prosecution were then examined but I shall not burden this narrative with a detailed account of their less important testimony. As at the first trial, the State Solicitor relied chiefly on the testimony of King, Arnold and O'Neill. The only piece of new evidence adduced was the shirt of Jeff David, which was introduced on the suggestion of the "volunteer" attorney who was assisting the Solicitor. It had been in the State's possession at the first trial but was not then offered in evidence.

Exhibited now, it was proved there were stains of blood upon it. No effort was made, except in that "volunteer's" argument, to prove it was human blood; but as it was shown that the stains were on the back of the shirt, and none on the front, and also that the stains were accounted for by the fact that Jeff David had that morning killed a hog and carried the carcass on his back, the attempt to claim that it was human blood was ridiculous. In my argument to the jury I treated that "bloody shirt" testimony with the scorn it deserved, then rolled the shirt up in a bundle and flung it with contempt in the face of that "volunteer" prosecutor, saying, "Take your bloody shirt, Sir, and be ashamed of yourself for offering it in evidence." This, I admit, was going too far, but I was furiously indignant and could not refrain. That incident and some other denunciating language I used came near to causing a duel.

The witnesses for the defense were then examined. My plan was not only to disprove the testimony of the State's witnesses and show that the theory that Jeff David was guilty had no foundation, but also to satisfy the jury by my after-discovered evidence that the murder had been committed by two men, a white man and a negro, with whom Jeff had no connection. The defense was based, therefore, chiefly on the testimony of Fuller, Nickles, Dr. Waddell and Shillito.

The plan of the locality and the plan of the Franklin house were also introduced and they aided greatly in making the testimony clear. The testimony of Fuller and Nickles as to tracks proved that King and Arnold had testified falsely. The double set of footprints going and coming between the tall pine and

Jeff David Case

the house; the finding of the bloody persimmon club; and of the two sperm candles; the out-going footprints showing that the murderers, throwing away in the yard the bloody club and the candles, stumbled in their haste into the pig-pens, then fled full speed across the ploughed field to the tree where the horse stood hitched; the size of the footprints indicating that they were made by a negro and a white man, made it clear that the State in prosecuting Jeff David was on the wrong trail, and had been misled and misinformed by King and Arnold.

Frank Fuller's testimony showing that the persimmon club must have been cut by a one-armed man, completely fascinated the Judge, the jury, and all who heard it. I have heard testimony given by many hundreds of witnesses, and I have read reports of many cases, and many books on evidence; and I pronounce Fuller's statement on the witness stand the finest piece of evidence I ever heard or read. As clear, convincing legal proof, it would be hard to find its match. And let me add, its weight and value were much enhanced by the modest, frank and manly demeanor of the witness. When he came down from the stand, Mr. Lyon, our Judge of Probate, himself a one-armed Confederate veteran, said to me, "You have not only acquitted Jeff David; you have also convicted a certain one-armed man!" I may here state that fortunately one of the jury was a one-armed individual.

It is proper that I should explain that Dr. Waddell was not a witness for the defense. He had been sworn by the State, and I was thus enabled to get from him, upright, unbiased man that he was, most valuable evidence for our defense in his cross-examination, evidence which the State could not question, he being a State's witness. You will recall what I have already quoted from him about the nature of the wounds on the heads of George and Drusilla Franklin, and what he said about the pool of blood in which the old woman's head had lain and had moved backward and forward on the floor--and about the drops of blood leading from her end of the supper table to the bed where her body was found.

Our witness, Bob Nickles, was particularly clear and emphatic in his testimony about the two sets of tracks in the ploughed field, the negro tracks at the tall pine tree, the finding of the bloody club and the sperm candles.

"The Franklins never used store-bought candles," said Nickles, "nor Jeff David, neither," he quickly added. He was sure the murderers had been plundering the house and hunting for the money half an hour or longer, "when something must have scared them," he said, "and they cut and ran as fast as they could, and flung away the 'simmon club and the candles just before they ran against the pig-pen." He was very positive that at the time King and Arnold

arrived on the scene, no mortal man could have found Jeff's tracks where those witnesses swore they did. It was noticeable that he always spoke of "the two men," "the men that killed the Franklins," "the murderers,"--using the plural--plainly showing his belief in Jeff's innocence.

George Shillito's testimony about the twelve knives and the twelve saplings they cut was listened to with breathless attention by all in the courtroom. He produced his written memorandum, made at the time he cut the saplings, numbering them from 1 to 12, and making the corresponding file-marks on the back of the big blade. When he came to Number 6, he was asked what the knife had cut; he answered: "This knife, Number 6, cut a persimmon sapling at a point about five feet from the ground, where it was three inches thick. The sapling was cut clean through."

"But, Mr. Shillito, Mr. Gideon O'Neill in his testimony swore that the stain on that knife blade was 'not at all like persimmon stain'--these were his words. What do you say to that?" I asked.

"Well," said Shillito, "I can't help that. That may be Mr. O'Neill's opinion, but I know that the stain on the blade is persimmon stain. This knife has never cut anything except that persimmon sapling. That was four days ago, and all the twelve knives have been in my possession since. Not a soul but Mr. Benet knew I had them, and not a soul has seen or touched them since, till today in the Court."

This evidence made a powerful impression on all who heard it. It may truly be said that the effect of it was both seen and felt. The foreman and several of the jury had jotted down on paper the answers made by Mr. O'Neill when he was examined about the stains on the twelve knives; and when Shillito said that Number 6 had cut persimmon, while O'Neill had sworn that the stain on Number 6 was "not at all like persimmon stain," I could almost hear a sigh of relief from the jury; I certainly saw on their countenances a look of satisfaction as they put their heads together and whispered and nodded.

The test of the twelve knives had dealt a crushing blow to Gideon O'Neill's pride of opinion. I learned afterwards from Bob Nickles that O'Neill quietly slipped out of the courtroom after Shillito left the stand, got into his buggy and drove away homewards. He had told Nickles he was going to camp on the Courthouse hill until the jury found their verdict of guilty; but he retired from the field completely crestfallen.

It is not necessary to say much about the several arguments to the jury. The first was made by the "volunteer" attorney; I have already said enough about him. He was followed for the defense by my young colleague who confined

Jeff David Case

himself to arguing the issues of law involved, leaving the issues of fact entirely to me.

What my theory of the murder has already been sufficiently indicated. My belief in Jeff David's innocence was firm and unshaken. And just as firm was my belief in the guilt of Martin, the one-armed white man and his unknown negro fellow murderer. The first part of my argument, therefore, was devoted to showing the jury that the evidence on which Jeff had been convicted had been successfully contradicted and the State's main witnesses discredited.

In the latter part I made plain to the jury my theory of the murder. I asked them, was there any man at that time in the neighborhood of the Franklins who had urgent cause for fleeing the State--had he already committed a homicide? Was he sulking in concealment in order to escape arrest? Was he in great need of money? Was he an one-armed man? Had he cut the persimmon club? Had he employed some negro man to help him to rob the Franklins who he knew had thousands of dollars in their lonely log cabin?

I then pictured the two burglars meeting at the tall pine tree, leaving the horse hitched there, stealthily approaching the cabin from behind, walking warily, for it was clear moonlight; the negro looks in at the back window; he sees old George Franklin and Miss Drusilla sitting at their supper, the old man's back being right at the front door as he sat in this chair, his sister facing him at the other end of the small table. The burglars see how easy it will be to strike the two old persons each a blow with the club--a blow that will render them unconscious, but need not be a fatal blow. No, the white man does not wish to murder his two old neighbors, but their money he must have. Nor must he be seen and recognized by them. The black negro, the blacker his face the better, must suddenly open the door and strike the stunning blows. So far, so good.

Old George and Drusilla are lying helpless and harmless and unconscious on the floor; no danger, they are quiet and still, now for the money. The white man has two candles; he lights them; the cupboard is searched, every drawer is ransacked, several trunks and boxes are burst open. The noise does not disturb the unconscious old man and his old sister, although they are being robbed of their long-hoarded money. The burglars soon discover rolls of many bills, the white man thinks there must be more hidden somewhere; here are some locked trunks and drawers; where are the keys? They must be in the old man's pocket; his pockets are quickly and carefully searched and the keys are found, and more money is discovered. The burglars are in the bedroom still searching in a trunk; a half-hour has passed; their search has been successful, and they are still coming upon rolls of greenbacks. The two candles give a bright light; the burglars are kneeling beside an open trunk; they hear a sound from the other *room; they look up and there stands poor old Drusilla Franklin! She has recovered consciousness; she sees the two robbers; she knows Martin; she calls his name; and shameful burglary has to be turned into hideous, cruel murder. The horrid deed--the double murder--is done in mad haste. The murderers flee from the house, the burning candles still in their hands; the one who has brained the aged victims still has the bloody club in his hand. The candles and the club are thrown away in the yard as the murderers, now in a frenzy of fear, make their way running at full speed towards the tall pine.*

But why unnecessarily prolong this story?--already so much longer than you desired or I intended. It must make you think of the red rose and the briar in the ballad of Lord Lovel, that "grew and they grew to the church steeple top, until they could grow no higher." Only remember there is no such limit to the growth of this narrative. I could easily make it much longer. Indeed, although you asked for "full details" I am leaving out many details of minor interest and importance. Enough to say that during my argument I felt encouraged by the close attention and evident interest of the jury. I believed they were adopting my firm conviction of Jeff's innocence and the guilt of the one-armed man and his negro confederate. Martin's name I, of course, did not mention, but I was sure the jury had him in their minds as I pictured the approach of the murderers, the robbery and the murder, the headlong flight . My argument lasted fully four hours. At the end, I apologized to the Judge and the jury for taking up so much time. "No apology is necessary for the jury," said the Foreman, Andrew Wardlaw, and his fellow jurors nodded approvingly.

Solicitor Orr closed for the prosecution. Our gigantic friend did his best, you remember his six feet five and massive build, his big, honest countenance and his bald head. Always strong before a jury on the facts, which he called "fax," he argued well. But he was handicapped, first by the weakening and discrediting of the State's witnesses; secondly, by the unexpected mass and weight of the new evidence for the defense; and thirdly by the hurtful interference of his "volunteer" associate. Sorry I was that Cothran was no longer Solicitor; it was over him I longed to triumph.

The trial had lasted three days; it was now half-past eleven at night of the third day when Judge Fraser charged the jury. The charge was brief, but clear and unobjectionable. Exactly at midnight the jury retired to their room to find their verdict. It was a chilly night, and I noticed that several of the jurors had sent for their overcoats. True, the jury-room was not comfortable; no fire or stove there; but the sight of the overcoats sent a chill through me. Did it mean the jury expected an all-night session, at best a failure to agree, a mistrial?

The Judge instructed the Sheriff that if the jury announced they had agreed

Jeff David Case

on a verdict, he should send for him and the counsel. Slowly I walked home, thinking many anxious thoughts, and feeling quite "let down" in mind and body. I waked no one in the house, but sat down at the fireside with a cigar and a glass of grog, to await the Sheriff's summons. Andrew Wardlaw's warning made me uneasy; had his true-blue Presbyterianism, perhaps his pride of opinion, withstood the effect of the new evidence for the defense? Was his belief in Jeff David's guilt still unchanged?

At one o'clock, here comes the Sheriff's deputy. The jury have agreed. "Any intimation? "No; just that they have agreed on a verdict. The Sheriff has gone to the hotel for the Judge; and the Solicitor has been sent for." How did I feel as we walked to the Courthouse? Do you know the sensation when your heart sinks until it seems to go down to your heels? It had been almost four years of discouraging struggle--and soon I would know.

The big crowd had gone home, but there was a surprisingly large number in the courtroom when the Judge and the Solicitor returned. The big hanging lamps had been put out; only two or three small hand lamps were burning; the room looked gloomy and cheerless. Before the Judge came I had overheard more than one remark like, "I'll bet the verdict is guilty."

The jury is brought in. They take their seats in a silence that is painfully solemn. In the dim light I cannot read their countenances.

The Judge: "Gentlemen of the jury, have you agreed upon your verdict?"

The Foreman: "We have, your Honor."

The Judge: "Mr. Clerk; publish the verdict."

The deputy clerk unfolded the record. He was known by me to be a strong believer in Jeff's guilt. He fumbled the paper in his excitement. He held a small lamp in one hand and proceeded to read:

"State of South Carolina, County of Abbeville. The State against Jeff David, indictment for Murder." Here he stopped, a startled expression on his face, looked at the jury as if surprised, then resumed the reading. "Verdict, Not Guilty,"--adding the formula, "That is your verdict and so say you all," the twelve jurors assenting.

The old prisoner was standing in the dock. I was standing on the floor at the side of the dock when the astonished clerk read the words, "Not Guilty." The poor old man threw his arms around my shoulders, weeping and sobbing and saying, "De Lord will bless you for dis. De Lord will bless you for dis." The Foreman of the jury told me afterwards that this touching incident moved all who saw it--that there wasn't a dry eye in the jury box.

Andrew Wardlaw also told me that when the jurors selected him as their

Jeff David Case

Foreman he asked them not to discuss the case with one another nor to express an opinion during the trial. To this they agreed, and they acted accordingly, so that when they retired to find their verdict no juror knew the opinion of any fellow juror.

Major Wardlaw told me he then said, "Now, gentlemen, before we begin to discuss the case, let us see how we stand. Let each write on a piece of paper 'Guilty' or 'Not Guilty.' Mr. Barnwell will act as secretary, and Mr. Morse will collect the ballots in this hat." The twelve ballots were prepared, dropped in the hat; opened and read. To the utter surprise and amazement of all, each one of the twelve ballots read "Not Guilty." Almost all the members of the jury had previously believed Jeff was guilty. While each found he had changed his mind, he did not think the others had changed theirs. They could hardly believe their ears heard aright when Ben Barnwell announced the result, "Guilty, None. Not Guilty, Twelve." The Foreman then said:

"It will never do, gentlemen, to go back to the Court and render our verdict right off. This is a very important case. The whole state is waiting to hear the verdict, and it will seem as if we were too hasty. I suggest that we stay in here at least one hour. We can still discuss the case although we have agreed on a verdict. But first let us write the verdict." And they did so. Here was a striking contrast with old "Jedburgh justice" under which the Scottish Borderers hanged a man first and tried him afterwards.

I must here add that Judge Fraser, when the verdict was announced, turned to the jury and said, "Gentlemen of the jury, it affords me great pleasure to assure you that in my opinion you have found a true verdict and done justice to this poor old negro."

When the Court was adjourned, the jurors came to me, each shaking hands with me and requesting through the Foreman that the twelve knives in evidence be given them as souvenirs of the famous trial, which was done.

As a precautionary measure, in case the once strong lynching spirit still existed, I deferred drawing the order discharging the prisoner and left him in the Sheriff's custody until morning, for safekeeping. His old wife, Mary, who had sat through the whole trial, was with him and went to jail with him that night in a state of happiness like the man in the Gospel, "walking and leaping and praising God."

The long four-year fight was ended. The victory was mine. And a great victory it was. Yet I was unconscious of any feeling of elation such as I have felt on other occasions of successful contest at the Bar. The uppermost sensation was one of sincere gratitude and profound satisfaction. Reaching home I sat in the easy chair at the fireside; the unfinished toddy was on the mantel-piece within reach. I would smoke a cigar, drink the toddy and go to bed. It was now nearly 3 A. M. At seven o'clock I was waked up by old Daddy Willis, rattling his dishes in the pantry. Physically exhausted I must have been, for I had gone to sleep in the chair without touching the toddy or lighting the cigar.

Any more details? Well, I may mention that old Jeff and old Mary begged to be allowed to serve me and my family like bond slaves as long as they lived. Their gratitude was pathetic. Of course, I could not accept their services. Mary stayed in our home with the servants for a month, until your grandfather, then a Justice of the Supreme Court, took them under his protection to Columbia to live with their son. I had been warned by Fuller and Nickles and also by Gideon O'Neil that it would not be safe for Jeff to return to his home at Indigo Springs. The lynching spirit might be aroused again.

What fee did I receive for my services you may ask? One malicious newspaper insinuated that it was the Franklin money that was paying Jeff's lawyer. It is--or was--a point of honor with South Carolina lawyers when appointed by the Court to defend a prisoner who stands in the dock in forma pauperis to accept the appointment without demur and do his duty without fee. But I have to confess I received a fee for defending Jeff David. His son, who lived in Columbia--Griffin, I think, was his name--came to me at my hotel there shortly after the first trial and paid me the sum of seventeen dollars and a half. Did I accept it: Certainly I did. I brought it home to Abbeville and gave it to poor old Mary the next time she came to visit Jeff in jail.

You should now ask, what did the defense of Jeff David cost me from first to last. It cost me, not counting my time in the 4-year fight, over seven hundred dollars. More than half of that had to be paid to the negro detective employed by Governor Hampton, for the Governor's contingent fund was exhausted, and I had advanced the money. That detective's work was worth exactly nothing. But Hampton had acted so handsomely in Jeff's behalf, I did not grudge paying his useless detective.

What became of Martin and the negro, the real murderers? Well, I had my thumb on them up to the last trial--Martin in Mississippi; the negro near Lake City, Florida. If Jeff had been found guilty a second time, I should have had them both arrested and brought to trial. With Jeff's acquittal my work in the Franklin murder case was finished. I learned afterwards that Martin moved to southeastern Georgia shortly after Jeff's acquittal. Years afterwards, the thick-skinned and shameless effrontery of Jim King showed itself by his coming to me

Jeff David Case

in Greenville one day and telling me he knew where Martin was, and actually asking if I would help him, King, to get Martin arrested and brought back!

What became of Jeff David? He lived for eight or ten years in Columbia, and died there. Business took me often to that town, and Jeff somehow always knew when I was at Wright's Hotel, and never failed to come to see me.

Let me close this narrative with a description of his personal appearance. Judge Mackey had called him the "black fiend." As a matter of fact, Jeff was not black; nor was there in his features nor his expression anything to suggest a fiendish disposition. His skin was that of a mulatto, of a ruddy brown color, more like a red Indian than an African. Indeed I am pretty sure if his parentage had been traced it would have been found that there was more Indian than negro blood in his veins. He was built like an Indian, was tall, straight, square-shouldered. He had very black hair--not woolly--and uncommonly bright black eyes. I never saw any but a kindly expression on his face. So, there you have a faithful picture of the "black fiend."

Mysterious are the ways of Providence--or Fate. An old negro, found guilty of a double murder, sentenced to death; five times respited under four Governors, saved from death by lynching by the Sheriff's vigilance; placed on the scaffold to suffer the agonies of a condemned man about to die; tried a second time; triumphantly acquitted. This old negro, innocent as the unborn babe, would have been hanged six weeks after the first trial but for the chance request King made of me to sign his petition for the reward when I happened to meet him in the courthouse corridor. Call it chance or decree of Providence, that casual request saved the life of Jeff David.

The man whom Benet told the jury was the likely killer was a one-armed man who had on Thanksgiving killed his brother – in –law in the neighborhood and had need of the Franklin money to flee the area. In Benet's account he chose to refer to him as "Martin," not his actual name. Both Abbeville papers on Dec. 5 1877 carried accounts of the same Thanksgiving homicide , (1) from the Abbeville *Medium: A Thanksgiving Tragedy. On last Friday T. C. Pinson died from the effects of a wound received on Thursday night at the hands of Keitt Ingram. The circumstances attending the fearful tragedy are somewhat as follows: Keitt Ingram has a store at Simms X Roads near Greenwood where he carried on a little retail trade in articles of every day consumption. He and his victim Pinson were cousins by blood and brothers-in-law by marriage. They had had a number of business transactions together and without any trouble or disagreement up to last Thursday night. Some times since it appears that Ingram and Pinson agreed to destroy all old notes and accounts each held*

The Thanksgiving Tragedy

against the other and in this way "strike a balance" and begin anew. Pinson kept one of his old accounts and on the day of the homicide proposed to have it entered as a set off against his account with Ingram for 1877. Ingram claimed that this was not according to the agreement made between them and that he would not consent to such a settlement. One word brought on another and frenzied by passion Ingram fired a pistol at Pinson and thus put an end to all further disputes on this subject. The ball entered between the last two lower ribs on the right side, pierced the liver, the large intestines, and kidneys; and lodged in the outer opposite fold of the abdomen. Pinson fell and Ingram fled. After suffering the most intense torture the unhappy man died on Friday night, about twenty-four hours after receiving his wound. An inquest was held over his remains by Trial Justice Rogers on Saturday. Dr. George H. Waddell made a post-mortem examination of the body and testified that the deceased came to his death from the pistol shot as above described. Pinson was about thirty years of age and left a wife and three children to mourn his taking off. Ingram is a one-armed man and is said to be a rather quarrelsome fellow. This makes the fourth death by violence in this county during the last month. Somebody will have to be hung and that quickly.

The Press and Banner *of the same date: "Another Deed of Blood. Another homicide has to be added to the already bloody docket of Abbeville County for the next court. The fatal encounter took place at Simms Cross Roads last Wednesday night between eight and nine o'clock. Thomas Pinson called at the house of Madison S. Ingram, who keeps a store at the Cross Roads. Pinson had been at Ninety Six and was returning homewards slightly under the influence of whiskey, Ingram possessed a promissory note of Pinson's which the later asked to see, and thereupon a dispute arose in the presence of Mrs. Ingram and a young man named King. Pinson made use of expressions in Mrs. Ingram's presence to which Ingram took exception and ordered Pinson out of his house. Pinson was armed with a stick and refused to go out. Ingram is a one-armed man, but he advanced toward Pinson to put him out. The latter raised his stick and Ingram retreated behind his store counter, telling Pinson not to advance or he would shoot him, Pinson gave no heed to the warning, said he could defend himself and still followed Ingram. Drawing a pocket pistol on him, Ingram fired. The shot took effect, and Pinson walked out on the piazza and immediately fell to the ground. Ingram ran to Mr. Henderson's house for help for the wounded man. Mr. Henderson came at once and Dr. Waddell was sent for.*

The wound was pronounced fatal. On undressing Pinson it was discovered that he had no fire-arms about his person. Pinson lingered in great agony to

The Burt – Stark House

Friday morning. After his death it was found that the ball had lodged in the liver. The deceased was a young farmer about twenty eight years of age, married and the father of three children. He was working a part of Mr. Wm Fouche's plantation on Saluda River. Ingram is a married man about thirty five years of age. He had disappeared . The wives of the two men are sisters..

On the 26th of Dec. the *Medium carried the announcement of "*The Price of a Man." *Governor Hampton has offered* the reward of one hundred dollars fort the apprehension and delivery in any jail of the State of M. S. Ingram, charged with the atrocious murder of Thomas C. Pinson near Greenwood on November 30. After the commission of this crime Ingram hung around home but managed to escape the efforts made for his arrest. Where he is now is not known – it is rumored that he is far on his way to Texas. In the Governor's proclamation the following description of the man which may lead to his arrest is given: *Said Ingram is 33 years old, grey eyes, light complexion, 5 feet 10 inches high, weight 160 pounds, speaks rapidly, right arm off near the shoulder, scar on the face. said to have been caused by gunshot.*

Chapter X **in Old Abbeville** dealt with the Lesley-Hoyt-Simmonds-Burt-Norwood- Calhoun-Stark House. The author wrote that "this house has long been the symbol of Abbeville, and its history has illustrated that of the town." The fifth paragraph of that chapter dealt with the second owner of the house, Rev. Thomas Hoyt who was there from 1855 to 1860. The author knew then that Rev. Hoyt had a family connection to Woodrow Wilson but did not know the details. Through *The Woodrow Wilson Papers* and other sources, he has learned that Thomas Hoyt was the first Mrs. Wilson (Ellen "Ellie" Axson Wilson's favorite "Uncle Tom." While Rev. Hoyt was in Abbeville he was a member of the board of trustees at the South Carolina College and in September, 1857 was elected to the vacant chair of Logic, Rhetoric and Philosophy of the Mind" on the faculty, but he declined. Hoyt left his pastorate of the Upper Long Cane Church to become pastor of the First Presbyterian Church in Louisville, Ky. His pro-Secessionist views caused him to leave his post in Louisville and to take refuge in Canada until the Civil War concluded. After the war he located in New York where he served for several years as president of the "gold board." which would later become the New York Exchange. When he re-entered the ministry, he became pastor of the First Presbyterian church at Nashville for eleven years (1872-1883)and later the Chambers' church in Philadelphia (1883-1901.)

From 1884 to his death in "Ellie's" exchange of letters with W. W. (Woodrow Wilson) Uncle Tom is noted. In 1884, ELA [Ellie Axson] wrote

The Burt Stark House

W.W. [Woodrow Wilson] "Uncle Tom is very anxious for me to spend the Xmas holidays with him, and I think perhaps I will." Three days earlier she had written that "I have surely struck a streak of luck at present! Who do you think is coming to New York[Ellie was in New York studying art] now, Uncle Tom and Aunt Sallie!" The next day she wrote W. W. from New York: "I told you I believe that Uncle Tom was coming yesterday. As I came rushing home from the sketch class (it is perfectly dark now at half past five, and I almost fly – think I make the distance in a minute and a half). I saw on our dark street a great figure looming up in the distance and I knew at once it must be him, no one else is so tall. He had come, for the second time, to take me up with him to dinner. So we had quite a family party; and of course I spent the day with them, too. I wish you knew Uncle Tom, he is just 'too lovely for anything.' "

On the 27th, Wilson replied "It makes me very happy to know that you are having such a delightful time with those who are so dear to you. By-the-way, little lady, would you like to be a near neighbor of 'Uncle Tom's' ". [He told her of his possibly taking up work at Bryn Mawr near Philadelphia.]

On Dec. 4, Wilson wrote ELA that "he knows she would be happier with him than with "Uncle Tom and Aunt Saidie or anybody else.." On Dec. 7, he wrote ELA, "It is probably best that I shouldn't make a point of meeting your uncle this time; because truly he and I am delighted that you are able to get away from your boarding house for a little while. I can't help feeling slightly aggrieved that he has spoiled my Christmas for me by claiming the little lady who is all the world – and more- to me and who alone would make the season a happy one by her presence. He is doubtless guiltless of all thought of me – and therefore of all thought of harming me in the matter, but it's true, all the same that I grudge him the privilege of having you at Christmas time."

On Dec. 8, ELA wrote W. W. that "I wish for the twentieth time that I had never promised Uncle Tom to spend Xmas with him! It would be so much nicer to spend it alone with you. . . Yes, Uncle Tom did think of you.. He said when he asked me 'I suppose Mr. Wilson will want to be with you, but he can come to Phila. as well as New York',."

After the holidays when Wilson had visited Ellie and her uncle's family, Ellie wrote " You seem to have had golden opinions from all of them. Uncle Tom is loud in your praise and Aunt Saidie keeps well up with him."

After Wilson had written somewhat critically of Uncle Tom on January 10th, 1885, he wrote ELA, "Were you hurt, my darling, by what I said about your uncle. It was thoughtless of me to write for your eyes a criticism of the uncle you love so much; but I talk to you as I would talk to myself – and I love you so much and with so thorough a sense of identification that I feel that "Uncle Tom' is almost as much my uncle as yours. So you must not think that my criticisms argue any lack of affection or respect for those you love."

On April 9, 1885. ELA wrote W, W. "by the way I had a dear little letter from Uncle Tom yesterday, and I believe I will enclose it – to eke out your short rations. I want you to know some of my relatives better and to read their letters, you know. " On the 13th, W. W. replied "This is a dear "little letter" from your uncle, and I most cordially approve of your sending me such letters as introduction of those of your relatives who are dearest to you. I love 'Uncle Tom,' because he loves you." On the 18th, W. W. wrote ELA from Phila., "Here I am at Uncle Tom's according to engagement. The rest have gone to afternoon service, inviting me to stay at home and rest."

Wilson found that he got along with Uncle Tom very well, though he found Hoyt's wife difficult. . He wrote EAW [E. L, Wilson] Aunt Saide "could not keep her temper in an equable poise. She knew everything about every topic that was broached; and I came away more disgusted and tired than ever by her shallow wit and surface information. Uncle Tom is either very blind or of a heavenly temperament, to stand as he does the kind of disagreement with which she treats some of his opinions. It would ruin me within a twelve months to live with such a woman." In July, 1888 Uncle Tom wrote Ellie when it was clear that Wilson was moving from his post at Bryn Mawr to Wesleyan University in Connecticut, He wrote "while I rejoice in the promotion of your dear husband, it is a real grief to me and all of us to lose you and him from our vicinity.. You are very dear to me, Woodrow has been exceedingly agreeable. In view of his leaving, I think it might be well for Woodrow to meet Mr. Wannamaker [John W., merchant and philanthropist] . The understanding I had with him was that on my return, I would introduce Woodrow to him; but now I fear this will not be practicable."

On August 27, 1888. Wilson wrote his old friend Robert Bridges. "A little scheme which is brewing here has been confidentially imparted to me which I am going to venture to tell you about, knowing that you will see how important it is to keep a secret for the present, lest it should miscarry, and yet wishing you to know and if you have anything to suggest, advise. My wife's uncle, Rev. T. A. Hoyt, who is pastor of the old Chambers Church in Philadelphia, went up to Princeton with me to hear Patton's address A week or so later he dined with John Wannamaker (who sent his sons to Princeton, you know, being a great Presbyterian) and told him what Dr. Patton had said about political science. 'Do you know.' said Mr. Wannamaker. 'I should like to endow such a chair as that.' They talked the matter over, Dr. Hoyt not in the least discouraging the idea, you may be sure, and Dr. H. suggested that he take me to see Mr. W. sometime on a a special conversation on the college's needs. Mr. W. assented; and in the Fall Dr. H. and I are to spend an evening with Mr. W. If he does endow, he will probably, from all indications, endow just the sort of chair I want in which case I shall certainly be a candidate. "

In 1860, Rev. Hoyt sold his house to Andrew J. Simonds of Charleston who had married his cousin Sallie, the daughter of John A.. Calhoun, the nephew of John C. Calhoun and the largest slave holder in the area. Simonds was put in charge of the Abbeville branch of the Bank of the State of South Carolina. In 1862, Simonds sold this house to Armistead Burt and moved to a plantation below town near where his father-in-law lived. Burt become the intendant (mayor) of Abbeville.

Burt never completely paid for the place, and he and his wife Martha (who was John C. Calhoun's favorite niece) enjoyed a somewhat lavish life style. In 1868, Simonds sought a settlement when he wrote Burt April 25th that *the house together with the furniture which I turned over to you cost me about $10,000 in gold. You have had possession of it for seven and one-half years for which I have received nothing. The payments which you made in Confederate money I call nothing, it being worth only five cents on the dollar. When payments were made in worthless currency, though asking that they not be paid, I did not refuse. I desire though that the debt not exceed $7,500. That amount I shall be glad to lend you at seven percent five years.. I want, in addition, a lien on Orange Hill (Burt's plantation], I will not disturb you in the full enjoyment of the property during your lifetime and no one will have a better claim to it than myself after your death.* (Letter is in the Burt Manuscripts at Perkins Library, Duke University.

In 1868 in part because of Mrs. Burt's health, the Burts moved to The Marshall House on the northeast corner of the Square where Mrs. Burts died shortly. James A. Norwood and his family became the fifth owner of the Lesley House. Andrew Simonds's mother-in-law, Mrs. John A. Calhoun's maiden name had been Sarah Mornin Norwood. While the Burts had no children, the Norwoods had five grown children(four daughters (two sets of twins) and a son).

The house next attracted the attention of the local newspaper on March 11, 1874 when the *Press and Banner* reported *the residence of James A. Norwood was entered last Sabbath night and robbed of goods amounting to more than two hundred dollars in value. The thief gained an entrance in a manner unknown to any of the household and the supposition is that he secreted himself in the house until dark and then went about his work of plunder. Mr. Norwood's room was searched – his watch (a valued time-keeper worth one hundred and seventy-five dollars) taken, his pocket book searched and emptied and the suit of clothes he had been wearing carried off. The thief went through the house and made a close search for valuables. After securing his plunder he took his seat on the front piazza of the house and went through the pocket book – throwing away notes, papers, etc., but holding on to the money. The robbery was committed about eleven o'clock, and was done with silence and dispatch. No clue has been found to the thief. Let him be caught if possible and let him be made an example of. Shall Abbeville rival New York in crime?*

Two weeks later (on March 25th) the *Press and Banner* reported *Thief Captured. Sanders, the man who entered Mr. Norwood's house in this place a few weeks since, and stole jewelry & clothing amounting to several hundred dollars in value, was caught at Athens , Georgia last week. He committed a robbery in Ruckersville and was traced to Athens by a Mr. Rucker and captured. He had upon his person Mr. Norwood's gold watch, gold spectacles, gold pencils and about thirty dollars in money. He was a hanger on of the show that exhibited a few days preceding the robbery. We suppose he will be brought to this place for trial.*

On December 9, 1874, the *Press and Banner* reported *Mr. James A. Norwood, an old, most respected citizen of this county, died at his residence at this place on Monday after a long and painful illness aged sixty-four. Mr. Norwood was born on his father's plantation on the Savannah river, in this county and has been a resident of the county during his whole life. He was the last of the family except one, Mrs. John A. Calhoun, his sister. Mr. Norwood was an educated man; a graduate of Athens, Georgia University. He was a farmer by occupation and one of the most practical and successful men in the county. Before the war he was very wealthy and saved enough from the wreck to make himself comfortable.. . his funeral will take place at Trinity of which he was a member.*

On January 12, 1876, the *Press and Banner* reported on James A. Norwood's property at the time of his death as including *the valuable improved lot in the town of Abbeville in the fork of the Greenville and Anderson roads containing five acres more or less containing the family homestead. Also three plantations (1) the White Hall tract on Vienna Road with 'elegant building' and 415 acres (2) the Young plantation adjoining the McDuffie plantation 600*

The Burt Stark House

acres, and (3) the McDuffie plantation in the Flatwoods on waters of Little River 4,200 acres.

On June 16, 1875, the Abbeville *Medium* reported on the death of the Norwood's daughter 'Miss Willie' at the residence of her mother. The *Medium* indicated that "Miss Norwood was one of the best of womanhood. She had no faults. Her life was like a beautiful picture without a blot upon its face. She was modest, intelligent and accomplished. In disposition kind and in everyday life a model to be copied. Wherever she went there was always a 'sweet attractive grace' which drew about her a host of friends and admirers."

The house itself attracted the admiration of the *Press and Banner*, Sept. 20, 1876, when the Wade Hampton Campaign came on Sept 16th to Abbeville. "Gen. Hampton was the guest of Hon A. Burt, at Mrs. Norwood's. The Abbeville Silver Cornet Band headed a procession which greeted Hampton at the Railroad Depot. In the parade route to the speaking the paper's account reported that "Mrs. Norwood's [house] was especially noticeable with the flags and transparencies at the gate and the brilliant lights at the house."

Sallie (Sarah) Norwood married E. B. (Edward Boisseau) Calhoun and the house next passed to the Calhoun family. Will Perrin in the 1930s wrote two articles for the *Press and Banner* about social events at his Aunt Sallie Norwood Calhoun's when he was a young boy. One, in Aug., 25, 1932., under the title "Memories" related an incident which occurred there. *Mr. Wister Archer was the first male teacher I had. He had a vicious temper. Mr. Archer married while he was here a most attractive young lady from Richmond, bringing her here as a bride. They boarded with Mrs. E. B. Calhoun, who lived in the house now occupied by the Stark family. It was the custom at that time for the young men of the town to call on New Year's day on the young ladies of the place, going from house to house. Cake and wine was usually served at each place.*

At the home of Mrs. Calhoun were her two sisters, Misses Lila and Bessie Norwood, two of the popular and attractive ladies of the town, so of course most callers came there to wish them a Happy New Year, and Mrs. Archer being a bride, she and Mr. Archer received with them.

Among the callers was Mr. Tillman Wardlaw, one of the beaux of that day, a man of courtly manners and a charming conversationalist who was seated next Mrs. Archer, and in his inimitable manner began to pay her flowery compliments as the wine probably loosened his tongue they were probably more eloquent than usual. Mrs. Archer was quite as sprightly in her repartee. Mr. Archer, who was listening from another part of the room, suddenly jumped to

The Burt – Stark House

his feet, ran to the fireplace, knocked with all his force on the mantel, exclaimed in his angriest tones, 'Mr. Wardlaw, Mr. Wardlaw, this has gone far enough.' Immediately the room was thrown into confusion, the ladies crowded about Mr. Archer, hustled him out of the room and upstairs to his bedroom; all the while he was beating with his fist against the wall as he ascended the stairs and uttering imprecations against Mr. Wardlaw. The poor little wife humiliated beyond the power of expression. Mr. Wardlaw and his friends left immediately and in a short time one of the friends of Mr. Wardlaw appeared at the house with a note for Mr. Archer which proved to be a challenge to a duel; whereupon Mr. Archer wrote an apology to Mr. Wardlaw which closed the incident."

In the *Press and Banner,* June 29, 1933, in "The Hermit of Millwood, " he wrote about James Edward Calhoun, the wealthy and eccentric brother –in-law of John C. Calhoun. He noted that *the only nephew and nearest living relative of Mr. Calhoun was Mr. Edward Boisseau Calhoun, who married my aunt, Mrs. Sallie Norwood. . . When he was nearly ninety years old he made occasional trips to Abbeville, about twenty miles from Millwood, coming in a schooner (covered wagon) until he reached the outskirts of the town when he would mount his horse which had been led behind the wagon and gallop through the streets to give the impression that he had ridden the entire distance from Millwood on horseback. On these visits he stayed at the home of his nephew, Mr. E. B. Calhoun, and I have been present on occasions which he would make a young daughter of the house, Cuddie Calhoun, play some kind of jig on the piano when he would take her twin sister, Saudee, to dance with him, holding her at arms length he would piroutte about the floor in a stiff jointed manner. He said he was dancing the ' Spanish fandango.'*

The *Press and Banner,* Feb 22. 1894, announced that *Misses Cuddie and Saidee Calhoun will open a dancing school soon at their residence, for the younger set of boys and girls.* On Dec. 12, 1894. The *Press and Banner* carried the sad news of *Death of Miss Cuddie Calhoun. The beloved daughter of Mr. E. B. Calhoun died at the family homestead at the village at noon on Friday Dec. 7, 1894. She had been a great sufferer for many weeks of disease* [unnamed]. *Funeral service in the Episcopal church and buried by relatives.* The grave marker lists her name as "Martha Maria Calhoun."

About a year later, Jan. 22, 1896. the same paper reported that *tomorrow at the home of Mr. and Mrs. E. B. Calhoun, Mr. A. M. Schoen and Miss Saidee L. Calhoun will be married by the Rev. Edward McCrady. The ceremony will be performed at eleven o'clock in the morning. The happy pair will leave at once via the S. A. L. for a month's stay in the land of Flowers. Only the relatives of*

The Burt - Stark House

the contracting parties will be present. Miss Calhoun is one of Abbeville's most beautiful and accomplished daughters and has many friends not only at her home, but all over the State. Mr. Shoen is a polished and affable gentleman, a native of Richmond, Va. He is a civil engineer on the G. C. & N. made this place his home for sometime. After the road was completed he took a course in electrical engineering, and as a proof that he is at the top of his profession he has a responsible and lucrative position with Eastern Tariff Association, as electrical expert, with headquarters in Atlanta, Ga.

The *Press and Banner*, March 4, 1903. reported that *last week the old historic Burt – Calhoun mansion was sold to Mr. J. S. Stark of this city for the sum of 5,500 dollars.*[**Old Abbeville** mistakenly says 1913] On Oct. 8, 1902, the *Press and Banner* had reported that "J. S. Stark offers house I now occupy for Sale. Can give possession Oct 1 – also I want the public to know thatI am in the stock business now and hereafter. J. S. Stark."

On June 11, 1903, the *Press and Banner* commented on "The Stark Mansion. The old Burt House famous for the last meeting of the Confederate cabinet, has been bought by J. S. Stark and he now occupies it as a residence. It has been painted and is wonderfully improved in appearance. It is snow white in color and the contrast with the green foliage of the surrounding trees is beautiful. There is not a modern dwelling house in town that will compare with this "mansion" in appearance.. Mr. Stark is a man of approved taste which has been shown in the way he has improved that place." Like the Calhouns before the Starks had twin girls but no other children. Like the Calhouns one of the twins married in the Burt-Stark house

The *Press and Banner*, Dec. 5,1927, carried the following story: *Wedding of Miss Frances Evelyn Stark to Mr. John Wesley McKee on Dec.4 at the home of the bride's parents by former pastor of Abbeville Baptist Church, Rev. Lamoreaux. . The spacious interior of the stately and historic old home, with its antique furnishings and its simple but effective arrangement of Smilex, pink Briarcliff roses and lighted pink tapers afforded a lovely setting for the event. In the ceremony room the bridal colors of green and white were used in the decorations. Forming an improvised altar before which the vows were spoken were two white pedestals, gracefully entwined with smilex and asparagus fern and adorned with handsome silver candelabra each holding five lighted tapers,*

Just before the ceremony, Mrs. W. E. Johnson played two piano selections, "To a Wild Rose" and "To a Water Lily" by McDonald and while the ceremony was being performed Shubert's Serenade was softly rendered."

Mr. J. W. McKee, Jr., a native of Abbeville County (Arborville) had been there about five years . . The *Press and Banner* on March 17, 1927. noted an

The Burt – Stark House

"announcement yesterday by Mr. J. W. McKee the first shipment of,Chevrolet cars are now on the road and are expected to arrive in Abbeville during the latter part of the week. Mr. McKee to be connected with the agency here & E. F. Arnold Co. (formerly Ford dealer)."

On March 18, 1937. The *Press and Banner* carried the following sad story: "John Wesley McKee, prominent Abbeville automobile dealer, died here Tuesday morning at 9:30 from pistol wounds. He had been in ill health for several months. Mr. McKee went into the bathroom of his house and a few minutes later a pistol shot was heard. A physician was called and Mr. McKee was found slumped to the floor with a pistol by his side. The news of his untimely death brought sorrow to the entire city.

" He was among the most progressive of Abbeville's citizens and was known throughout the section.. From young manhood was connected in some way with sale or manufacture of automobiles. . . . was head of the McKee Chevrolet company at the time of his death. He was married ten years ago to Miss Fannie Stark and since that time had made his home in the Burt house, the home of his father-in-law, Mr. J. S. Stark. He was a member of the Methodist church but attended the Abbeville Baptist Church with Mrs. McKee."

Fannie's twin sister, Mary married Dr. T. L. Davis and lived in Tennessee until 1945. The *Press and Banner*, Feb. 8, 1945 carried the following story: *Dr. T. L. Davis To Make Home Here. Dr. Thomas Lyles Davis, who had made his home in Chattanooga for a number of years in the practice of eye, ear, nose and throat medicine has retired and has come to Abbeville to make his home. He is a son-in-law of J. S. Stark who at Christmas time presented Dr. Davis and Mrs. Davis with one of his Flatwoods farms, and the doctor is enthusiastically launched on the direction of farming.*

" *In the Flatwoods farm there are seven hundred acres, with nine tenants and usually yields around one hundred bales of cotton. . There are fifty head of white face cattle on the farm and last year there was sold six hundred dollars of hay, reserving enough to feed ten mules and fifty cows. In 1944 he made five hundred bushels of corn. There are fifty acres of original forest on the Flatwoods farm.* Unfortunately. Dr. Davis' farming career was cut short with his death of Oct, 1947. His widow Mary Stark Davis had reached the age of 103 when she died at the Burt-Stark house.

Slaves and Masters: The Slave Experience in an Ante-Bellum Upcountry South Carolina District (Abbeville)

Next to church and family, slavery was the most important institution in the life of the people of Abbeville District during the century which followed the first white settlement. By 1860, almost two-thirds of the people of the district were slaves, and two-thirds of the free families owned slaves. During the 1850s, almost two-thirds of the people of the district were slaves, and two-thirds of the free families owned slaves. During the 1855 Fourth of July celebration at the Marshall House in Abbeville, the leading citizens followed a sumptuous meal with toasts to "the Day We Celebrate,: "the Memory of George Washington"; "the Memory of John C. Calhoun (drank standing up and silently)," "the Union," and "the Constitution ." The sixth toast was to "the Institution of Slavery: Sanctioned by Religion and Policy. Its preservation, at all hazards, is essential to the interests of the South.."

What were the beginnings of slavery in the district? One fanciful version was given by W. Pinckney Starke in his "Account of Calhoun's Early Life," which was published by the American Historical Association in 1899 as a preface to a collection of the great statesman's letters in its annual report. Starke grew up in the area, and he was probably relating a local or family tradition when he wrote, *On returning home from his legislative duties in Charleston, Patrick Calhoun brought home on horseback behind him a young African, imported in some English or New England vessel. The children in the neighborhood, and perhaps many of the adults, had never seen a black man. Mr. Calhoun gave him the name of Adam, and in good time got a wife for him. At the time of John Caldwell's birth, Adam had a family coming on, one of whom, named Sawney, was a playmate for Mr. Calhoun's boys.*

A half century later, Robert L. Meriwether in his study of the settlement of this area estimated that there were approximately 300 slaves in the South Carolina backcountry in 1756 when the Calhouns first migrated to the Long Canes. He thought that these slaves were principally brought into these lands from the low country, but some were brought down by the settlers from Virginia. The colonial authorities did not wish to encourage the importation of slaves into the backcountry because of security problems, and the South Carolina General Assembly excepted slaves from the fifteen year tax exemption given new settlers in the frontier region.

Yet even before the first settlers brought in slaves, there were earlier slaves who had been the porters and other servants of the Indian traders, and sometimes these traders settled on farms. One such example was John Vann who settled on the east side of the Savannah across from the mouth of Georgia's Broad River. In 1751, even such a seasoned frontiersman as James Francis of Ninety Six described Vann's companions, three Negroes, a mulatto (apparently free), and a

Slaves and Masters

half-breed Indian, all so unsavory "that there is not three families on Saludy would suffer any of them to remain four and twenty hours on their plantation." In the summer of 1781, it was reported that Indians had stolen some Negro slaves and in other instances "seduced" them to run way from their owners. Some of the runaways told the Cherokee leaders "that there was in all the Plantations many more Negroes than white people, and that for the sake of Liberty they would join them."

In November, 1751, Governor James Glen negotiated a treaty with the Cherokees which provided that "if any Negro or mulatto [sic] shall desert from his master and shall fly to the Cherokee country, the Indians shall do their utmost Endeavor to apprehend him, and shall deliver them to some of our Traders or bring him to Charles Town for which they shall have a Reward, and no Trader shall carry into the Indian country any Negro or other slave. Still four years after the first Cherokee War, a low country clergyman noted in his journal in September, 1764 that he had heard from his Long Canes friends who "have now a great company of negroes among them. . . and are very much exposed to both the Creek and Cherokee Indians."

During the years of the American Revolution, the backcountry slaves often proved pawns in the struggle or simply victims. For example, in one of the first violent incidents, the Cherokees in July, 1776 killed five Negro slaves as well as five of the children of Captain Aaron Smith who lived on Little River a short distance below the Indian Boundary. Tories sometimes stole the settlers' slaves, especially when their owners were away in service to the patriot cause. A tradition which came down in the Calhoun family dealt with one of Patrick Calhoun's slaves who was supposed to have formerly been an African prince. When Calhoun's slaves were seized and carried off to St. Augustine, the ex-prince escaped and returned to the Calhoun Settlement. He told the Calhouns where their other slaves were being held and went back with them to retrieve them "except the man who told the Tories where they could find the slaves whom Mr. Calhoun had hid in a swamp."

Like other patriots, the Rev. John Harris had his slaves stolen away by the Tories who transported them to Florida. Mary E. Davis wrote that in this incident *a negro woman was chased by them for three days with her child in her arms. At last she was caught and carried to the Indian nation, but made good her escape, leaving her child behind. The child was finally rescued by Colonels Pickens and Anderson, and is still [1862] living.*

Slaves and Masters

In another case, soon after the Revolution, Robert Anderson recovered two slaves who had been taken from Martha McCoy, widow of an Indian trader, by tracking them down in Virginia. He had bought the rights to them. In a third incident, he went into Georgia to recover several slaves which were stolen during the war, and later he engaged in a prolonged dispute in equity court with Joseph Calhoun over their ownership.

Although a number of slave holders in Abbeville District emigrated in the 1780's, such as Andrew Pickens and Robert Anderson, at the time of the first federal census (1790), there were 333 heads of family who owned slaves. This was approximately one fourth of the 1,338 families in the district. One fourth (87) of the slave holders owned only one slave, and another one fourth (96) owned two or three slaves. The one-sixth (56) with the most slaves held half of the total. Richard A. Rapley, the Commissioner in Equity and an English born lawyer, owned the highest total (57); and he was followed by Davis Moore with 39, James Lincoln, Esq. with 33, and Patrick Calhoun, Esq. with 31. Seventh with 25 was Adam Craine Jones, Esq., who like James Lincoln had been a delegate to the South Carolina Convention which ratified the new United States Constitution (they both voted against it).

In the 1800 census, there were 604 slave holding families out of 1,827 white families, and there were nearly three thousand slaves (2,964) in the district. Almost half of the slave holders (278) held only one or two; at the opposite end of the spectrum, the top hundred held about half of the total. Rapley was still the leader with 58, followed by William Shaw, another English born lawyer who lived at Cambridge.

One of the slave holders (with only one slave), the Rev. Alexander Porter, in 1814 led a colony of approximately 170 from the Lower Long Cane and Cedar Spring and Due West congregations to Preble County, Ohio because of their opposition to slavery. In 1805, the Rev. Robert Wilson, pastor of the district's largest and most influential church, the Upper Long Cane Presbyterian Church, also left for Ohio because he found "highly distressing" the reopening of the slave trade by the South Carolina legislature and thus felt that would "render the prospect of usefulness in the ministry (in my view) very small." Wilson later served as president of Ohio University in Athens.

Slave holders were faced with the question of whether they could free some of their favorite slaves. Unfortunately, the manumission records of the district were lost, but some evidence survived in probate records. State laws made this difficult. For example, when James Brownlee died in 1802, his will left his property, including two slaves, to his wife for a life estate. He asked that his two sons, George and Joseph, emancipate the slaves at their mother's death.

Slaves and Masters

Their sister Nancy and her husband William Richey were mindful of this provision in her father's will, and since they were leasing the slaves (now three in number) when Mrs. Brownlee died, they claimed ownership on the basis of an 1800 state law which disallowed emancipation except by legislative act and provided that illegally freed slaves could be seized. Their action, taken on the advice of John C. Calhoun, then practicing law in Abbeville, was upheld by the courts.

Edward Hooker, a Yale graduate who came to teach at Cambridge (a state college which operated for a short time near Ninety Six), attended a local July 4th celebration in 1806, and he was struck by an irony. Later he wrote in his journal, "The tables were served by Negro slaves under the superintendent of the managers. What an incongruity? An Independence dinner for freemen and slaves to wait upon them – I couldn't keep the thought out of my mind the whole time I was there feasting."

If such thoughts occurred to any of the natives, they were not expressed. A steadily increasing percentage of them became slave holders. By the time of the census of 1810, the number of slave holding families had increased to 857. and the slave total in the district was 6,672. In 1820, for the first time two of the districts' planters reported 100 or more slaves; Charles W. Bulagh held 122 and Richard Rapley held 100. In March, 1823, the administrator of Rapley's estate inventoried his slaves who then numbered 90. Twenty three were listed individually; the rest were arranged in eighteen family units. All were listed by name followed by birthday (except for eight whose age was given by years) and assessed value. The oldest was about 78, the youngest who was named Rapley was only nine days old.

In 1820, there were 1200 slave owners in the district who held a total of 13,106 slaves. By 1840, the number of slaves surpassed the white population by 13, 148 to 13,880, and in 1850, there were 1600 slaves owners with a total of 19,262 slaves. Reuben Robertson, a free black who lived at the mouth of Turkey Creek in Abbeville District, held 50 slaves in 1850, the most of any free black in South Carolina, and only 51 of the 1,300 slave owners in the district owned more than 50 slaves. Ten owners held above 100 slaves, fifty four held about 50 slaves, and one (George McDuffie) held above 200 (202).

Slaves and Masters

McDuffie had earlier experimented with supplying slave labor for William Gregg's textile factory at Vaucluse (near Aiken), and he became known as a proponent of the use of slave labor in manufacturing. He was known as a generous slave master. An observer in 1840 testified that McDuffie was careful not to overwork his hands, and even in the busy seasons he reported that he had seen "some of the most active of them returning from the field and the completion of their tasks at 3 o'clock in the afternoon (March 19, 1840). In 1856, at the settlement of McDuffie's estate, his 210 slaves were sold in lots to a Western planter for $140,000. His friends were gratified that his slaves were not divided.

The McDuffie slave prices illustrated how the value of slaves had risen by the 1850's. When Rapley's slaves were valued in 1823, the average value was only about $200. F. P. Robertson, who often served as auctioneer for the district slave sales (which were held along with the other estate and public sales the first Monday in each month at the court house), reported to the *Banner* in 1859 that in 1845 at the sale of the estate of Major Broyles, he sold 35 Negroes, including a distiller, two shoe makers, two house girls, two weavers and seamstresses, two blacksmiths, a good cook, two wagoners, and a number of fully grown and likely field hands at an average price of $449, less than half the average price which slaves were bringing fourteen years later. In 1857, the *Banner* noted that a thirteen year old girl brought $1300. In January, 1860, the 90 slaves of the W. W. Belcher's estate sold for an average of a $1,000. *The Independent Press* pointed to what it called "the tall prices" which district slaves were bringing, and commented that "it shows what we have often asserted, that the howl and rant of 'abolitioners' abroad can never affect the confidence of our people on the stability of the institution."

A citizen of "education and intelligence" wrote J. Foster Marshall, the district's state senator, in 1856 in support of a move to reopen the slave trade. *Slavery,* he wrote, *is quite indispensable to Southern civilization. . . . As the best type of labor for our climate, I know that you will appreciate it as a heaven-sent agency in the growth and culture of the great staples of the country. Slavery exists of right and necessity, because it harmonizes with the teachings of both natural and revealed religion. . . . Would to God that I may live to see the day, when every freeman can sit at leisure under his own vine and fig tree, and listen to the merry song of his slave while doing the labors of the field..* During the 1850's the natural increase in the district's slave population was five times that of the white population. In 1853, for example, the excess of births over deaths for the slaves was 393, for the whites it was only 75..

Slaves and Masters

As the black population came to double that of the whites, the latter became uneasy about rumors of slave uprisings. In the Spring of 1851, Samuel Agnew, a student at Erskine College, noted in his diary reports of a "rising among the blacks" in Abbeville. His father, a Due West physician, later served as a juror in the trial which followed, and he recorded what his "Pa" said about the case. The Abbeville newspaper reported that three slaves were found guilty of "counseling [slaves] to run away," and the jury sentenced Austin, a slave of Mrs. Allen, and Asa, a slave of T. E. Owen, to 150 lashes, administered at the rate of 24 every other day, followed by banishment from the state. Taffy, a slave of John White, was given only 25 lashes and discharged. He was judged guilty only of being in bad company and under the influence of liquor. *The Banner* reported that there was much feeling in Abbeville that the two leaders clearly planned an uprising, and the public was upset that they were not executed..

Sometimes rumors appeared to have been without basis. For example, in January, 1861, an Erskine College student from North Carolina wrote a friend back home that *during Christmas time there was a great deal of excitement here in town* [Due West]. *An insurrection was expected on the week before Christmas . . . There was 15 negroes arrested and put in jail. Also a white man who was supposed to be at the head of the business.*

The fear of slave uprisings reached a peak in the immediate pre-war years. *The Independent Press* in October, 1857 observed that intemperance was on the increase among the Negroes in the community, *and they assuredly have facilities for procuring liquor which did not exist formerly. We have been credibly informed that there are several places within the corporate limits where liquor is positively retailed by negroes. . . at any time they can procure orders signed by white men to the grocer. We advise masters to look into this if they do not wish their negroes ruined. This is infinitely worse than downright abolitionism.*

In 1858, the new town council was elected on a wet or license platform; and, when whiskey became legally available for whites, it also became quite accessible for slaves. In January, 1860, James M. Perrin wrote that "for twelve months past drunkeness has been a common evil among our negroes . . . . Scenes of riot and debauch have occurred in our streets, and even the sanctity of our churches have been invaded." Yet, it developed that the town council could only punish the offender, not "the source of the evil."

Thus near the end of 1859, an extra-legal group was formed when a number of "worthy and respectable citizens" of the village resolved themselves into the Abbeville Vigilance Committee. This committee claimed two objectives: "1st.

Slaves and Masters

To prevent improper meddling with our slaves by suspicious persons" and "2d. To prevent the liquor traffic with them." The committee sent Perrin to talk with J. & W. Knox, the liquor dealers in the village, to inform them of the evils of "the order system" and to ask them as "good citizens" to close down their cellar from sundown to sunrise, to sell spirituous liquors to no Negro on any man's order, and to sell to no "irresponsible, worthless white man." The Knox brothers complied with his request, but "some of the good people of the country" complained. Perrin's answer was, "To you in the country it is a small matter to ride a few miles to purchase in person the liquor you wish. To the citizens of this village it is a matter of vital importance to have their negroes sober and obedient."

In February, 1859, at Millway, a public meeting adopted resolutions proposed by Dr. J. W. Hearst "to ferret out all illicit traffic between white persons and negroes . . . [and proposed] that in paying our negroes for their crops of corn and cotton, or any other products of their labor--such as brooms, baskets, collars, etc.--we will in every instance accompany the money with a written order to trade to that amount and no more."

By this time the slave patrol came under increased pressure. In July, 1859, a former militiaman declared in a letter to the newspaper that "our slaves no longer fear the patrol and are permitted to roam where they please. We know plantations of negroes which have not been patrolled for years,". Mrs. Lydia Calhoun Starks told the WPA interviewer that she was "born in Avonville [Abbeville] S. C. and belonged to Mr. James Taggart who owned from 25 to 30 slaves, and he "wus jes' as nice ter 'em as he could be." Taggart would not allow the patrol to come on his plantation to whip his slaves, but Mrs. Starks said she could remember seeing "the ole overseer" on the plantation adjoining "jes' whipping dem po' ole slaves till dey couldn't even stan' up."

In October, 1859, a captain of a slave patrol in Abbeville was tried for shooting and wounding a Negro who was trying to escape. In charging the jury, the judge explained that the law did not allow the patrol to use a deadly weapon except in cases of self-defense. The defendant was convicted, but as the wound was slight and there were mitigating circumstances, the fine was only $5. (The same court also dealt with the case of two "respectable" physicians who disinterred the dead body of a Negro for the purposes of dissection. They plead guilty to the indictment, and alleged, in extenuation of the offense, that it was done with the design of advancing their professional knowledge, the Negro having been a patient of one of the two, and his disease presented some "peculiar symptom," so they were simply performing a post-mortem examination. The judge was sympathetic.

Slaves and Masters

In November, 1859, there was a citizens meeting in Abbeville to consider "a suspicious character in Abbeville named James L. Woods . . . with whom there was a woman who called herself his wife. Also a young man and one or two children." The town council had warned them to leave and they agreed, but later refused. Six citizens observed Woods talking with a slave "using certain incendiary language . . . and endeavoring to excite him to insurrection by expressing a hope that the negroes would rise, and murder every citizen of this place." They were arrested and taken before the magistrate who committed them to jail. In February, 1860, Charles Ward was lynched in Greenwood for tampering with the slaves of several citizens.

Slave owners often lived in fear of violence. When John Baxter Bull left his Willington plantation in 1846 on a business trip to Charleston, he advised his wife, "Be sure to have some good and decent white person with you always. Do not venture to stay alone." Bull might well have been influenced by what happened to his brother some seven years earlier.

On December 27, 1838, a servant found William A. Bull dead in the public road near his house, "killed as was supposed by a fall from his horse, as his foot was fastened in a stirrup." However, as his neighbor Mary Moragne wrote in her journal, "the poor creature had been *murdered* by his own Negroes during the night . . . [It was learned] that two of his Negroes fell upon him with clubs last night, as he was returning about nine o'clock from his usual visit to his plantation. They dispatched him with five or six ghastly wounds on the head, and then dragging him through the woods past his house, it appears that Dick, his body servant, brought them his horse ready saddled, and then placing his *right* foot in the *left* stirrup. . . . they dragged him along the road 'till the stirrup gave way."

On December 10, 1847, Leonard Wideman who lived in the lower Long Cane area was killed at night by his servants about a half mile from his home. He was choked and beaten to death. The servants moved his body some distance in an effort to make it appear as if he had been thrown by his horse and dragged for a time. Four of his Negroes were tried for the offense, and three were executed. Before he was hanged, one of them confessed that he and his two brothers had not only murdered their master, but that they had killed a former master. Wideman's estate administration showed that he owned 109 slaves.. In an apparent reference to this case, George McDuffie in January, 1848 wrote Henry H. Townes in Calhoun Mills about the execution of three slaves for killing their master. He said "they regard themselves as martyrs in the cause of liberty and say that they cheerfully die to better the condition of the other blacks on their plantation." In December, 1847, James L. Petigru, who had gotten some news about the case, commented in a letter to his sister at Badwell on Buffalo Creek near the Wideman plantation, "I could have wished more particulars of L. W.'s fate, at which I do not wonder. Even the lowest people may be raised by despair to the commission of great crimes." Petigru's nephew who edited this series of his letters added a note that "'L. W.' was a neighbor who had been murdered by his Negroes."

In the upper portion of the district in September, 1854, Jesse Maddox, overseer for Larkin Barmore, was killed by three of Barmore's slaves. He was killed with an ax, thrown into a creek, and then drug into the woods. Three slaves were implicated, but the youngest was reprieved. One of the other two fled the area for a few days, but was caught. They were hanged near Donnaldsville before a crowd estimated to be between 2,500 and 3,000 in number.

Slave execution followed a careful process. For example, the Abbeville *Banner* in April 1847 reported that "a Negro boy belonging to William Pratt is lodged in jail and will be hung on May 14 for burning the stable of Mr. John Clinkscales." However Judge David L. Wardlaw overturned the sentence, because "this [the State v. Giles, a slave of William Pratt] is a second trial, of which the proceedings are now before me, and I regret to perceive, that in a matter so important, as every matter affecting the life of a human creature must be, notwithstanding the plain directions given in the Magistrate Act of 1839; there are yet many and great errors in the proceedings." He ordered a new trial by Magistrate John Eli Ellis, Esq.. Others objected to the slow process of law. In the later issue of the *Banner* cited above, the editor complained that a slave of Faris [Phares] Martin, who had earlier been sentenced to imprisonment and whipping for striking his master, was being held but not whipped. He added, "Is this the proper way to have the laws respected and obeyed?".

In February, 1846, the Abbeville *Banner* reported that two Negroes belonging to Gen. McDuffie were killed on Friday last by two others who were acting in the capacity of drivers.. the murderers have been committed to jail, and will soon be put on trial, when all the facts in connection with it will be developed., In November, 1849, the Edgefield newspaper reported that one of the two slaves suspected of stealing a considerable quantity of gold dust from their master's gold mill," had died as a result of whipping by two young employees of William Dorn. James Coleman and Richard Griffin, the latter from Georgia, " in endeavoring to abstract the truth" from the slaves "did not nicely measure the extent of the punishment inflicted and the Negro died." The two men ran away to Georgia. It was an open secret that some white men

Slaves and Masters

carried on a very intimate relationship with slave women. Mrs. Lucy Haddon in her 1857 suit in equity for alimony vividly described the behavior of her husband, Abraham Wilson Haddon. He owned sixteen slaves, but her concern was primarily with his relationship with two domestic servants, as follows:

[She testified that] *her husband . . . has lavished his time, money and attention upon his domestic slaves, Cloe and Jane and upon lewd and unchaste white women in the immediate neighborhood to the great grievance of your Oratrix* [Mrs. Haddon], *and furthermore that for years past he has notoriously indulged his libidinous desires upon his said domestic slaves Cloe and Jane, kept them as his mistresses and by them has become the father of several children. . . . that in and about the year 1846, her said husband first gave evidence of his want of proper respect for her position and feelings as his wife as also of the actual perpetration of violence to and upon her person, that about the aforesaid year your Oratrix was in her kitchen superintending, as was her duty in preparation of breakfast for the family, that whilst so engaged she directed her cook Cloe (the kept mistress of her said husband) to remove her children who were about the fireplace and the cookery further away from the same, whereupon the said Cloe became vexed and in a loud voice began to insult your Oratrix by giving to her impudent and disrespectful speech during which her said husband entered the kitchen, espoused the cause of the said slave and not only ordered your Oratrix out of the said kitchen, but angrily seized her person, and with rudeness and violence threw your Oratrix out of the door of the kitchen, and then and there choked her to the great pain, injury and insult of your Oratrix and to the manifest delight of the said Cloe who was knowingly permitted by the husband of your Oratrix to laugh at and to treat with levity the insolent and undutiful conduct of her said husband, furthermore that soon thereafter and on another occasion your Oratrix was chastising the said Cloe, when she threatened your Oratrix to stamp her into the earth . . . . the said Cloe, encouraged and emboldened by the conduct of your Oratrix's said husband, and with his knowledge, procurement and approval repeatedly took and used the clothing of your Oratrix against her wishes and on two occasions in a fit of anger and passion tore the dresses from the person of your Oratrix. . . . [and] possessed herself against the wishes of your Oratrix of her keys, to wit, the keys of the house, closet, drawers and trunks, and made an improper and unwarrantable use of the same to the knowledge of your Oratrix's husband . . the keys . . . have been for the last five or six years in the sole custody and keeping of her said husband and his said slaves and mistresses Cloe and Jane . . . upon whom he has for a period of years lavished his caresses, his moneys and his time, and for whose sable embraces your Oratrix alleges and charges her said husband has left your Oratrix's bed repeatedly in the night time, preferring with them to luxuriate in his lusts and to revel in their caresses. Your Oratrix further alleges, avers and charges that by the slave Cloe her said husband is the father of four children and by the said slave Jane he is the father of one child, that with the said slaves he has for years past spent most of his time by day and by night.*

Sometimes old and helpless masters came to be entirely dependent upon their domestic slaves. One example is that of George McDuffie who in 1850 held 201 slaves, but whose declining health soon made him an invalid. The son of James H. Hammond remembered how McDuffie paid his father a visit at Redcliffe (below Aiken) "unexpectedly coming in a four horse carriage with no attendants except a negro woman and negro boy, who seemed to be leading him about the country as their fancy moved them."

An interesting and even bizarre case involved what was commonly called "the Tucker Will case;" and, even though Tucker lived in Laurens District, the case involved a large slave holder in the Flatwoods section of Abbeville District, W. W. Belcher who was suing to uphold the provisions of Tucker's will which would have given him the estate. The equity court record summarized the facts as follows:

Tucker was about eighty years of age, altogether unlettered, and of a mind, originally feeble, impaired by age and disease. . . . His neighbors dealt with him in small matters of trade, but usually through the agency and under the supervision of some of his slaves . . . in his small purchases . . . he asked for the articles of merchandise, but one of his slaves, generally George, would make the selection. He was unmarried and excessively fond of his slaves and indulgent to them; indeed, they fared better than he himself. . . . His slaves, especially George, had great influence over him and he anxiously desired their emancipation at his death. Of defendant Belcher, he knew nothing. . . except from the representations of George, in these particulars, apparently truthful, that Belcher was . . . the kind master of many slaves. George was a cabinet maker, and had worked at his trade for some years in the neighborhood of . . . Belcher, and had there taken a wife. . . . George was shrewd and intelligent, had been taught to read well, and he enjoyed the confidence of his master. . . in 1854, he drove his master . . . to the house of [a neighbor] Blakely, and producing the bill of sale of that date, in Belcher's handwriting, and $900 in bank bills, and Tucker acknowledging the previous payment of $100 to him by George, Blakely attested as a witness the mark of Tucker to the bill of sale, and delivered it to George. At the time, George said that $700 of the money belonged to himself, and that he had borrowed $200 from Belcher, and

Slaves and Masters

thereupon Tucker returned $200 to be repaid to Belcher, and Blakely, as Tucker's agent, took possession of $700. . . . [Another neighbor] *attested . . . two or three days after . . . he was sent for to Tucker's house, when Tucker said, in the presence of George, I wish you to draw a bill of sale to Belcher for my other slaves. I wish my negroes to be free at my death, and not to serve another; and George has told me that Belcher would befriend him and the other negroes by taking them to a free state. Witness said to George, you are Belcher's property, and George replied, I am not afraid; Belcher is too good a man not to do what he has said, and he will contrive a way for my escape. . . . Witness drew up a deed of gift from Tucker to Belcher of the former's land and negroes, and George, from his own money, paid $1.50 for the service, but the matter was not then consummated.*

[In June, Tucker] *executed a paper, purporting to be his last will . . . whereby he attempted to bestow his whole estate. . . upon Belcher, "a perfect stranger," also a bill of sale of all* [seven slaves] *remaining in his possession* [reserving a life estate] *. . . on the same day Tucker bought his burial clothes . . . selected by George. . .. George remained for about two years* [in Belcher's possession] *and disappeared . . He was much attached to his wife. There were reasons which induced her owners to give their active or tacit consent to her leaving the state. The defendant* [McKelvey, the administrator of Tucker's estate] *has no doubt she did so about April, 1856, and that George went with her (probably to Pennsylvania) . . . not in pursuance of any understanding . . .with Tucker. Tucker died in 1855, and his will was set aside. McKelvey, the administrator, was proceeding to sell the* [seven] *slaves.*

Belcher's bill versus McKelvey was dismissed, and the bills of sale to Belcher of 1854 were declared void under the South Carolina Act of 1841 to prevent emancipation. George and his wife, however, had already escaped..

Kenneth M. Stampp in his history , *The Peculiar Institution, Slavery in the Ante-Bellum South* (1956), gave prominent notice to another benevolent Abbeville slave holder, as follows:

John Clark, a small, obscure slave holder who lived in Abbeville District, South Carolina, provided a striking example of inconspicuous paternalism. Clark, a childless widower, resided on his estate "without the society of white persons." To his slaves, twelve in number, he was "indulgent to a degree hurtful to his pecuniary interest and he regarded them as objects of care and regard. His will stipulated that his slaves were to be kept together on his land, the proceeds from their labor used for their comfort and support. Clark's heirs contested the will on the grounds that it would emancipate the slaves illegally, but the probate court denied that it violated state law.

Slaves and Masters

This decision was as unique as the will that precipitated it. Masters who ignored the demands of discipline by flagrantly violating slave codes, who elevated their slaves to virtual freedom, who treated them with utter disregard for their status as property, and who strictly regulated their use when bequeathing them to heirs, are justly celebrated in the folklore of slavery. But they are celebrated because their conduct was so abnormal. Had other masters imitated them, the slave system would have disintegrated--and a nation might have been spared a civil war.

Stampp cited a WPA typescript of the district's *Judge of Probate Decree Book, 1839-1848*, and an examination of all of Clark's probate records reveals a somewhat different story. As Stampp noted, Clark did will twelve of his slaves to his nephew with the provision that they be kept together on his 273 acre farm. In addition, he made special provision for two older slaves (not included in the twelve above) Jesse and Jinny to whom he gave his bed, bedstead, and furniture. He asked that his nephew and the two friends whom he named as executors manage the estate with the proceeds "to be supplied to the support of the said two old Negroes and also for the comfort and the support of the other Negroes named above (the twelve willed to his nephew). In addition, in a provision not noted by Stampp who apparently had not seen the full text of the will, he declared, "I will that my negro man Jack, his wife Louise and son Washington and also my negro man Andrew, William, and Charles be sold. . . those having wives not to be sold far from them and also having regard to good masters."

It must be noted that Belcher and Clark's generosity toward their favored slaves was not unique. According to the traditions of the Lesley family, David Lesley, who became the Ordinary (judge) of Abbeville District in 1841, saw a house on a journey up the Hudson River valley, and he sent his slave carpenter, Cubic, on horseback up to New York to survey the house. Cubic and his fellow slaves then built the house in Abbeville which later became locally famous as the Burt-Stark House in which President Jefferson Davis held his last Confederate war council in May, 1865 .

Slaves most commonly appeared in wills and estate settlements as the bulk of a deceased person's personal property, often as much as 80 to 90% of the total. Also, the wills sometimes indicated the dying master's concern for the fate of his favorite slaves. For example, in 1821, John Campbell requested that his children not separate husbands and wives in the sale of his slaves and that his "house woman" Cloe have the liberty to choose her own master.. Cador Gantt, a Baptist minister, in 1846 asked "that his negro woman Phillis be left as free as the laws of the country will admit of and $50 and a guardian for her

Slaves and Masters

government." Williamson Norwood, the fourth largest slave holder in the district in 1840, in his will on July, 1848 wrote, *I am extremely desirous of setting free my negro woman Rachael and her children Ashbury and Catherine also Delia and her child Malancton but as the laws of the State do not at present permit me to do so I give the said negroes in trust to my son James for their use and benefit requesting he will see carefully to their interest and benefit and if opportunity should offer to the education of the children as he may think best by removing them or any of them to the free states.*

Perhaps the most gentle of all the slaveholders in the district were the Petigru family, James L. Petigru and his sisters, Mrs. Jane G. North and Miss Mary Petigru. The latter two lived at the family homestead, Badwell, in the lower part of the district; and, although James L. Petigru's law practice and family kept him primarily at Charleston, he still maintained a great interest in Badwell. He was philosophically opposed to slavery, but his practical concern was to be a good master. On Christmas, 1835, he wrote, *the only thing to flatter my vanity as a proprietor is the evidence and striking improvement in the moral and physical condition of the negroes since they have been under my administration. When I took them they were naked and destitute. Now there is hardly one that has not a pig, at least, and with few exceptions, they can kill their own poultry when they please.*

Tom and Prince were inherited by Petigru's mother from her brother Joseph Gibert. About four years after her death, Prince, whose wife belonged to a neighbor, came to Petigru and said that as he had been a faithful servant, he wished to be free, and he was freed in 1830. When Tom was asked if he wished to be freed, he replied that he preferred his present lot. So with his wife and children, he was always a privileged resident at Badwell with his own house, field, pony, cow, pigs, chickens and also "his jug." At his death, his grave was placed in the family cemetery with a tombstone marked with a warm tribute inscribed on it to him "as a friend" who was "buried like a Christian."

Petigru's sisters indicated a similar concern for their servants in 1860 when they were forced by hard times on the farm at Badwell to decide to sell Isaac, the coachman. Mary Petigru wrote her sister Adele Petigru Allston at Georgetown (wife of ex-Governor R. F. W. Allston), "I ask'd the boy if he is willing to be sold to you as a coachman he said quite willing, as well he might be, he has proved himself so far, an uncommonly good and valuable servant." Jane G. North also wrote to urge the sale, because "I would like for you to have the boy, it w'd be promotion for him and I think he would make a good servant for you, and he is willing to go, has no wife."

Mrs. North's servants sometimes took advantage of her soft rule. As she wrote her neighbor, John B. Bull, one of them named Felix had a wife and four children, but had got "into the habit of running about the country to the neglect of his family at home." She had found that he spent half of his time on Bull's place and even kept half of his clothes there "in charge of a woman called Louisa." She requested that her neighbor take measures *to prevent his being so well received on your place--I have told him that he must give up this sort of life, and he promises fair but that is all--he does not know of my writing to you and it would be better perhaps if he did not know it and took the prohibition as coming from you--it will certainly be more effectual, for he thinks it right to evade my orders whenever he can.*

In November, 1858, the Calhoun Mills Agricultural Society which was composed of some of the largest slave holders in the district engaged in a discussion of the subject, "The Management of Negroes." A committee which included President Armistead Burt and Secretary Octavius T. Porcher was appointed to produce a report which was a summary of the discussion. The report noted that although "there was a division of sentiment and diversity of practice in reference to nearly all the details," there was clear agreement about the evils of "running about at night: and "promiscuous intercourse of the sexes" among slaves. The conclusion was that "we know of no greater safeguard against this than the sacredness of the marriage relation which should be encouraged among them as much as possible."

This subject was often in the minds of masters. In 1859, James L. Petigru wrote his daughter, "I was rendered very sorry by a letter on Saturday from one Clinkscales, who says he has Sammy's wife, and rather than part them offers to buy or sell, the wife would be of no use to me and I have no right to sell Sammy, for he belongs to Ma, and I more than doubt whether she would be as willing to make a sacrifice for the marriage union as I." The following year his sister Mary wrote from Badwell that the family servants "are very quiet more so than usual I think," and she described the preparations for a slave wedding which she pronounced "quite a great occassion [sic]."

Slaves and Masters

William Hunter, an ex-slave living in Arkansas told a WPA interviewer that his mother came for *Abbeville, S. C., a Negro trading point. When she was put on the stand my father went to McBride* [his master] *and asked him to buy that woman for him a wife. He said she was a might pretty young woman.* McBride *bought her. . . My mother was mixed with the white race. She was a bright Woman.*

Professor John G. Clinkscales in his affectionate picture of the slaves on his father's plantation near Antreville, *Down on the Old Plantation* told the story of one runaway from the plantation named Essex. Essex lost in a contest with his fellow slave, Griffin, a teamster, for the hand of "Little Cindy." He was so disappointed, as he later told his master, that he might have tried to kill Griffin if he had not run away. At any rate, he stayed away for three years hiding along the Savannah River above Augusta. Eventually, a slave girl on a plantation which he visited at night betrayed him in a fit of jealousy, and he was lodged in jail. Back home, the Clinkscales family remembered him saying, "Dat gal tell on me. . . . I could fool de dogs, but when dat yaller gal tell dem white folks, dey trap me." Essex managed to regain his status with his old master who later made him the foreman on the plantation.

Runaways were a common feature of slavery in the district. Mary Moragne wrote in her journal on April 24, 1837, *this morning Will was brought home, after an absence of seven weeks, having been taken by Mr. Cobb at Abbeville Co. H. yesterday evening. He came straight to my mother, whose gentle heart he well knew, and plead for mercy. She couldn't forgive the puppy, but she begged hard for him,, and he was let off with 50 lashes.* In September, 1841, she noted that her brother had flushed a runaway from their strawpen and sent for 'the slave dogs,' but the dogs finally lost the track."

M. E. Hollingsworth in a memoir written about his ante-bellum childhood remembered that Alex Connor's two sons, Bill and John, owned the only 'negro dogs' in the Abbeville area. He noted that the Connor dogs had a ferocious reputation and were supposed to be able to track down runaways even if they hid among the other slaves in the fields. Few slaves were willing to risk possible death. Hollingsworth knew of only one successful case, that of Ned, a slave of Mrs. Fanny

Slaves and Masters

Allen, who ran away during the war to the Yankee lines and returned after emancipation.

Hollingsworth also wrote that a few months before the surrender in 1865, three slaves, charged with rebellion against their master, Alex Conner, were tried by a Mr. McClinton, a trial justice, and executed at the seven mile post on the Snake Road below Abbeville near the Connor place. In addition, he also said that a few months before the Confederate surrender, three Negroes were taken from the jail in Abbeville to a point near Island Ford and executed for the murder of an old man named McClinton.

In the *Press and Banner*, January 26, 1916, Hollingsworth recalled a practice which he saw during the Civil War in the town of Abbeville in which slave speculators brought their cargoes in "very large covered wagons. . . They were brought into town like droves of cattle, horses and mules, and sold, battered or exchanged.. The women and children rode in these wagons, while the boys and men walked. There were from two to four men at the tongue to guide, while a long chain was fastened to the end, as there were breast chains, not single trees, as now used, and the men strung out on either side of the chain, did the pulling. . . They usually remained two or three weeks, or sufficiently long to sell or exchange those brought for others, and would frequently leave with about the same number. . . If an owner here had a delicate slave or an unruly one, or for any other cause, they were taken to the camp to sell or exchange just as is now done on the bone yard. The value of a slave was lessened if it was known they were purchased from a speculator.)

Annie Groves Scott at the age of 93 told a WPA interviewer that she had been born in 1845 at "Lyonsville, S. C. (Lowndesville) and that her parents belonged to "Squire Tom Grant" (Gantt). Mrs. Scott recalled how well she was treated as a young girl and raised up with her owner's sons Dick and Larry Gantt. However, she also told about how her *"Uncle Bill Grant [sic] schemed out to run off and got as far as the river [the Savannah], but the water was high and he couldn't get across it. He hid around the brush and pretty soon the hounds was after him, and the patrollers, too, with bull whips that they carried all the time. Anyway,*

Slaves and Masters

them hounds track Uncle Bill to the river and smell him out where he is hiding. They tell about it after they come back to tell Master Grant [sic] his slave is dead. "They dogs got him," one of the men say, "they got him so good he is tore to pieces..

R. R. Hemphill in a memoir about his boyhood referred to a tradition of a attempted runaway at Due West in the 1850's. A poor white man, whom he recalled was known simply as "Tennessee" Wilson, made a coffin, put a slave in it, and set out on a wagon to carry the slave to freedom in the North. He was caught and never returned to Due West On the eve of the Civil War, the Abbeville papers reported an incident in which authorities found a cave in the upper part of the district with cooking utensils and provisions stored in it. A watch soon discovered two slaves belonging to Dr. Yarborough and T. C. Perrin, and, when they attempted to get away, both were shot and one was killed.

Newspapers regularly ran notices of rewards for runaways, and sometimes the ads were revealing about both the slaves and their masters. Two striking examples were the following:

$20 Reward for a runaway from Abbeville, the property of Susanna Hill, a negro man named Gabriel. He is of bright complexion, quick spoken, has a scar on one of his cheeks, and has a piece of one of his ears bitten off. The forefinger of his right hand is stiff in two joints, toward the end. He went off about the last of March, 1838 with a white woman, who calls herself Sally Hunt, alias Sally Simpson. This woman had three little white girls with her. She and negro Gabriel can both write a good hand. The negro is a great gambler. Nelia Vines, Abbe., Jan. 26, 1839.

100 Dollars Reward. Runaway from the subscriber on the night of the 22d of April [1858], my negro boy Sam. Sam is about 25 years old and weighs 160 lbs., well developed about the hips, and is 5 feet, ten or eleven inches high, usually wore his hair twisted in strings. On examining his mouth (the cavity being one of the very largest) you will find one jaw tooth out, the clothes he wore off were really worn. Possibly he has a new Sunday suit, as he says he bought one on Christmas. Sam may be in the neighborhood of Due West. Mrs. Lindsay owns his father; or he may be in Elbert or Heart [Hart] Co., Ga., is well known in the Dark Corner, Anderson Dist. I will give $20 for the delivery of Sam on my farm, or $10 for confinement in any jail, so I may get him, or $100 for his head without the body, if it cannot be obtained otherwise. Lewis C. Clinkscales, Mountain View, S. C.

At least one slave owner used runaways for his own devious purposes. James L. Petigru in the Fall of 1861 wrote his daughter about the story of Daniel

Slaves and Masters

Neu (usually spelled New) and his slaves. New lived at the cross roads about five miles east of Badwell, and local tradition had it that he had once been a pirate. Petigru thought that in 1861 he owned a small farm and 15 slaves (the slave census of 1850 listed him as owner of 41 slaves). "His children of both colors grew up together in equal dirt and squalor," Petigru wrote. New always kept runaways at his farm; and at his trial in September, he openly boasted that "one nigger in the bush was worth three in the field." His slaves preyed on the neighborhood and stole cows, pigs, and even clothes off wash lines. When two of them were caught, the people of the neighborhood wished to lynch them, but Petrigru secured their indictment as nuisances and New for maintaining a public nuisance.

New obtained Edward Noble for his defense, but Petigru pursued the case through to conviction. New was ordered to sell his Negroes out of the state, and he himself given 30 days to leave the state. Petigru reported that although New made a display of moving some things across the Savannah River, his family stayed at the old place and it was said that he frequently returned.

Some slave masters devised incentives to encourage their slaves to work. "Ninety Six" described such a system on his Cambridge farm in 1839, as follows:

*Yesterday morning at broad daylight, my hands (20 in number) entered the cotton field. The result at night, weighed by my overseer, in the presence of Mr. H. and myself, was 3,302 pounds net cotton, an average of 160 pounds per hand. . . . The premium was a gallon whiskey and a pound of tobacco. The officers of the day were Slim-sides and Mucklejohn. And I will venture to say no two Indians ever acted with more caution in the selection of their combatants for a **ball play**, than did these two sable generals. I visited the field about sun rise. The generals, surrounded by their own soldiers, had posted themselves on opposite sides of the field. I could not hear a word, save now and then issuing from mouth of one of the commanders-in-chief. . . . At night, the prize was given to Muckle-john, and his brave boys, in the 'midst of shouts, hurrahs, hallooing, singing and dancing; while mortification and distress seemed depicted in the countenance of the vanquished party. Poor Slim-sides (I was sorry for him) preemptively refused to drown his deep-felt sorrow, with 'a drop o' whiskey, o' tautingly offered him by his victorious opponent.*

Whiskey was a dangerous tool. Mary Moragne noted that her father's overseer secured a gallon of whiskey for a log rolling. When the hands began their work, the overseer began to drink the whiskey himself, and when dusk came and the slaves were fed and began their "ball," their master of ceremonies was drunk. He did arouse himself at 9 p. m. when he gave the slaves warning of the "patrol" which caused the dancers "to scatter through the hollow like wild fire."

Mary Moragne's own concern for her family's slaves was in sharp contrast to that of the family's overseer. When she went through a religious experience in June, 1839, she was walking alone and came upon two older black women at work in her mother's field. "One of them asked me what I had been doing there; the other said she hoped I had been out in the wilderness to pray--that it was time I was seeking a *home* and that was the right way to seek it." When she told them that she had, the two began to testify to their own religious experiences, and Mary left them thinking that "they too were my sisters."

Four months later, Mary Moragne attended a Methodist camp meeting and was disgusted by "the moaning and screaming" of the Negroes and found that they kept this up until daybreak. In September, 1841, Mary heard a Negro at the slave quarters singing "Come humble sinner in whose breast." He was singing from a song book, and he would stop when he came to a hard word, and not begin again until he had mastered it. It led her to write in her journal, "He has taught himself to read and though he is considered the worst negro on the plantation, he may yet be a chosen vessel of grace." This thought led her to add, "Every day of my life I only weep and mourn that I am able to do nothing for the souls of these poor creatures. They are so separated from us by the forms of society that it seems impossible for me to get at the opportunity of instructing them--and 'alas' we have such a diffidence in speaking of these things."

The churches of the district consistently tried to develop the moral discipline of their black members. The Turkey Creek Baptist Church minutes recorded the experience of one church. On October 6, 1777, "Br[other] Dick an ethiopian offered, was received, next day baptised [sic], and took a seat with the brethren." Although cited several times for various acts of misbehavior, Dick remained an active member until January 9, 1808, when he was charged with having "married a second wife while first was still living--publicly excluded." On May 11, 1822, one of Turkey Creek's slave members was cited with absenting himself from his master, and again in December, 1827, the congregation excluded Jack for "absconding from his master, it not being his first offense of this kind."

In the Turkey Creek church, blacks were more often the subjects of discipline than whites. On October 11, 1823, the church minutes noted that "some difficulty existed among Robert Robertson's black people," and the congregation appointed a committee to inquire about it and to settle it. On November 1, 1824, the committee reported that it had been settled. In April,

Slaves and Masters

1829, there were charges against a black member, Ned, and when Ned's owner would not let him come to the church to answer the charges, the church sent a member to see his owner. The result was the exclusion of Ned for passing counterfeit money and disobedience to the church.

The Little River Baptist church in the upper portion of the district had similar problems with its black members. On December 18, 1830, it recorded that "our black Brother Jim is charged with knowing of his fellow servant stealing from his master and not informing his master of the same." At its next business meeting, the congregation on January 15, 1831, "took up the charge against our black brother Jim and acquitted him of the charge." On May 11, 1827, the congregation received "a report against our black brother Reuben" and appointed two members to investigate. Two months later on July 14, 1827, it reported that "the case of Reuben being charged with threatening to give his young mistress a good whipping and calling her a bad name and his persisting in an evil spirit for which cause he is excluded."

The churches were also interested in teaching the Bible to the slaves. When South Carolina made it illegal to teach slaves to read, the Rev. W. R. Hemphill and his congregations of the Cedar Spring's and Lower Long Cane Associate Reformed Presbyterian Churches petitioned for repeal of the law. Although no action was taken on this and similar petitions, Hemphill continued to instruct his single slave in the scriptures despite some unspecified threats by authorities to charge him with violating the law. In 1854, Robert A. Fair, Esq. addressed the Abbeville District Bible Society on the subject of "Educating our Slaves," and the society printed his address and distributed it.

The Rev. Jimmie Moore, Methodist, conducted a Sunday school class for little Negro boys. Since they could not read, Moore gave them questions and directed them to seek the correct answers by asking whites. On the next week he would catechize them. Many masters undertook to do the same. Mary Moragne noted how Dr. Moses Waddel, after he lost his mental powers, continued to try to catechize his servants even though he could not himself remember the correct answers.

The Rev. G. W. Moore, Methodist, and the Rev. John McLees, Presbyterian, were among those ministers who were appointed to preach to the slaves as domestic missionaries, and they agreed to divide the territory of the Savannah side of the district. In April, 1847, the Rev. McLees noted in his diary that he had pursued this work for a full year, but he could not be sure that his efforts had had any success.

During the excitement of the Compromise of 1850 debates, President R. C. Grier of Erskine College became involved in a controversy which resulted from his teaching the Bible to his slaves. The Rev. Grier rented one of his slaves named George to Lemuel Reid who lived south of Due West, and Mr. Reid overheard the slave tell his servants that just as surely as God had freed the people of Israel from their Egyptian masters, he would one day free them. Reid quickly reprimanded George and sent him home. Soon the incident led to several letters in the *Banner* about how a slave owner was teaching his slaves dangerous ideas. Grier defended himself against the charge that he was advocating abolition, but admitted that he was teaching his servants the Bible. One of his critics, James Fair of the Upper Long Cane Presbyterian Church and an early trustee of Erskine, maintained that it was "peculiary [sic] important the President of an Institution of learning in the South, should not only be sound on the question of slavery, but above suspicion."

The outcome was that George was tried and sentenced to 39 lashes, and, unless his owner sent him out of the state, he was to receive 300 more. The district sheriff who administered the lashes was A. C. Hawthorne, a Due West hotel keeper and long time Erskine trustee. Since he thought that "friends and patrons of Erskine would desire correct information," Grier gathered all the records of the affair and published a broadside "To the Public." He explained that his chief motive was to prevent harm to the college from an adverse public reaction.

George was exiled to Mecklenburg in North Carolina which was Grier's ancestral home. According to the Hemphill family tradition, Erskine professor W. R. Hemphill made a trip to Columbia and got a pardon from the governor, and George Grier was returned. to Due West.where he spent the rest of hi slife.

Seven years later, in a case in Abbeville involving murder among slaves, two of the most important lawyers in the area stood for the prosecution and defense. The *Independent Press* (October 2, 1857) carried the following account: *"The trial of the boy Josh, belonging to Dr. S. S. Marshall, for the murder of Andy, a slave of Mr. Abram Lites, was held in this village on Tuesday last, before Wm. M. Haddon, Esq., the magistrate, and resulted in his conviction of manslaughter. The prosecution was conducted by General McGowan and the Defense by Col. Orr (Marshall's brother-in-law), who each delivered elaborate speeches on the occasion. The boy was sentenced to six months imprisonment, and to receive 600 lashes, to be given twice a month,50 lashes at each time."* Orr had been the Speaker of the U. S. House of Representatives.

Slave Holders of Abbeville District, 1790-1860 and Largest Property Holders - 1860

The following lists of slave holders in Abbeville District are arranged alphabetically and were taken from the printed federal census of 1790 and the manuscript censuses of 1800-1860. The 1790 list includes all slave holders, the 1800 and 1810 lists include all owners of three or more slaves, the 1820, 1830, 1840, 1850, and 1860 lists include all owners of five or more slaves. I have followed the spelling in so far as I could decipher it and in some instances placed a ? mark, and in other instances I probably should have added question marks. I am also aware that in some instances the census taker may have placed the slaves under the name of an overseer or guardian. Also some owners held slaves in other districts or states, and there were slaves in the district whose owners were not resident here.

The 1790-1840 lists were taken from the family census records, and the 1850 and 1860 lists were taken from the slave census records In 1790, there were 333 heads of family who owned slaves, and this was approximately one fourth of the 1,338 families in the district. One fourth of the slave holders (87) owned only one slave, and another fourth (96) owned two or three slaves. The one-sixth (56) with the most slaves held half of the total. Richard A Rapley, the Commissioner in Equity and an English born lawyer, owned the highest total (57); and he was followed by Davis Moore with 39, James Lincoln, Esq. with 33, and Patrick Calhoun, Esq. with 31. Seventh with 25 was Adam Craine Jones, Esq., who like James Lincoln had been a delegate to the South Carolina Convention which ratified the United States Constitution (they both voted against it).

In the 1800 census, 604 of the 1,827 white families held slaves, and there were nearly three thousand slaves (2,964) in the district. Almost half of the slave holders (278) held only one or two; at the opposite end of the spectrum, the top hundred held about half of the total. Rapley was still the leader with 58, followed by William Shaw, another English born lawyer who lived at Cambridge.

In the 1810 census, the number of slave holding families had increased to 857, and the slave total in the district was 6,672. In 1820, for the first time two of the district's planters reported 100 or more slaves; Charles W. Bulagh held 122 and Richard Rapley held 100. In 1820, there were 1,200 slave owners in the district, and they held a total of 13, 106 slaves. In 1830, Edward Collier was reported as the owner of 121 slaves.

Slave Census

By 1840, the number of slaves surpassed the white population by 15,148 to 13,880, and four owned more than a hundred (James Edward Calhoun (153), David F. Cleckley (148), George McDuffie (135), and Williamson Norwood (106). By 1850, there were 1600 slave owners with a total of 19,262 slaves. Ten owners held above 100 slaves, fifty four held about 50 or more slaves, and one (George McDuffie) held above 200 (202). The others were, as follows: James Edward Calhoun (183), R. E. Belcher (140), Charles T. Haskell (138), John C. Martin (132), Major B. Clark (114), James Norwood (113), James F. Watson (109), John A. Calhoun (103), Joel Smith (100).

In the 1860 census, two thirds of the families held slaves and and almost two thirds of the district's population were African-American slaves. An examination of the estates of the wealthiest planters in the district indicates that from 80 to 85% of their wealth was found in their slaves. Nine owners held more than a hundred slaves: James Edward Calhoun (201), James A. Norwood (195), A. H. Morton (170), Charles T. Haskell (160), John A. Calhoun (155), Augustus Marshall Smith (135), Henry C. Cabell (127), Thomas C. Perrin (130), Robert M. Palmer (107). Others clearly owned more than a hundred when their holdings elsewhere were added. For example, J. Foster Marshall, who owned 97 in Abbeville District, held a large number in Florida on his sugar cane plantation, and Augustus Marshall Smith owned over a hundred on his plantation in Arkansas.

Abbet, James	3
Agnew, Elizabeth . .	7
Aldrige, Nathan, Senr.	2
Alexander, James . . .	1
Allen, Robert	1
Anderson, Walter	4
Barksdale, Allen . . .	1
____ Hickerson . . .	26
____ John	20
____ Richd.	4
Barmore, James.	3
Barr, Elizabeth	5
Baskin, Hugh.	3
____ Prudence	2
____ Capt. Wm. . . .	7
Bates, Fleming	5
Beard, Jno. Bat	14
Beesley, Edmond . . .	5
Bell, Jerremiah	2
____ Joseph.	2
Blair, Saml..	1
Bowie, John, Esq. . . .	19
Bowman, Jane	4
Boyd, Robert	1
____ Wm.	1
Brannon, Jno.	4
Brazell, William . . .	2
Brown, Cornelius . .	16
____ David	1
Brownlee, George . .	1
____ James	3
____ Jno.	2
Burtin, Joseph	14
____ Jno.	1
____ Joseph	2
Bushelon, Joseph . . .	1
____ Mary Ann	1
Butler, Thomas	2
Campble, James . . .	5
____ Margaret	4
Carmichael, Elinor . .	4
Carson, Wm.	1

Chalmers, John. . .	13
Childs, Harry	6
____ James	2
Clark, Alexr.	3
____ Mary	7
____ N. Thomas. . . .	4
Cochran, Andw. . . .	3
____ Richd.	1
Coldwell, Charles . .	1
____ James	5
____ Jno.	2
____ Jno., Senr. . . .	2
Colhoun, Angus . .	3
____ Jno.	1
____ Capt. Jno. . . .	3
____ John	3
____ Capt. Jos.	3
____ Pat, Esq.	3
____ Wm., Jr.	1
Colyer, Elizabeth . . .	14
____ Wm.	7
Conn, George	1
Conner, George	16
____ John	15
Cowin, Elinor.	2
Cox, Wm.	3
Crage, Rhoda	1
Crawford, Elizh.	4
____ Joseph	3
Cullins, James	1
Cummins, Rev. Francis. .	2
Cunnigam, David	10
Davis, Moses	3
Dela How, Dr. Jno. . .	14
Devaul, Michael	4
Devenport, Charles. . . .	22
____ John	5
Dodson, Enoch.	3
Donalson, Matw.	1
Dorris, Wm.	2
Drake, Thos.	1
Duglass, Hugh	71

Abbeville District Slave Holders

Dunlap, Wm.	5	____ John	2
Eddings, Benjn.	13	____ Thomas, Sr.	5
____ Wm.	1	Harris, Handy	5
Edward, Thomas	29	____ Henry.	2
Edwards, Andw.	2	____ Mary	6
____ Matw.	4	____ Thomas.	2
Elgin, Ann	3	____ William	9
Ellice, Joseph	2	Heard, Charles	1
Ellinton, Enoch (Wd)	1	____ George.	3
Elliott, Alexr.	7	____ John (FW)	2
Farrer, Barret	2	____ Wm., Junr.	1
____ John	6	Hearse, Jno.	4
Figgs, Jessiah	1	Heckleman, Michael	1
Foster, John	22	Hill, Jessey.	.6
____ Robert	3	____ Capt. Nil	3
____ Saml., Senr.	1	Hodges, James	4
____ Saml., Sr.	3	____ Wm.	1
____ Thomas	4	Houston, Cathrine	2
Gallaspie, Ann	1	Howard, Benjn.	8
____ David	1	Huggins, Wm.	2
____ James	2	Hughs, Rebecca	1
Ganes, Wm.	1	Hullin, William	8
Gant, Jno.	6	Hunt, Saml.	3
Gibert, Peter	2	Huston, Saml.	2
Gibson, Elias	1	Hutchison, William	3
____ Patk.	2	Irving, Jno.	2
____ Robert	5	____ Joseph	5
Gill, Daniel	11	Johnston, James	2
Glasgow, Mary	1	Jones, Adam C., Esq.	25
Glover, Frederick	9	____ Adam Cr., Jr.	3
Goodman, Wm.	4	Kerr, Mary	7
Gouge, James	1	____ Wm., Jr.	1
Gowdey, James	7	Kilpatrick, Andrew	1
Gray, James	1	King, Philip	1
____ John	3	Kirkwood, Robert	1
____ William	1	Lawson, Jones	3
____ Wm.	1	Le Roy, Philip.	1
Green, Jno.	6	Lee, Andrew	6
____ Peter	11	____ Thomas	4
Griffin, Robert	3	Lemaster, Joseph	2
Hall, Revd. Robert	5	Leslergett, Lewis	24
Hamilton, Andw.,Esq.	4	Lessley, Wm.	3
____ Archd.	1	Liddle, Raichel	2

Lincoln, James, Esq.	33	Milligan, Joseph . .	8
Lindsey, Ephraim . .	1	Mitchell, Tanner . .	14
Linton, Saml. . . .	4	Moore, Davis	39
Livingston Thomas. .	8	____ Elijah	6
Lockridge, Jas., Sr. .	1	____ John. . .'. . .	1
Logan, Isaac	3	Morris, Joseph . . .	1
Long, Henry	4	Morrow, Jno.	1
____ James	7	Murrey, Jno. . . .	1
____ John	7	Nash, Jno.	4
____ Nicholas	4	Nichels, Wm. . . .	6
____ Wm.	7	Nickels, Julius, Sr. . . .	8
Lord, Wm.	2	____ Wm.	8
Love, James	4	Noble, Alex.	20
____ Wm.	3	____ James	16
McAddams, Jno. . .	2	Norris, Jno.	1
McClaskey, Alexr. .	1	____ Patk.	4
McClinton, Robert,Sr.	2	Norwood, Capt. Jno. . .	3
McConnell, Jno. . . .	2	Oliver, James . . .	4
McCurdy, Elijah . . .	4	Patten, Arthur	6
McDonnald, Wm. . .	2	Patterson, George . .	1
McDowel, Alexr. . .	1	____ James	4
McElwee, James . .	1	____ Josiah	2
McFerrin, James . .	1	____ Wm.	9
McGaw, Capt. Jno. .	4	Pettegrew, William . . .	5
McKean, Wm.	1	Pettigrew, Ebenezer . .	8
McKinley, Wm. . . .	17	Pickens, Abraham. . .	1
McKinsey, John . . .	3	Pickins, Wm. G.	1
McMaster, ____ ll . .	1	Pollard, Robt.	2
McMullin, Rev. Peter	3	Ponder, Jas.	2
McMurthrey, Wm. . .	1	Porter, Elizth.	1
McMurtrey, Saml. .	3	Posey, Richard . . .	2
Maddin, Wm.	1	Pratt, Wm.	5
Martin, Jno.	16	Pressley, David	7
____ Roger	3	____ David	1
Mathews, Isaac . .	2	____ Wm.	2
____ Philip	2	Pullim, James	1
Mattison, Jno. . .	3	____ Jno, Sr.	15
Meriweather, Capt. Jno.	13	____ Jno., Junr.	1
____ Dr. Zachy. . .	4	Quce, Jno.	3
Merser, Robert . . .	1	Raglin, Jno. R.	4
Michel, Mary	15	Rapley, Richard A. . . .	57
Mickel, Benjn. . . .	14	Ravlin, Jno.	4
Miller, Jno.	1	Ray, Thos.	1

Abbeville District Slaveholders

Razor, Luke . .	1	____ Wm.	1
Reed, Joseph . . .	9	Watkins, Henry	2
____ Capt. Saml .	2	Watt, Andw.	1
Rice, Gery	3	____ Saml., Esq. . . .	4
Richey, Robert.	1	Weed, Rubin.	1
Robbison, Jno. . . .	4	Weems, Bartw . . .	2
____ Wm. . . .	12	____ Thos.	6
Roberts, Peter .	2	Wetherall, Jno., Esq .	8
Rogers, Anne. .	4	White, James	1
Roseman, James . . .	9	____ Wm.	1
____ Capt. Saml. . .	3	Whitfield, George . . .	24
____ Serah	3	Wideman, Henry	5
Ross, Andw. . . .	3	____ Adam	2
Russell, Dr. Timothy	8	Wildear, George . . .	5
Saylor, Lenord . . .	4	Williamson, Wm. . .	3
Scott, Wm. . . .	7	Wilson, James	4
Shanklin, Thomas. .	2	____ Nathaniel.	1
Shard, Wm., Esq. .	8	Wimbish, James.	5
Sharp, Jno.	5	____ Meldrid	19
Shottwell, Hannah . .	6	Winn, Thomas. . . .	23
Shirley , Jno.	1	____ Wm.	6
Sims, Nathan. . . .	4	Woods, Wm.	5
Smithers, Gabriel. . . .	7	Yewel, James . . .	8
Speers, Wm.	6	Young, Francis . .	3
Spruill, Jno. . .	2		
Standard, Daniel ..	1	**1800 Census**	
Stanfield, Wm.. . . .	3	(owners of three or more)	
Stewart, Robert. . .	3		
Tawnehill, Jas. . . .	1	Aldridge, Nathaniel .	. 3
Taylor , Andw.	1	Anderson, Kathrine . .	6
Terry, Robert	2	____ Walter	7
Thompson, Moses .	3	Ansley, William	4
____ Peter . . .	7	Arnold, John	6
Trimble, Esther .	1	Baird, James	17
____ Joseph . . .	5	____ Matt	13
Tylor, William . .	1	Baldee, William	4
Vernon, James .	5	Ball, John	5
Viccory, Wm. . .	4	Barksdale, Fanney . .	8
Wakefield, Jane . . .	1	____ Hickerson . . .	26
Walter, Linord. . . .	8	____ John	4
Wardlaw, Hugh, Esq.	8	____ Richard	7
____ Jno.	6	____ William	3
____ Lydia . . .	6	Barmor, James	7

Bartee, Thomas	9
Baskin, Prudence. . .	3
_____ Sarah	3
_____William . .	11
Bates, Fleming . . .	10
Bleckley, John. . .	22
_____ Joseph	7
Bell, Duke	13
_____ Jeremiah . . .	5
_____ John, Junr. . .	4
_____ Joseph . . .	3
Blain, William . . .	3
_____ William . .	10
Bostick, Stephen	3
Bowie, John, Senr . . .	22
Bradley, James . . .	5
Brazeal, Enoch .	8
Brennan, John . . .	10
Brightman, Thomas .	4
Brooks, Christopher .	3
Brown, Joseph	4
_____ Peter	8
_____ William	8
Brownlee, William .	3
Burton, Allen	7
_____ John	5
_____ Joseph	8
_____ Josiah	5
Bynum, Jessey . . .	6
Cain, William . . .	4
Caldwell, James . .	4
_____ James	6
Calhoun, Joseph. .	5
_____ Martha	25
_____ William, Jr.	6
Callahan, William	4
Campbell, James . .	7
Carson, John	12
_____ Robert	6
Chambers, Pye . .	5
Chetum, Robert . .	5
Childs, Benjamin .	3
_____ James	3

_____ John	9
_____ Judea	4
_____ Judey	4
_____ Nimrod	3
_____ Rubin	9
_____ William	18
Clark, John	4
Colbert, John	8
Coleman, Peter . . .	5
Collier, Edward . . .	8
Conidrey, John	10
Conner, George . . .	26
_____ John	25
_____ Lewis	3
Cook, Joseph	4
Covington, Feby . .	6
Cox, William	7
Crear, Thomas B. .	8
Criswell, Joseph . .	5
Cummins, Rev. Francis .	8
Cunnigem, Jane	14
_____ Margret	5
Davis, Robert.	7
_____ Robert	5
Duval, Michael, Senr . .	10
Devinport, Charles . .	30
_____ Susannah	12
Dodson, Enoch	5
Donaldson, Mathew	4
Druman, Benjamin . . .	4
Duglas, Archibald.	3
_____ Jane.	3
Dunlap, William. . . .	6
Edwards, Ambros.	10
_____ Elizabeth	8
_____ James	3
_____ Joseph	7
_____ Mathew	5
_____ Thomas	5
Egnew, James	4
Elgin, Robert	8
Ellington, Fanney . . .	5
Emerson, Thomas . . .	4

Abbevile District Slaveholders

Eskridge, Richard	7	Henderson, Robert . . .	10
Flatcher, William	3	Herd, George	4
Forrest, James	4	Hill, Joseph	12
Foster, James	8	____ Joshua	12
____ John	10	____ Wil	6
____ Robert, Senr. . .	3	Hodges, John	5
____ Samuel	4	Houston, Alexander .	3
Frazier, Donald . . .	17	____ John	3
Fushee, Charles . . .	7	____ Abraham	8
Gains, Henry	3	Huggins, Patsy . . .	5
____ Jonadab . . .	5	Hunter, Alexander .	3
Ganes, Richard . .	6	Huston, James . . .	3
Garvin, Daniel . .	5	Hutchinson, William	4
Gee, Nevil	3	Hutton, Joseph . . .	3
Gibert, Peter . .	8	____ William	10
____ Peter, Junr.	16	Irving, Joseph	4
Gibson, Robert . . .	4	Jack, John	7
Gill, Daniel . .	14	Jackson, Abel . .	9
Gillaspie, David . .	3	Jent, John	12
Glover, Allen . . .	9	Jentry, Hezekiah . . .	10
____ Benjamin . .	15	Johnson, Charles . . .	4
____ Drury	3	Johnston, Zilpha	7
____ John	5	Jones, Adam Cr., Sr. . .	28
Goodman, William .	6	Kain, James	3
Gowdy, James	9	Kirkwood, Robert . . .	3
Graves, Joseph . . .	6	Lawson, James	5
Gray, Andrew . . .	6	Lee, Andrew	9
____ John	4	Leroy, Philip	3
____ Robert . . .	4	Lilly, David	7
Green, James . .	3	Linton, Samuel	12
Hacket, Martin .	6	Lipscomb, Joel	10
Hamilton, Andrew .	8	____ Nathan	13
____ Archibald . . .	4	____ William	7
____ John	4	Livingston, Thomas . .	16
Harris, John	5	Logan, Isaac	7
____ John	15	____ John, Senr.	5
____ Handy	5	Lomax, James	8
____ Richard	5	Long, Gabriel	4
____ Richmon . . .	5	____ James	10
____ Thomas	3	____ John Reid . . .	9
Hawthorn, James . .	7	McClinton, Robert . .	3
Hearst, John	6	McCurdy, Anney	3
____ Joseph	3	McDonald, William . . .	3

-75 –

McGehee, Carr . . .	14	Pascal, Samuel . . .	9
McKinley, Mary . . .	14	Patterson, George . . .	3
McMasters, William .	5	____ William	16
____ William	6	Perrin, Catherine . . .	5
McMullin, Peter	4	Pickens, Andrew . . .	3
Maddox, Hanby . . .	7	Pollard, Richard . . .	9
Martin, John	12	____ Robert	7
____ Robert, Junr. . .	3	Pool, Micajah . . .	8
____ William . . .	3	____ Thomas	9
Mattison, Benjamin . .	5	Posey, Richard	3
____ John	9	Presley, David . . .	3
Maxfield, John	5	____ John	3
Meriweather, John . .	13	Prince, Edward, Junr. .	4
____ Joseph	5	____ Edward, Senr . .	15
____ Mary	27	Pullum, Sarah.	14
____ Nicholas	24	Rapley, Richard A. . .	58
____ Zacheri	9	Ravlin, Mary . . .	5
Miller, Ebenezer	6	Rayford, William . . .	10
____ John	6	Razor, Cristion. . . .	4
Milligan, Hugh	5	Reid, Hugh	9
Mitchel, Benjamin . .	16	____ Samuel	5
____ Daniel	3	Reynolds, Benjamin .	9
____ Randal	4	____ Larkin	6
Mitchell, Lewis . . .	3	Rice, Levi	5
____ William . . .	5	Richards, William	3
Moore, Alexander . .	10	Richey, James, Senr. .	3
____ William	5	____ Robert	5
Moragne, Peter . .	13	Richmond, John . . .	5
Morrah, Hugh. . .	4	Robertson, John	10
Moseley, Charles . .	7	____ William	26
____ Joseph	9	Rogers, Peter	4
____ Richard	16	Rosemond, James . . .	9
Murrey, Tidus . . .	10	____ Samuel.	6
____ Ruben	3	Sample, Robert	3
Nichols, Julius, Junr.	9	Sanders, John	7
____ Julius, Senr. . .	7	Saxon, Samuel	19
____ William	9	Scoggins, John	3
Nickery, William . .	4	Shanklin, Thomas . . .	5
Noble, Alexander . .	22	Shaw, William	40
Norris, Elizabeth . .	3	Simmons, Robert	3
Oliver, James	10	Sims, Nathan	7
Partlow, John . . .	3	Smith, Augustin	4

____ Robert	5	Wideman, Henry	8
____ Robert. . . .	4	Wildridge, Gibson . . .	10
____ William . .	6	Williams, Samuel	4
Stetham, Charles . . .	5	Wilson, Henry	36
Stone, William. . . .	6	____ James	8
Street, William	3	____ Littlebury	14
Swain, Robert	5	____ Thomas	4
Swansey, Rosannah . .	7	Wimbish, Alexander. . .	4
Swindle, George . . .	13	Winn, Abner	4
____ Thomas	9	____ Lettice	20
Tatom, William	5	Worrell, Amos	5
Terrey, Benjamin . . .	8	Wright, Pleasant . . .	3
____ Terrey	8	____ Robert	8
Tompson, Moses . .	10	Yarborough, William .	3
____ Samuel . . .	7	Young, Francis	7
Tomson, John	11		
Tribble, Joseph. . .	4	**1810 Census**	
Troutman, John	5	(owners of 3 or more)	
Turner, Abednigo . .	15		
Vernon, James, Senr. .	4	Adams, Benjamin . . .	15
Vicory, William. . . .	4	____ John	9
Wade, William. . . .	10	____ John	8
Waller, Benjamin . .	13	Adamson,Jas.	4
____ John	19	Agnew, Andrew	5
____ John N. . . .	6	____ James	7
____ Leonard . . .	14	____ Samuel	3
Wardlaw , Hugh . . .	9	Aikens, Robt.	4
____ James	8	Alexander, Jane . . .	7
____ John	11	Allen, James	3
____ Nancy	7	Alston, James	10
Ware, Edmond . . .	4	____ Nathaniel . . .	12
____ William	4	Anderson, Jacob . . .	20
Watson, Christopher . .	5	____ Richard	5
____ James	8	____ Robert	3
Watt, Samuel. . .	15	____ Robert	3
Watts, James	4	____ Samuel	9
Weatherall, John . . .	17	____ Thos. J.	7
Weed, Martha	3	____ Walter	5
Weems, Elizabeth	3	Ansley, Thomas.	3
____ Margret	3	Armstrong, John	8
Weldon, Antony	3	Arnold, James	16
White, Francis	12	____ John, Senr.	8
____ George	5	____ John P.	6

____ John P.	4
____ William P. .	8
Ball, Peter	3
Barber, Nathaniel.	6
Barksdale, Henry. . . .	5
____ Joseph. . . .	5
Barmore, James	12
____ William.	4
Baskin, John.	7
____ Thomas	8
Bass, William.	5
Bastee, Thos.	7
Bates, Margret . . .	14
Battes (?) James . .	5
Beard, James . . .	33
____ Mary	8
Bell, Abraham . .	5
____ Duke	12
____ Jeremiah . . .	8
____ Jno.	7
____ Joseph . . .	4
Bickley, James . .	4
____ Joseph . . .	28
Bigbey, William .	5
Bigby, Archabald .	8
Black, Robert . .	4
Blain, William .	4
Bluford, William.	6
Boles, Isaac C. .	3
Bones, James . .	12
Boniat, Elizabeth . . .	8
Bowie, George	14
____ John, Sr.	26
Boyd, John	5
Brannon, John	29
Brightman, George .	20
____ Thos.	12
Brooks, Christopher.	7
____ John	20
Brown, John	5
____ Peter	10
Brownlee, George .	10
____ George, Junr.	5

____ James	16
____ John	4
____ William . . .	17
Bugg, Susannah C. . . .	8
Burt, Moody . . .	18
Burton, John	17
____ Jonah	3
____ Joseph	3
Bushell, John C. . . .	9
Cafians (?), William. .	11
Cain, William	16
Caldwell, Charles . .	4
Calhoun, Alex	3
____ Ezekiel	5
____ Ezekiel, Junr. .	3
____ James	24
____ John	4
____ Joseph	12
____ Patrick	19
____ William	9
____ William, Junr.	18
____ Wm. (Saluda) .	9
Cameron, John . . .	4
Campbell, James . .	7
Carr, David	3
Carson, Giles.	8
____ Jas.	51
____ John	21
Casey, Thomas . . .	9
Chalmas, Henry J. .	16
Chastain, Jas.	3
Chatham, Thomas . . .	3
Cheatam, Robert. .	6
Childs, John . .	17
____ John, son of Jas.	4
____ Thompson . .	5
____ Walter	12
____ William . . .	9
Chiles, Benj. . . .	7
____ Maj. John . . .	11
____ Judith	10
Chitam, Robt.	16
Clarke, John . . .	7

Clary, Nochel (?) . . .	5	Devenport, Charles	4
Clay, John	17	_____ Elizabeth . . .	10
Coalman, Peter . .	13	Devlin, Jas., Junr. .	4
Cobb, James	12	Dickson, Starling . .	4
_____ Thomas	6	Dixon, Hugh	4
Cochran, Jos., Esq. .	4	Dobbs, Jesse	5
Cofer, Agripa . . .	5	Dodson, Enoch	5
_____ Joseph	13	Donnal, John	6
Colbert, John . .	8	Douglas, Archibald. . .	23
Collier, Edward	43	Downey, John	12
_____ James . . .	57	Dozier, A. G. . . .	13
Colwell, David .	6	_____ James	3
_____ John	3	_____ Mark	4
_____ William . . .	6	Drummond, Moses. .	3
Conley, George . . .	7	Dubose, Joshua . .	25
Conner, George. . .	28	Dunlap, William.	5
_____ John	3	Dusset, Plesent. . . .	7
_____ Lewis	3	Duvall, Michael. . .	3
_____ Robert	10	_____ Saml. . . .	13
Cooper, Jacob . .	4	Dye, Randolph. . .	3
_____ Joseph. . . .	4	Eaves, Daniel . . .	7
Cothin, Harison . .	4	Eddings, Elizabeth . .	8
Covinton, Joseph B. . . .	3	Eddins, Joel	7
_____ William . . .	16	Edwards, Ambrose . . .	12
Cowen, Isaac	21	_____ Thomas . . .	21
_____ Saml., Senr . . .	4	Ellington, Dice . . .	3
_____ Samuel . . .	4	_____ John	5
Cox, James	7	Ellis, Robert	4
_____ Margret . .	19	Eskridge, Richd.	5
Craig, Rhoda .	3	Finch, John	4
Creagh, Thos. B.	19	Findley, Thomas . . .	10
Criswell, Geo.	8	Finey, Robt.	3
_____ Joseph	5	Finney, Benjamin . . .	6
Croford, Agnes . . .	3	Forrest, James	10
Crymes, Jno.	19	Foshee, Chas.	14
Culpepper, Jas.	29	Foster, James	24
Cunningham, David .	15	_____ Joseph	26
_____ James	6	_____ Joseph	24
_____ Robt. A.	10	_____ Robert	4
Davis, Eli	12	_____ Samuel, Senr. . . .	4
_____ Joseph	5	Frankling, Asa	4
_____ Joshua	5	_____ William B.	5
_____ Robert	12	Frazier, James. . . .	11

Fuquay, Seth . . .	6	Harris, John	8
Gains, John D.	17	___ John	20
___ Richard	7	___ Richd.	4
___ Susanah	8	___ Richmond . . .	9
Gant, Mary	3	___ Samuel	12
Gayle, Billips	11	Hatten, Benjamin. . . .	8
___ Jno	27	Hears, John	3
Gent, Daniel. . .	4	Hearse, Jos.	4
Gibert, Peter	14	Henderson, James . .	7
___ John S. . . .	3	___ Jas.	9
Gibson, Robt. . . .	7	___ Jno.	3
Gilaspie, David. . . .	5	___ Margret	4
Gilbert, Stephen. . . .	9	___ Nat.	11
Gillam, William . . .	13	___ William	7
Glover, Allen . . .	17	Hendrick, William . . .	4
___ Benjamin . .	53	Herd, Geo.	7
___ John	13	Herse, Joseph	15
___ John F.	13	Hester, Henry	5
Goodman, William.	5	Hill, Benjamin	4
Graves, Joseph . . .	21	___ Jos.	24
Gray, Andrew	10	___ Joshua	15
___ James, Senr.	5	___ Thomas . . .	10
___ John (Sadler) .	4	___ Uel	16
___ Rebecka	4	___ Wm., Senr. . . .	4
___ Robert	8	Hind, Richard	9
___ Thomas . . .	6	Hirst, Richard . . .	9
___ Thomas. . .	7	Hodges, John . . .	8
___ William. . .	7	___ William . . .	6
Green, James . . .	5	Holiday, Wm. . . .	4
Griffin, Adim. . . .	7	Houston, Joseph . . .	3
___ Jice	12	Howlett, Penne . . .	3
___ Richd. . . .	17	Hughs, Jas., Senr. .	11
___ S.	3	Hunter, Alexander .	8
Hackett, Frances . . .	5	Huse, James.	18
Hackney, Joseph. . . .	14	Hutchison, James. .	3
Hall, William	10	Hutton, Joseph . . .	11
Hallums, Basel	14	___ Rebecker. . . .	4
Hambleton, Alexander.	5	Jacobs, Mary	9
Hamilton, Alexander . .	11	Jewell, Thos.	7
___ Andrew.	15	Johnston, Henry . . .	8
___ Mary Ann	5	___ Henry	4
Haney, Mary	4	___ James	3
Harkann, James . .	7	___ Jonathon	3

Abbeville District Slaveholders

____ Zelpha . . .	13	McCaslin, Robert . . .	5
Johnstone, Benjamin .	13	McClinton, Robert. . . .	3
____ Charles . . .	4	McClurg, James . . .	7
____ Snellen . . .	5	McComs, Andrew. . .	3
Jones, Adam Cr. .	25	McCoppin, William. . .	4
____ Benjamin	6	McCord, John, Senr. . .	3
____ Dudley.	4	McCron, Edward . . .	5
____ John, Junr .	5	McCulloc, James	4
____ Margret. . .	6	McDonald, Irish Wm. .	4
____ Nelson	9	McGaw, William	10
____ Steven . . .	4	McGee, John	9
____ Thomas . . .	6	____ Mical	3
Key, James	3	____ Michel	3
King, Philip . . .	3	McGehe, Meredith . .	19
Kirkwood, Robert . . .	11	McGehee, Carr	40
Lasley, William . . .	3	____ Charles	15
Lattimore, Clement. . .	10	____ Dabney	5
____ James	4	McGill, William . .	5
Lawson, Jesse . . .	5	McGowin, Elizh . . .	5
Leavengston, Bruce . .	6	McKenny, Roger . . .	8
Lebil (?), David . .	3	McKinley, Archabald . . .	4
Lee, Andrew. . . .	3	____ James.	3
____ Thomas . .	10	____ John	5
____ William . .	11	____ Robert M. . . .	5
Lesley, Joseph . . .	3	McMasters, William .	9
Levengston, Nancy .	22	McMurtry, John	3
Linsley, John . . .	9	McNeal, John	7
____ Robert. . . .	4	McRacken, James .	14
Linton, Samuel . .	34	Madison, Benjamin. .	18
____ Samuel . . .	5	____ John	3
Loftis, Martain. .	5	Maddox, Jane.	6
Logan, Andrew . .	11	Mains, James . . .	3
____ Clem. . . .	6	Marshall, Geo. . .	3
____ Eli, Senr .	6	Martain, Bird . . .	5
____ Isaac	5	____ Martha . . .	18
____ John	11	Martin, Bird	4
____ John (SM). . .	7	____ Jacob	6
Lomax, George. .	4	____ John	30
____ James. . . .	16	____ John	9
Long, John R. . . .	8	____ Thomas	17
McCalla, John . . .	6	Mason, John C. . . .	22
McCanal, Joseph .	4	Matheson, Frances . .	9
McCaller, John . .	3	Mathews, Ann. . . .	3

Maury, Benjamin . .	3
____ Titus	15
Maxwell, Chas. . .	3
____ George . . .	6
Maye, Robert . .	9
Meek, Elinor . . .	7
Melwail, William . .	3
Merina, Isaac . . .	8
Merino, Peter	11
Meriweather, John . . .	28
____ John H.	7
____ Joseph. . . .	14
____ Nchs	25
____ Zach	3
____ Dr. Zach	22
Merriwether, Zacariah.	3
Miller, Ebenezer . . .	5
____ John	8
____ John	3
____ John H.	6
____ Joseph	3
Miles, Lewis. . . .	7
Milligan, Andrew . .	7
Mitchel, Martha . . .	3
Mitchell, Benjamin	20
____ Kaziah	9
____ Lewis	14
Monday, Harison . .	5
Montague, John . .	8
Moor, Frances	14
Moore, John	5
Morina, Francis . .	9
Morrow, Hugh . .	11
____ John . . .	3
Moseley, Henry . . .	4
____ Joseph . . .	9
____ Richd., Junr . .	3
____ Richd., Senr.	19
Mucklevany, Samuel	4
Murine (?), John .	11
Nash, Abner	5
____ Ezekiel	5
____ Nimrod . . .	4

____ Polly H. . . .	14
____ Rubin	8
Nealy, John . . .	5
Newby, John N.	8
Nibs, Wm., Esq .	6
Nichols, Wm., Junr. .	17
Nicols, William . . .	10
Noble, Alex . . .	4
____ Ezekiel . . .	13
____ James	11
____ William . . .	11
Norris, Andrew . . .	17
____ John . . .	3
____ Wilson	3
Norwood, Isham. . . .	6
____ Nathaniel	5
____ Williamson . . .	25
Olliver, William. . . .	4
Owens, Richd.	6
Pace, John	8
____ Silas	4
Parmer, Martain . . .	3
Partlow, Capt. John .	7
Paskil, Firba	5
____ Milton	10
Patterson, Jas.	4
____ Jonah . . .	10
____ Josiah, Junr. . .	3
____ Thomas	3
Paul, Andrew	7
Pedigrew, James . .	3
Perrin, Samuel . . .	13
____ William	6
Pettis, James	4
Piles, Rubin	13
Pollard , Robt. . . .	20
Poluse, Austin . . .	5
Pool, Abram P. . . .	8
____ Leah	17
Poole, Micajah . . .	12
Porter, Elizabeth . . .	4
____ Hugh	17
Posey, Benjamin. . .	4

Abbeville District Slaveholders

____ Richard	8	____ James	3
Powers, John	34	Sales, John	4
Presley, D. . .	8	____ William . . .	6
____ David, Junr.	4	Sample, Alexander . . .	9
____ David, Senr. . .	7	____ Robt. . . .	8
Prince, Edward. . .	6	____ Wm.	6
____ Edward, Jr. . .	11	Sanders, John. . .	7
____ Hudson . . .	5	____ Joseph	5
Pucket, Dabney	20	Savage, Samuel. . .	29
____ Jas.	8	Saxton, Benjamin. .	17
Pullain, Jas.	3	____ Samuel	28
____ Sarah	13	Scogan, Jno.	5
____ Zach	6	Scot, Agnes	6
Quinn, Charles . .	3	Scott, William . . .	15
Raford, William P.	11	Scuddy, Augustian . . .	8
Ramsay, Saml. . .	13	Scudy, John	14
Rapley, Richard A. .	65	Sevenston, Henry . .	3
Rasor, Christian .	9	Shackelford, Nathan .	32
Read, Hugh	9	Shanklin, Thomas. . .	10
Renche, Sarah . .	7	Shealy, Samuel . . .	13
Reynolds, Benjamin .	22	Shelworth, Thomas. . .	6
Rice, Zeri	6	Shotwell, Hanah . . .	14
Riley, William . . .	5	____ John	5
Ringold, Richd . . .	5	____ Robert	5
Ritchie, James. . .	5	Sifford, Royal M. . . .	4
____ Nancy	12	Sims, Lewis	3
____ Robert	9	Smith, Fanney . . .	6
Roberts, George. . . .	7	____ John	4
____ Leroy	4	____ John B.	7
Robertson, Isham . .	5	____ Moses	3
____ John	24	____ Moton.	17
____ Peter	3	____ Peter	8
____ William . . .	7	____ Robert	50
____ William . .	60	____ Robert	4
Rogers, Peter B.	7	____ William	23
Roman, Abraham Senr. .	3	Speed, Robert	43
____ Robert	7	Spence, John H.	3
Rosman, Nathaniel J. .	6	Spruill, George	4
____ Robert	7	Stallworth, Thos. . .	6
Russel, David . . .	4	Stansfield, Sarah	8
____ Mathew . . .	5	Stark, Charles	7
____ William . . .	3	____ Jeremiah	3
Russell, Elizabeth . .	4	Staturn (?),Charles .	4

Stephens, Edmund	7		____ Jas.	16
____ John. . . .	6		____ Moton	7
Stephil, Philip	3		____ Steven	5
Stewart, John	13		____ William	16
Stuart, Alex . .	4		Watt, Samuel	4
Swain, John .	4		Weams, Margret . .	4
____ Robert	5		Wedgeworth, James .	4
Swansey, Dr. Saml. . .	4		Werrel, Amos	8
Swilling, John	7		Wertlaw, Hugh . . .	3
Tagard, David . .	3		____ John	7
Tagat, Moses . . .	8		____ Joseph . . .	8
Talloon, Charles . .	8		Wetherell, John . . .	18
____ Sarah	8		Whipple, Malcom .	4
Teary, Benjamin . . .	3		Whistler, Bert . .	3
____ Jeremiah . . .	17		White, Durett . . .	5
Tennent, William . . .	25		____ George . . .	9
Thomas, David . . .	6		____ Margaret. . .	6
____ Wm. S. . . .	3		____ Robert	10
Thompson, Margret. . . .	4		Whitfield, George . . .	5
____ Moses	7		Whitlow, Saml. . . .	8
____ Samuel.	9		Widman, Adam . . .	7
Thrift, Archibald . . .	14		____ Leonard	5
Thurman, Robt. . .	7		Wignn, John	11
Tilman, Edmon . .	23		Williams, James . . .	3
Travis, Donald . .	28		____ James, Senr.	11
Trimble, John. . .	7		Willis, Robert . .	6
Vernon, William . .	3		Wilson, John. . .	4
Vicary, Betty	4		____ Sally	4
Waddle, Moses . . .	16		Wimbish, Benjamin .	4
Waldin, Lucy	3		____ Samuel . . .	9
Walker, John . . .	3		____ William	5
Waller, Leonard . . .	14		Winn, Letice.	15
____ Thomas B. . .	11		Wirtlaw, Robert. . .	12
____ William. . . .	15		Woods, Susanah C. . .	8
____ Wm., Junr. .	7		Wooldridge, Gibson . .	10
Wardlaw, James . .	19		____ Robert . . .	5
____ John	6		Wright, John L. . .	4
____ Joseph	10		____ Pleasant. . . .	4
____ Jos., Junr. . . .	14		Yancey, Benjamin C.	5
____ Wm.	3		Yarborrow, William . .	10
Ware, Edmond . . .	10		Yeldell, Antony. . . .	5
____ William . . .	13		Young, Francis, Sr. . . .	11
Watson, Elizabeth . . .	12		____ Robert . . .	11

Abbeville District Slaveholders

_____ Samuel	7	Bell, Abraham	5
_____ William	3	_____ Elizabeth . . .	8
_____ Wm.	7	_____ Jaramiah . . .	14
		_____ Joseph F. . .	8
1820 Census		Bickley, Frances . .	17
(owners of 5 or more)		_____ James	5
		Bigbee, Archabald .	12
Abney, Micajay . . .	17	Black, Robert F. . .	8
Adams, Alexander . . .	22	Bonner, Samuel . .	10
_____ Benjamin . . .	25	Bonniat, Elizabeth . .	8
_____ Jesse L.	10	Botts, Thomas	5
_____ John	15	Bowie, Alexander.	8
_____ Lucy	5	_____ George	20
Adamson, Lydia . .	5	_____ John	8
Agnew, Andrew . .	10	_____ John	39
_____ James	10	Brewith (?), Samuel . .	6
Agnon, John	5	Brightman, Thomas . .	14
Aiken, Robert . .	12	Brooks, Sarah	10
Allen, Bannister .	7	_____ Wesley	18
_____ John L. . . .	13	Brown, Peter . .	5
Alston, James . .	13	Brownlee, George . .	9
Anderson, Jacob .	5	_____ John	6
_____ Samuel . . .	9	_____ William . .	19
_____ Walter	8	Buchanan, Robert . .	10
Ansley, David . . .	5	Buford, William . .	11
_____ Thomas . . .	7	Bulagh, Charles W.	122
Armstrong, John .	15	Bull, William A. .	32
Arnold, James . .	24	Bullard, William . .	8
_____ John	14	Bullock, Bartlett S.	7
Askins, Thomas .	5	_____ Benjamin F. .	5
Ausburn (?), Samuel	5	_____ Mary	22
Bagot, Randolph . .	7	Burnett, John J. . .	12
Baker, Alpheus . . .	7	Burterson (?), John. . .	7
_____ Joseph	9	Burton, Benjamin. . .	5
Bard (?), John . .	10	_____ Beverly	6
Baremore, James .	20	_____ John	24
_____ Nancy . . .	6	Bushell, Jesse C. . . .	18
Barmore, Peter .	5	Butler, James	19
Barr, William H. .	6	Cain, Mary	12
Barron, Uriah . . .	6	Caldwell, Abigail . .	5
Baskin, James H. .	6	_____ Abigail	7
_____ John	10	_____ Elizth.	6
Belcher, Washington	22	_____ Samuel	9

_____ William H. . . .	10	
Calhoun, Alexander .	7	
_____ Ezekiel	9	
_____ James	28	
_____ Joseph	12	
_____ Nathaniel . . .	7	
_____ Martha	18	
_____ Patrick	42	
_____ William . . .	31	
_____ William . . .	11	
_____ William . . .	20	
Calvert, Jesse . . .	5	
_____ John	16	
Cambell,	12	
Cameron, John . .	5	
Campbell, James .	8	
_____ John	17	
Carder (?), William .	7	
Carson, James . . .	5	
_____ John	20	
_____ William . .	15	
Caruthers, James W.	14	
Cason, Larkin	6	
Cater, Richard B. . .	17	
Chatham, John . . .	7	
_____ John	12	
_____ Robert . . .	15	
Cheatham, Peter .	13	
Cheves, John . . .	5	
Chiles, Benjamin .	11	
_____ John	26	
_____ Judith	12	
_____ Judith . . .	9	
_____ Larkin . . .	5	
_____ Thomas . .	19	
_____ Thomas W. .	16	
_____ William . . .	24	
Clark, John	9	
Clay, Edward . . .	5	
_____ Simeon . . .	5	
Clinkscales, Francis B.	8	
Cobb, Charles	5	
_____ William	12	

_____ Thomas	9
Cochran, John	9
_____ William	7
Collier, Edward	82
_____ Edward W.	15
Colt, Palnick S. . . .	8
Conner, Francis . . .	19
_____ George, Junr. .	12
_____ George, Senr. .	30
_____ John	26
_____ Lewis	8
Cooper, Agrippa . .	8
Cothran, Samuel . .	14
Covington, Richard .	17
_____ William	9
Cowan, Isaac	34
_____ Samuel	7
Cox, Margaret	25
Crawford, James . . .	32
Creagh, Thomas B. .	34
_____ Thomas B. . . .	30
Crenshaw, Stephen . . .	26
Creswell, Elihu	22
_____ George	14
_____ Joseph	7
Cromer, George . . .	18
Crymes, John	21
Culpepper, Joseph .	24
Cummings, Thomas .	5
Cunningham, David .	21
_____ Robt. A. . . .	20
_____ William	11
Danelly, Isra	8
Dansby, Charles . .	5
Daricott, Hulbert . .	7
Davenport, David R.	9
Davis, Chesley . . .	7
_____ Eli S.	17
_____ Elizabeth . . .	7
_____ Ephraim . . .	6
_____ Garah	20
_____ Joseph	12
_____ Joshua	8

Abbeville District Slaveholders

____ Nancy	13		____ John	25
Devinport, Lucius C.	20		____ William . . .	5
Delph, Henry . . .	7		____ William . . .	12
Devlin, James . .	5		____ Willis	16
Dickson, Hugh .	9		Golaspie, David . .	11
Dodgen, Ollyman	6		Goode, Lewelling . .	15
Donald, John . . .	6		Goodman, Thomas . .	5
____ John	8		Gooldshey, William .	13
____ West	5		Gordon, Robert C. . .	12
Douglas, Donald .	8		Gray, Frederick	22
Dozier, James . .	14		____ Frederick, Junr. .	6
Dubose, Joshua .	12		____ Frederick, Senr. .	5
Duvall, Sarah . .	7		____ Rosanna	5
Eakins, Joseph .	6		Grey, Mary	12
Edwards, Ambrose .	18		Griffin, David . . .	12
Ellington, John . .	12		____ Ira	26
Ellis, Robert . . .	9		____ Richard	32
Finney, Benjamin .	9		____ Vincent	9
Forrest, Elizabeth .	14		Grigsby, John . . .	13
Foshee, Charles . .	19		Groves, Joseph . .	28
____ John	11		Hacket, Robert . .	5
Foster, Elijah	6		Hackett, Martin . .	11
____ Hannah	6		____ William . . .	8
____ Joseph	19		Hagood, John . . .	10
____ Robert	14		Hainy, Mary . . .	7
____ Samuel . . .	8		Hallams, William. .	11
Franklin, Sarah . .	5		Haloway, John . .	9
Franks, John . . .	5		Hamilton, Alexander .	6
Fraser, Mary A. .	20		____ Andrew	11
Frasier, James . .	14		____ Thomas T. . . .	7
Gaines, Hiram . .	5		Hammond, William .	5
Gamble, James .	7		Handy, Isham . . .	7
Gans, James . . .	5		Harper, Lindsay . . .	7
Ghent, Daniel . .	5		Harr, Charles	9
Gibert, Joseph B.	11		Harris, John	7
____ Stephen . .	15		____ John	12
Gilbert, John L. .	21		____ John G. . .	7
Giles, Andrew . .	7		____ Richmond. . .	19
Gillam, David . .	5		____ William . .	25
Gillebow, Peter .	6		Hathorn, Lany . .	7
Glenn, James E.	22		Hatten, Benjamin .	12
Glover, Jacob H.	9		Heard, James P. . .	16
____ Jared	7		Hearst, Jesse	10

____ John . . .	13
____ John . . .	6
Hemphill,Margaret .	6
Henderson, Eleanor .	6
____ Margaret . . .	8
____ Simeon . . .	13
Herring, William B.	13
Herron, Thomas . .	7
Hester, Henry . . .	18
Hill, Benjamin . .	6
____ Joseph . . .	31
____ Joshua . . .	18
____ Uel	21
____ William . .	9
Hodges, George M.	9
____ John	10
____ William, Sr.	7
Holloway, John H. .	10
Hopper, Samuel . .	17
Houston, Alexander .	10
____ Oswald	5
Hubbard, James . .	5
Hughs, James . . .	25
Hunt, James	17
Hunter, Alexander .	6
Hutton, Joseph . . .	15
Jackson, Mathew . .	8
Johnson, Benjamin .	5
____ Elizabeth . . .	11
____ Henry	12
____ J. H.	7
____ Jonathan . .	9
____ Sugar	8
____ Warren B. .	6
Johnston, Henry .	11
Jones, Benjamin .	20
____ Dudley . . .	6
____ Isaiah . . .	8
____ John	5
____ Stephen . .	6
____ Thomas . .	5
____ Thomas . .	10
____ William T.	6

Jordan, Bartholomew . .	5
Kay, James	7
____ Robert	9
Kerby, John	5
Lassiter, Isaac	14
Latimer, C. T.	25
Lee, Stephen	18
Lesley, Robert H. . . .	8
Lesly, Joseph	6
Levillin (?), John . .	6
Leroy, Philip,Sr. . . .	10
Lewis, William B. .	6
Liddell, James	6
Lindsay, John	16
____ Robert	6
Linsey, Thomas . .	6
Linton, Samuel . .	42
____ Samuel, Junr. .	11
Lipscomb, Joel . . .	18
____ John	21
____ Nathan . . .	50
____ Thomas . .	23
____ William . .	5
Lites, Abraham .	5
Livingston, Bruce .	9
____ Bruce	11
____ Nancy	23
Logan, Andrew . .	21
____ Barbary . . .	28
Lomax, Aron . . .	5
____ George . . .	12
____ James	15
____ James, Junr. .	21
____ William	5
Long, Gabriel,Senr.	9
____ Thomas	8
McCalla, John . . .	16
McCaslan, Robert .	6
McClesky, David H.	8
McClune (?), James . . .	20
McClurg, Margaret. .	6
McComb, John. . .	20
____ Rebecca	5

Abbeville District Slaveholders

McCord, John, Junr. .	6		Mitchel, James	11
McCracken, Elizabeth	18		Mitchell, Benjamin . .	5
McDaniel, William .	11		____ Francis	24
McGaw, William . .	43		____ Judith	6
McGehee, Carr . .	43		Moore, Nicholas . .	6
____ Joanna	14		____ William	6
____ Meredith . .	9		Moragne, Isaac . . .	19
____ Michael . .	9		____ John	43
McGill, William .	7		Morah, Hugh	22
McKellar, Donald .	8		Morris, Samuel . .	6
____ Peter	7		Morrow, John . . .	8
McKinley, Robert M.	7		____ William . . .	8
McMasters, William .	16		Moseley, Joseph . .	5
McMears, William .	8		____ Richard, Sr.	19
McMurtry, John . .	9		____ Richard H. . . .	10
McQuerns, Elizabeth	6		____ Tarleton	13
Maddox, Augusta . .	10		Mosely, Henry . . .	10
____ Richard	9		Murray, Benjamin .	6
Madison, Francis .	7		Myrrick, Lyttleton . .	39
Marion, Nathaniel	44		Nash, Reuben	18
Marsh, John . . .	10		Nibbs, William . . .	9
____ Thomas . .	11		Nichols, John . . .	24
Marshall, George .	16		Noble, Ezekiel . . .	14
____ Isabella . . .	7		____ Patrick . . .	14
____ Samuel . . .	27		____ William . . .	13
Martin, George W.	20		Norris, Andrew . .	23
____ Jacob	16		____ Henson	5
____ James	29		____ John	12
____ John	13		____ Joseph . . .	5
____ Thomas P. .	24		Northcutt, Benjamin.	5
Mathews, Luke .	7		Norwood, Williamson .	52
Matterson, Benjamin	26		Oliver, John	11
Maxwell, Charles . .	10		____ John C.	7
Meriwether, Joseph .	15		Osborne, Thomas . .	10
____ Mary	6		Pace, John	20
____ Nicholas . .	9		Partlow, John	16
____ Zachariah .	6		Pascal, Milton . . .	24
Miller, Allen T. .	6		Patterson, James . .	70
____ George . . .	9		____ John	13
____ John	7		____ Josiah	11
____ Rachel . . .	8		____ Josiah, Senr. .	21
____ Samuel . .	7		____ Samuel	5
Milligan, Andrew .	12		____ Thomas	5

Pelot, Charles M. . .	9	Roberts, Benjamin . .	14
____ John F.	19	____ George.	14
Pennal, James	5	____ Lucy	6
Perrin, Samuel . . .	23	Robertson, John . . .	35
Perry, Simson	5	____ Mary	55
Pert, James	7	____ Michael . . .	6
Pettigrew, William .	7	Robinson, Richard . .	5
Phelps, Mary Ann .	8	____ Robert	70
Piles, Minian. . . .	6	____ Samuel	5
Pollard, Robert, Junr.	25	Rogers, Peter B. . .	9
Pool, Robert . . .	16	Rosemond, Mary . .	5
Pope, Sampson . . .	14	____ Samuel	5
Porter, Hugh	5	Russel, Josiah. . .	14
____ Hugh	6	Rutledge, Rasor . . .	6
____ John	6	Sail, James.	9
Postell, James .	53	____ John	9
Power, John, Sr. .	81	Sample, Alexander . .	17
Pratt, Joseph . . .	6	____ Barbary.	17
Pressly, David . .	7	____ John B.	5
____ Samuel . .	9	Sanders, Donald H. .	13
Prince, Edward .	10	____ Rebecca	6
____ Lucy . . .	14	____ Thomas A. .	17
Pucket, James .	9	Sanderson, Richard.	6
Puckett, Dabney .	24	Saxon, Benjamin H .	17
Pulliam, James .	12	Scott, William . . .	17
____ Stephen . .	5	Scudday, A. E. . . .	10
____ Zachary . .	19	Shackelford, Mordecai .	7
Pyles, William . .	8	Shackleford, James .	48
Raford, William P.	21	Shanklin, Thomas . . .	6
Rambert, Andrew .	29	Sharp, Henry	6
____ James	20	____ Robert C .	5
Ramey, John . . .	8	Shirley, Benjamin .	5
Ramsay, Samuel .	20	____ Joshua	8
Rapley, Richard A.	100	Shoemaker, James . .	5
Ravlin, John . . .	8	Simmons, John	5
Razor, Christian .	16	Sims, Lewis . . .	5
Reaves, George W. .	6	____ Thomas . . .	5
Reid, Henry	15	Slappy, Jacob . .	20
____ Samuel . . .	6	Slinkelas, John . .	7
Reynolds, William	9	Smith, James . . .	5
Richey, James, Sr. . .	5	____ John . . .	9
____ Margaret	8	____ Martha	34
____ Robert	5	____ Peter, Senr. .	13

Abbeville District Slaveholders

Name		Name	
____ Robert	7	Waller, Benjamin	8
____ William	31	____ Leonard	20
____ William W. .	42	____ Sarah	13
Speed, Michael . . .	11	Wardlaw, James . . .	38
____ Robert	6	____ John	24
Speer, Alexander .	15	____ Joseph	27
____ John	7	____ Polly	10
____ William, Junr. .	9	Ware, Edmond	27
____ William, Sr. .	11	____ James A.	28
Spraggins, William .	10	____ John	5
Sproull, James	18	Watkins, Robert	24
Stallsworth, William	7	Watson, James	35
Steger, Robert M. . .	5	____ Richard	23
Stewart, Alexander . .	17	____ Stephen. . . .	11
Stiefel, Philip . . .	8	____ William	19
Stuart, Larkin . .	15	Watt, Samuel L. . . .	8
Swain, John . . .	12	Weatherall, George .	8
____ Robert . . .	5	____ John	22
Swift, Jonathan .	6	Wedgeworth, James	10
Taggart, James .	8	Weems, James . . .	11
____ Moses	11	Wharton, Nancy . .	11
Talbert, John . . .	41	Whipple, Malcom .	9
____ Joseph . . .	6	White, Francis	8
Tennent, Martha .	21	____ John.	13
Terry, Benjamin .	9	____ John M.	5
____ Jeremiah L.	11	Whitton, Sarah . .	12
Thomas, David .	7	Wideman, Adam . . .	7
____ John, Junr. .	20	Wier, Thomas	5
Thompson, Eliza.	10	Williams, Agnes G. .	5
____ Moses	14	____ James	5
____ Nancy	10	____ John	6
____ Sarah	8	Wilson, Henry . . .	16
Tilman, David . .	11	____ Job	14
____ Edward . . .	15	____ John	14
____ Hiram . . .	17	____ John, Senr.	9
Townsend, Nath. W.	5	____ Samuel . .	8
____ Nath. W. . . .	5	____ Sarah . . .	13
Tritt, Ward	8	Wimbish, Benjamin .	8
Tullis, Aaron . . .	5	____ Didama	17
____ Moses . . .	8	____ Francis S. . . .	7
Turnbull, Jane .	9	____ William	14
Turner, Robert	6	Winn, Lettice	16
Vaughn, James . . .	7	Woods, Susan C. . .	13

Wooldridge, Martha . .	9
Wooldrige, Thomas . .	5
Wright, Martha . .	18
Wynn, Lewellyn .	13
Yarberry, John F. .	5
Yarborough, William	12
Yeldon, Anthony . .	6
Young, Francis, Junr.	8
_____ Francis, Senr. .	16
_____ John	8
_____ Robt. . . .	23
_____ Samuel . .	6
_____ Samuel . . .	11

1830 Census
(Owner of 5 or more slaves.)

Adams, Elizabeth . .	12
_____ Jesse S.	19
_____ John	8
_____ Lusey	9
_____ Savage . . .	9
_____ William . .	5
Adamson, Jonathan .	7
Adkins, James	7
_____ Thomas	11
Agnew, Andrew . .	18
_____ James	24
_____ Samuel . . .	24
Akin, William . .	6
Allen, Banester . .	23
_____ John	9
_____ John L.	52
_____ Robert . . .	8
Alston, James . .	48
Anderson, Archabald	7
_____ Richard L. . . .	6
_____ Samuel , ...	7
_____ Thomas	27
_____ William, Senr..	11
Ansley, Margaret . .	7
Appleton, Grigsby .	7
Arnold, A. B.	18

_____ Archabald	10
_____ Hart P.	22
_____ James	58
_____ Gacareah	8
Atkins, Frances	8
_____ James	8
Baker, Alpheus	10
_____ Joseph T.	8
_____ Samuel T.	7
_____ William F.	14
Banks, Nathaniel	16
Barmore, Lucy	5
_____ Est. James B. . . .	17
_____ Larkin	5
Barns, Mercer	12
Barr, William H. . . .	12
Barrat, John P. . . .	43
Bartin, James H. . . .	10
Baskin, James H. . .	10
_____ John	12
_____ John A. . . .	15
Bearden, Eli	7
Beasley, Jesse . . .	8
_____ William	5
Beckley, Francis . . .	8
Belcher, Washington . . .	38
Bell, Abraham	10
Bellanger, Peter	11
Belot, Jacob	6
Bevel, Peter.	10
Bever, Peter	10
Bigby,Archd.	11
_____ George	8
Blain, Mary	23
_____ Robert A.	16
Blain, Mary . . .	5
Blake, John	11
_____ John, Sr.	5
_____ William N.	10
Bonnett, Johne J.	21
Boole (?), Agnes . . .	10
Boosman, Susan . .	7
Boozer, Henry	7

Abbeville District Slaveholders

Boshell, Jesse C. .	32	____ Joseph, Junr. . . .	5
Bosnan (?), William.	9	____ Martha	10
Bowey, Arthur	21	____ Nathan	17
Bowie, Alexander .	28	____ Patterick	42
____ Langdon. . . .	6	____ Thomas P.	31
____ Samuel	16	____ William	29
Boyd, Robert	7	____ William	43
Branian, Thomas .	5	Calvert, Hugh A.	5
Brock, Georg . . .	7	____ Jesse	17
____ James L. . . .	5	____ John	22
____ Thomas . .	6	Cameron, George I. . . .	7
Brooks, Stanmore	20	Campbell, W. S.	47
____ Wiley	48	Camrin, John	15
Brown, Eliza . . .	6	Canida, John	6
____ John	7	Cannon, Nathaniel . .	9
Brownlee, George .	13	Carson, James	24
____ George	24	____ Martin H. . . .	5
____ John	6	____ Thomas	15
____ William . . .	22	____ William	16
Buchanan, James. .	6	Carter, William . . .	6
____ John	10	Casey, John	14
____ Robert	15	Castin, John	6
____ William	5	Chaney, Nathan . . .	8
____ William	10	Charter, Richard B. . .	32
Bull, William A. . . .	48	Chetam, Martha . . .	5
Bullock, Elizabeth .	17	Chetham, John . . .	13
Bunton, Isaac . . .	29	____ Nancy	25
Burley, John F. .	8	____ Richard	7
Burt, Asa	19	Chevis, Martha . .	5
____ Armistead .	6	Chiles, John	27
Burton, John . . .	25	____ Milton	5
Busby, Edmond .	5	____ Robert	30
Caldwell, Georg .	11	____ Thomas . . .	28
____ James	10	____ William . . .	25
____ John G. . . .	6	Chitham, ____ter . .	9
____ Samuel . . .	10	Clark, John	10
____ William H.	12	____ William . . .	6
Calerhan, John . .	6	Clinkscales, Francis .	17
Calhoun, Ephraim . .	6	____ John . . .	16
____ James	28	Cobb, Charles . .	8
____ John C. . . .	34	____ Erman . . .	7
____ John Ewen .	9	____ James . . .	53
____ Joseph. . . .	22	____ Sarah . . .	6

Collier, Edward . .	121
Colman, John T.	16
____ Nancy . . .	23
Connor, Elizabeth .	8
____ Francis . . .	57
____ George . . .	12
____ Paul M. . .	11
____ Wesley . .	17
Cook, Philip . .	9
Cooper, Agripa .	16
Cothran, John .	15
____ Mary Ann .	16
Cotrell, Thomas .	5
Covington, Richard	29
Cowen, Isaac	43
____ James	5
____ James	5
____ Samuel	2
____Samuel	9
Crafford, Arabelar . . .	13
Crawford, Mary	19
____ Mary.	10
____ Robert A.	10
____ Robert F.	12
____ Samuel	11
____ William	5
Criswell, Sarah . . .	22
Cromer, Elizabeth .	22
Crossen, Hugh . . .	15
____ Robert	9
Cruse, Stanley . . .	6
Cullins, Charles . .	9
Cunningham, John .	15
____ Robert A. . . .	22
____ Thomas	9
____ William	16
Curnee, William . .	5
Dabbs, Elizabeth .	7
Dabs, Elizabeth . .	9
Davis, Chesley . .	15
____ E. S.	17
____ Ephraigan . .	12
____ Fleming . . .	14

____ Joseph	27
____ Joshua	11
____ Samuel	6
____ Thomas	8
____ Thos. N.	11
Defer, David B.	20
Dendy, Charles	18
Devinport, Sqe (?) . .	63
Devlin, James	12
Dickson, Hugh	19
____ John	5
____ Thomas	7
____ Thomas	7
Donald, John	10
Donnal, John	8
Donnald, Margaret . .	6
Dosier, James	26
Douglas, Donald . .	24
____ Thomas	6
____ William	7
Downey, Sarah . . .	20
Dowtin, Thomas P. .	9
Drennan, William T. .	6
Drinkard, Martha B. .	5
Dubois,Joshua	17
Dun, Robert	7
Dunn, William . . .	10
Eakins, Joseph . . .	15
Eddings, William .	42
Edwards, Elizabeth .	14
Ellis, John E.	5
____ John L.	9
____ Robert, Junr. .	11
____ Robert N. . . .	6
English, Daniel . . .	6
Evans, William . . .	16
Fair, Archible	10
____ James	17
Fewer, Henry	5
Fooshe, Charles B. .	11
____ John	20
____ Sarah	21
Foster, Elizabeth . .	25

_____ Joseph	20	Hacket, Ann	12
_____ Joseph	5	_____ Martin	19
Franklin, Asa . . .	8	Haddon, Abram . .	9
_____ James	14	Hagan, Edward . . .	5
_____ Sarah	8	Hall, David	8
Frasier, James . .	16	_____ Joseph	16
Frazier, John G. .	25	Hametion, Thomas I.	10
Fuller, Raison (?)	12	Hamilton, Alex . . .	26
Gaines, Elizabeth . .	13	_____ Andrew, Senr . .	10
_____ Thomas A. . .	13	_____ William	5
Gains, Larn	5	_____ William	10
_____ Richard	6	Harmon, Thomas . .	15
Gary, William L. .	16	Harper, Linsey	8
Gauden, Robert C.	23	Harris, Elever	7
Gent, Jesse	9	_____ John	13
Gibert, Sarah B. .	24	_____ John C.	6
Gibson, Rober . .	7	_____ Mary	5
Gilabow, Peter . .	9	_____ Nathaniel . . .	5
Giles, Andrew . .	12	_____ Richmond . . .	7
Gilbert, Jane . . .	6	_____ Thomas	5
Gillam, James . .	53	_____ William	50
Gillaspa, David .	12	_____ William H. . .	16
Gillian, James . .	21	Harthorn, Leney . .	5
Glasgow, James .	10	Haselet, Nancy . .	5
Glenn, James E. .	11	Henderson, Ann . .	9
Glover, William H.	8	_____ Richard	9
Goldin, Reubin . .	11	_____ Samuel	6
Gray, Frederick . .	26	Herndon, Stephen . .	35
_____ Henry (A) .	46	Hickley, Thomas. .	23
_____ James . .	9	Hill, Benjamin	42
_____ James A. .	9	_____ Hamilton	8
_____ James A.	7	_____ Joseph W.	8
_____ Jane . . .	9	_____ Joshua	13
_____ John . . .	7	_____ Martha	13
_____ John F. .	24	_____ Samuel	7
_____ Sarah . .	5	_____ Uel	21
_____ Thomas J. .	10	Hobbs, Burrel	9
Green, Robert H. .	7	Hodges, A. J.	10
Griffin, Est. of I .	33	_____ Gabriel	11
_____ James F. . . .	18	_____ George W. . . .	26
_____ Richard . . .	56	_____ James, Sr. . . .	5
_____ Vincent . . .	32	_____ John	9
Groves, Joseph . .	29	Holaway, George .	15

Holloway, John . .	16	Key, Robert	12
Hopper, Elizabeth .	12	Kirkpatrick, William H.	6
Horbot (?), Robert .	10	Kirkwood, Hugh	11
Hose, Henry	6	Knew, Daniel	5
Houston, Alengnear	22	Klugh, P. D.	27
_____ James	9	Lasetor (?), B. H. . . .	18
_____ Oswell . . .	5	Lasiter, Isaac	27
Howy, John B. .	10	Lasley, Joseph	5
Hucison (?), Meriman	18	_____ Robert H. . . .	17
Huckbay, George W.	7	_____ William	11
Hughey, John (S) . .	15	Latimore, Clemment .	16
Hughs, James	16	_____ James	12
Hunt, Eliza	41	Leak, Samuel	6
Hunter, Alexander .	43	Lee, Stephen	19
Huston, James A. .	5	Leroy, Isack	6
Irwin, Samuel . . .	7	_____ Philip	5
Jacks, Samuel A. .	16	Lesley, David	5
James, Samuel C.	5	Levingston, Agnes .	10
Johnson, Henry .	20	Lewis, Elizabeth . .	6
_____ James	11	Liddle, Sarah	22
_____ Jonathan . .	10	Lifford, Joel A. . . .	5
_____ Lemuel . . .	8	_____ Obedience . . .	6
_____ Patrick . . .	8	Lindsay, Robert . . .	19
_____ Robert R. .	7	Linsey, James	10
_____ Sarah	11	_____ John	13
_____ Sugar	19	Linton, H. S.	11
Johnstone, John .	10	_____ Thomas I. . .	13
Jones, Adam C. .	5	_____ William N. .	6
_____ Benjamin . .	7	Lion, Noah	6
_____ John (S) . .	5	Lippford, Dewey . .	6
_____ Robert . . .	10	Lipscomb, John. .	46
_____ Stephen . .	12	_____ Est. of T. . . .	28
_____ Thomas . .	10	Lites, Abram	11
_____ Thomas . .	12	Livingston, James . .	7
_____ William T.	10	_____ Jno. F.	11
Jordan, Barth. .	14	_____ Thomas	5
_____ Jonathan .	13	_____ William	22
_____ Samuel . .	15	Lockhart, Joel	9
Kay, Charles . .	26	Logan, Andrew . . .	19
_____ James . .	9	_____ Barbara	30
_____ John . . .	5	_____ John	19
_____ Wm. W. .	15	_____ Telar	7
Keller, David . . .	12	Lomax, Aron	11

_____ Georg . . .	11	Mance, Andrew	12
_____ James, Junr. .	59	Mantz, Christopher .	14
_____ James, Senr. .	40	Marion, Nathaniel . .	70
_____ William . . .	13	Marner, Thomas . . .	6
_____ William, Senr.	6	Mars, John A.	7
Loveless, William .	19	Marshall, George . .	27
Luyllen, John . . .	10	_____ Isobela	19
Lyons, Elijah . . .	16	_____ John	13
_____ Elisha	6	_____ Samuel	58
McCallister, William .	7	Martin, George W. . .	16
McCaslin, Robert . . .	7	_____ Jacob	18
McCelister, William .	19	_____ James	6
McCelvey, John . . .	10	_____ John	6
McCeterick, James .	6	_____ John C.	39
McClinton, Robert .	5	_____ John C.	6
McClusek (?), David H.	7	_____ Nancy	18
McCollister, David .	6	_____ Nancy	21
McComb, Ketty . .	13	_____ Pharis	6
_____ William . . .	5	Mathews, Luke . . .	9
McConnall, John .	9	Mathison, Heggerson .	14
McCord, John . . .	13	Matterson, George . .	9
McDonald, William, Sr.	5	_____ John	16
McDuffie, George . .	34	_____ William	11
McFarlin, James . . .	5	Maxwell, Charles . .	9
McGaw, William . .	49	Mealy, Thomas . . .	6
McGee, Mical	13	Meouts (?), Nathanile	9
McGehee, Adison .	23	Merane, Milly	5
_____ John	15	Meriwether, Martha .	21
_____ John, Sr.	17	_____ Mary	11
_____ Meredith . . .	27	Miller, Allen T. . . .	11
_____ Sharlotte . . .	22	_____ Andrew	5
McGill, William . .	6	_____ Ebanazer . .	7
McGilleand, John .	9	_____ George A. . . .	14
McKellar, Donald .	17	_____ Rachel	9
McKelvey, James . .	9	_____ Samuel	10
McKinney, Robert W.	5	Mincham, Joshua .	13
McLaurin, John . . .	6	Mitchel, Francis . .	24
McMullin, Archble .	6	Mitchell, James . .	16
McNear, Margrit. . .	7	Moore, Hylam . . .	5
Madden, Richard . .	21	_____ Robert (S) . .	7
Maddox, Augusta .	16	_____ William . . .	9
Mager, John P. . . .	7	Morgan, Malon . . .	6
Malden, Archibald .	6	Morighn (?), John .	42

Morrighey, Isaac . . .	28
Morris, Benjamin . .	55
____ Samuel	5
Morrison, John V. .	19
Morrow, Hugh . . .	13
____ James	6
Mosely, John W. .	5
____ Tarden	8
Mosley, Henry . .	21
____ Joseph . . .	8
Murry, James . .	10
Myrrick, Tarlton .	30
Neely, Charles . . .	15
Nelson, Henry . . .	17
Noble, Ezeke . . .	7
____ Mary	32
____ Mary H. . .	26
____ Patrick . . .	41
____ William P.	12
Norrel, Joseph . .	7
Norris, Eli	21
Northcutt, Benjamin .	8
Norwood, Daniel . .	15
____ John	9
____ Williamson .	99
Oliver, Alexander . .	9
Orsburn, John . . .	7
Owen, Thomas E.	9
Paget, John	6
Parker, John W. .	9
____ Thomas . .	32
Parsons,Mary . .	5
Partlow, John . .	48
Pascal, Milton .	17
____ Samuel . .	5
Patten, Archd. .	7
____ William . .	32
Patterson, James .	9
____ James	104
____ Joseph . . .	10
____ Josiah, Esq.	5
____ Thomas . .	5
Paul, Sarah . . .	10

Pedegrew, William . .	6
Pelote, Charles M. . .	17
Perrin, Abner	23
____ Eunice	43
Perry, Benjamin . . .	12
Persell, William . .	8
Pert, James	5
Peterson, Q. Clenanaer	6
Petigrue, William . . .	7
Pettigrew, Robt. . . .	6
Pettis, Anno (?) . .	6
Piles, Lewis	12
____ William . . .	15
Pinchback, William . .	53
Pool, Abraham	15
Porter, John	19
____ Samuel	5
Power, Henry F. . .	8
Powers, John	7
Prat, Elizabeth . . .	8
Prater, James W. .	12
Pratt, Sarah	10
Presly, John B. . .	5
Pressly, David . . .	6
____ George W. . .	13
____ John T. . . .	11
____ Samuel . . .	29
Prince, Edward . .	5
____ Hugh M. . .	5
____ Hutson . . .	6
____ Leney . . .	16
Pucket, Frances . .	5
Pulliam, James . .	18
Pullum, Larkin . .	5
Pullock, Agnes . .	11
Quarles, Robert G.	15
Raborne, David . .	7
Radly, Robert . . .	8
Raford, William P.	24
Ramey, John	9
____ Samuel	6
Ramsay, Daniel. . .	13
Rasor, Ezeal	20

____ John	8	____ Stephen	6
Ravlin, John	5	Runnels, John V. .	6
Ray, Silas	6	Sample, Barbara . .	27
Reagan, Paul R. . .	6	____ Isaac	12
Reed, George	16	____ James	20
Reede. Henry	9	____ John B. . . .	13
____ John S. . . .	17	____ John N.	16
Reid, Samuel	12	____ Washington. .	6
Reves, George W. .	12	Sampson, William .	11
Reynolds, Bennet .	9	Scott, Alexander . .	9
Richey, Jas. W. L.	10	____ Archble	7
____ John	6	____ John	11
____ John	11	____ Mary	28
____ Joseph . . .	11	____ William B. . . .	26
____ Margaret . .	9	Scudday, A. E. . . .	9
____ Mary	6	Selva, Owen	5
____ Robert (BL) .	16	Shackleford, James .	67
____ William	7	____ Mordica	7
Ridell (?), Francis .	7	Sharp, Henry	7
Riley, Andrew . . .	6	____ Robert C. . .	12
____ Thomas . . .	5	Shirley, Nathaniel .	6
Roberts, Georg . .	7	Simmons, Lewis G.	25
____ Jane	8	Sims, Thomas . . .	6
____ Lucy	6	Smith, Charles . . .	9
Robertson, Andrew .	34	____ James	13
____ Delpha . . .	6	____ Joel	29
____ Hugh (Le) .	24	____ Moses	14
____ Moldan (?) .	5	____ Peter (S) . .	10
____ Reuben . . .	13	____ Robert . . .	10
____ Richard . . .	6	____ Robert . . .	6
____ Samuel . . .	9	____ Thomas . .	23
____ Thomas . .	43	____ William . .	9
____ William . .	5	____ William . .	16
Rodgers, Peter B.	12	Speer, Alexander . .	35
Rolen, William .	6	____ George W. . . .	5
Rolin, Nathaniel .	5	____ John	13
Roman, John . .	7	____ William	9
____ Thomas . .	7	Spence, Robert . . .	7
Roof, John	5	Sproull, Rebecca . .	37
Ropp (?),Grisham . .	13	Stallsworth, Thomas .	7
Rosaman, Samuel .	8	____ William	11
____ Thomas . . .	14	Stark, Charles	19
Ross, Dorothy . .	7	____ Wiett	46

Starke, Reubin . . .	74	Vines, Jabish	11
Staunton, Joseph . .	7	Wair, Albert N. . . .	6
Stewart, David	7	____ Edmon	57
____ John	21	Waddle, Isack . . .	10
Still, Richmond . .	14	____ Moses	44
Sturdman, Alexander S.	22	Wakefield, Hezekiah .	10
Sullivan, D.	12	Walker, Henry . .	10
____ Elisa	7	____ John	6
____ Seaborn . . .	15	____ Sueley (?) . .	6
Sumner, Benjamin . . .	16	____ William . .	5
Swain, Anna	10	Wallace, Robert . .	14
____ Robert	6	Waller, Albert . . .	35
Sybert, George . .	8	____ Nancy . . .	11
T_____, Richard M.	24	Wallis, Robert	5
Tagart, Moses	14	Wardlaw, David L. . .	24
Taggart, James . . .	7	____ James	56
Talbert, John . . .	5	____ Joseph	44
Tarrant, Robert . . .	8	____ Mary	11
Tegue, Eliza	14	Ware, James . . .	5
Tennent, Martha .	12	____ John . . .	9
____ Wm.	13	____ William . .	11
Thisttin (?), Gabriel .	17	____ William . .	26
Thompson, Samuel .	14	____ William	6
Timmerman, Lemmie .	10	Watkins, A. P.	8
Tinch, Margaret . . .	9	Watson, James	35
Tolbert, Dan . . .	5	____ Stephen	11
____ Nancy	16	____ Terry	33
____ Robert	13	____ William	30
____ William . . .	10	Watt. Samuel W.	14
Tolman, Edward . .	20	Weatherall, Elizabeth .	20
Tomkins, Samuel .	5	____ Marshall . . .	8
Tragan, Frances . . .	7	Weems, Agnes	8
Travis, Joseph . . .	17	Wells, Mary	6
Tribble, Lemuel . .	8	White, Daily	6
Tucker, Robert C. .	22	____ John	18
Tullis, J. C.	9	Whitlock, Thomas L.	12
Turnbull, Jane . . .	6	Whitten, Isack Y. .	17
Turner, John, Sr. . .	9	Wideman, Adam . .	8
____ Robert	12	____ Henry	7
____ Robert	12	____ John	16
____ William . . .	10	____ Lenard	15
Vernon, Sarah . . .	5	____ Leonard	26
Vickry, Dines . . .	6	Wiley, Davis	5

Abbeville District Slaveholders

Williams, David . . .	7
_____ James	5
_____ John	18
_____ Ludwell	6
_____ M. G.	7
_____ Thos. W.	24
Williamson, Saunders	25
Willson, James . .	5
_____ John	8
_____ Margret . . .	18
Wilson, Elizabeth .	5
_____ James . .	7
_____ Robert . . .	8
Wimbush, Frances .	8
_____ Totter C. . . .	11
Winbush, Peter . .	12
Winslow, Dabney .	6
Wright, Daniel . .	18
Yarborough , Moses	11
_____ William . .	29
Yeldell, Robert .	9
Young, Goleslaw .	23
_____ Jane	13
_____ Martha . . .	10
_____ Robert . . .	11
_____ Samuel . . .	10
_____ Valentine . . .	9
_____ William	16

1840 Census
(owners of 5 or more)

Adams, Elizabeth . .	28
_____ Jesse L.	23
_____ Jno.	15
Adamson, J. B.	11
Agnew, Enoch	10
_____ Isaiah	7
_____ Jas.	24
_____ Saml.	8
_____ Samuel	35
Aiken, Jos.	13
Akim, Joseph	5
_____ Joseph, Sr. . .	20

Allen, Banister . . .	24
_____ J. N.	10
_____ J. S.	80
_____ Sarah . . .	6
Alston, Jas. . . .	8
_____ Jas	69
Anderson, D. . .	24
_____ R. L. . . .	5
_____ Saml. . . .	13
_____ T.	9
_____ W.	14
_____ W. C. . . .	19
_____ Walter . . .	5
Appleton, Grigsby .	10
Armstrong, H.	6
_____ John	15
_____ W.	5
Arnold, A. B.	52
_____ A. B.	8
_____ Archibald . . .	46
_____ Frances	9
_____ Hart P. . . .	7
Ashley, Wm. . . .	16
Atkins, David . . .	13
_____ Francis	15
_____ Rosa	10
Baker, A.	13
_____ Jas. T.	20
_____ Samuel S. . .	13
Baremore, Mary . .	6
Barksdale, S.	27
_____ Wm.	81
Barmore, E.	5
_____ L.	10
_____ Wm.	18
Barnett, J. J.	21
Barr, W. H.	17
Barrat, Thomas . . .	15
Barrett, John P. . . .	32
Barton, John A. . . .	25
Baskin, F. Y.	6
_____ J. H.	18
_____ Jas. S.	17

____ John	15
Beard, C. F.	6
____ Henry	5
____ Samuel	14
Beazly, Willison B.	12
Belcher, R. E. . . .	24
____ W. W.	7
____ Washington .	62
Bell, J. F.	14
____ Jas. E. G. .	7
Bentley, H. . . .	5
Bigby, Arch . . .	16
____ Geo.	15
Binnett, John . .	8
Black, E. . . .	8
____ James .	8
Blain, Mary .	8
Blake, John . .	10
____ Wm. N. . .	18
Boag, S. W. . . .	8
Boozer, Henry . .	13
Bowie, William .	18
Boyd, J. L. . . .	28
Bozman, Jas. . .	11
Bradley, A. . .	6
____ Jno. . . .	16
____ Wm. . .	13
Brady, R. . . .	25
Branch, Franklin .	5
Branson, Eli S. .	5
Branyan, Thos. . .	8
Britt, J. B.	10
____ John B. . .	75
Brooks, Henry . .	8
____ S. B.	40
____ Wm.	23
____ Wm. B. . .	32
Brown, Jas. . . .	7
Brownlee, G. W.	6
____ Geo	20
____ J. B. . . .	15
____ John . . .	27
____ R.	5

Buchanan, Daniel . . .	9
____ E.	8
____ F. A.	6
____ Nancy	6
____ R. E.	5
____ Wm.	7
Buckham, Wm. . . .	18
Bulger, D. S.	56
Burt, A.	6
Burton, Caleb . . .	7
Butler, William . .	5
Byrd, Thos. B. . .	43
Cain, Samuel . . .	30
Caldwell, Edney . .	19
____ Hariot	13
____ J. G.	18
____ Jas.	23
____ John	7
____ Norwood . . .	26
____ Robert	20
____ Thos.	13
____ W. H.	5
Calhoun, Agnes . .	7
____ Downs	48
____ E. R.	11
____ Edward	22
____ Francis	43
____ Jas.	32
____ Jas. E.	153
____ John A. . . .	21
____ Nathan	23
____ P.	47
____ S. A.	24
____ W. H.	8
____ Wm.	76
____ Wm. M. . . .	13
Callaham, B. . . .	5
____ J.	11
Calvert, J. M. . .	21
____ John	28
Campbell, Wm. .	7
Carson, M. H. . . .	8
Carter, David	5

____ Larkin . . .	13
Cason, B.	7
____ Jas.	8
____ Mary . . .	11
Cheatham, John C.	14
____ Martha	6
____ Peter	15
____ Thos.	35
Childs, Robert . .	25
____ Wesley . . .	19
Chiles, James M. .	34
____ Jno.	38
____ M.	10
____ Thos. W. .	35
____ William . .	20
Chipley, J. L. . .	6
Clark, Hardy . . .	13
Clarke, M. P. . .	12
____ Wm.	14
Cleckly, D. F. .	148
Clinkscales, F. B. . .	29
____ G. B.	7
____ J. B.	5
____ John	23
Cobb, Andrew . .	5
____ Charles . .	11
____ Edmond . .	10
____ Nathaniel .	10
Cochran, John .	15
Conner, Elizabeth	6
____ P. M. . . .	20
Connett, Drayton .	10
Cook, Jas. . . .	8
____ S. B. . . .	5
Cosby, Robt. .	6
Covin, D. . . .	10
____ L.	8
Cowan, Jane . .	11
____ Jas.	19
Cowin, Saml. .	23
Cox, G.	27
Cransion (?), G. J.	15
Crawford, G. B. .	11

____ Mary	20
____ R.	5
____ Thos.	10
Crews, Stanley . .	19
Cunningham, John .	13
____ Sarah	9
____ Thomas . . .	13
Danely, J. E. . . .	7
Dansby, J.	12
Davis, C.	26
____ Ephraim . .	11
____ J.	9
____ J. A.	6
____ John . . .	11
____ R. M. . . .	16
____ Thos. . . .	7
Dawson, John . .	8
Dendy, Charles . .	41
Deracoat, A.	10
Devall, Jas. O. . .	21
Devlin, James . .	17
____ Jas. J. . . .	8
____ Robert . . .	14
Dickson, Hugh .	38
____ Thos. . . .	10
Donald, J. A. . .	6
____ John	20
Donaldson, D. .	6
Doudin (?), T. P. .	26
Downey, S. . . .	5
____ Sarah . . .	7
Drenon, W. F. . .	15
Drumond, Ephraim .	5
Dubose, Joshua . . .	23
____ Joshua W. . . .	7
Duglas, Wm.	9
Dunn, Robert . . .	8
____ William . . .	7
Eddins, William . .	55
Edmunds, S.	16
Edwards, Amus . .	7
____ Mary E. . . .	57
Ellis, Jas. C. . . .	5

Name		Name	
____ John E.	9	____ George. . . .	18
____ John L.	17	____ J.	14
____ Margaret . . .	14	____ J. F.	10
____ Robert	13	____ Jas.	15
English, Danl. . .	9	____ John	9
Fair, Jas.	30	Graves, Thomas . .	28
Fife, Samuel . .	14	Griffin, Larkin . . .	33
Finley, Jane . .	27	____ Richd.	82
Fisher, Stephen .	5	____ T.	8
Foshee, Chas. B.	14	____ Vincent . . .	44
____ John, Sr. . .	35	Groves, Jos. . . .	25
____ John W. . .	6	____ R. N.	9
____ Sarah	17	Hackett, An . . .	14
Foster, J. E. . . .	14	____ Martin . .	31
____ Joseph . . .	35	Haddon, A. W. . . .	5
Franklin, John .	5	____ Abraham . . .	10
____ Sarah . . .	5	____ J. F.	6
____ Williston W.	5	Hagan, Edward . . .	8
____ Wm. . . .	7	Hampton, E.	8
Frashier, James .	36	Hall, William . . .	7
____ T. S. L. . .	10	Hamilton, J. A. . .	6
Frasier, J. G. . .	22	Harden, J. G.	9
____ M. A. . . .	19	Hardy, M.	8
Fulton, T.	5	Harkness, Robert E. .	11
Gaines, Elizabeth .	13	Harper, L.	8
____ Richd.	14	Harr, Francis. . .	6
Gary, Thos. R. . .	25	Harriman, Thos. . .	29
Ghent, Jesse . . .	15	Harris, E.	6
Gibert, J.	17	____ Elizabeth. .	91
____ Jas. F. . . .	38	____ M.	16
Giles, Andrew . .	19	____ N.	11
Gillebeau, Peter .	15	____ Richmond . .	13
Gillespie, A. . . .	9	____ T. L.	7
Gilliam, David . .	11	____ T. W.	60
____ James	60	Haskell, Charles R.	92
Gilmer, Robert . .	10	Hawthorn, A. C. . .	8
Golding, Griffin .	9	____ D. O.	12
____ M.	18	____ John	7
Gordon, Robt. C. .	35	____ Thos.	5
Goree, Isham . . .	6	____ Thos.	5
Graham, Wm	6	Hazelet, A.	6
____ John . .	5	Hearse, John	26
Gray, E.	15	Henderson, An . . .	13

Abbeville District Slaveholders

Henry, Francis	5		____ R. D.	9
Herd, An	9		____ S.	21
Herndon, Stephen .	57		Jones, A. C.	9
Hill, J.	20		____Benjan. F. . .	15
____ Martha . . .	14		____ E.	35
____ Richard. . .	7		____ J. P.	7
____ Richmond .	14		____ Jas. Y.	9
Hodges, A. F. . .	17		____ M.	28
____ Gabriel . .	18		____ Pinkney. . .	11
____ Geo. W. .	35		____ R.	16
____ Robert . .	6		____ Robert . . .	30
____ Saml. A. .	16		____ Thos.	30
Hoges, William .	5		____ Wm. T. . . .	23
Holeman, E. P.	6		Jordan, Bart. . . .	27
____ J. W. . . .	11		____ Jonathan . . .	40
____ R. S. . .	8		____ Saml.	27
Hollaway, Geo . .	32		Kay, Charles . . .	5
Holmes, W. .	18		____ James	15
____ Wm. . .	26		____ John	10
Hopper, Elizabeth .	17		____ R. H.	11
Horton, Jno. (?) .	54		Kellar, David . . .	20
Hose, B.	6		____ John	5
Houston, A. .	28		Keller, John	24
____ J. D. . .	7		Kennedy, I.	8
Huckabee, G. W.	12		____ Jno.	10
Huckerby, J. . .	9		Killingsworth, J. .	7
Hughey, Joseph .	5		____ N.	15
____ Vachel . . .	5		Kinman, Saml. . .	6
Hunter, Alexander .	61		____ Winniford . .	12
____ Marion . . .	21		Kirkpatrick, W. H. .	14
Hurst, Jno.	69		Klugh, P. D.	47
____ Jno. W. . .	18		Laramoor, Jas. . . .	16
Hutchison, M. . .	25		Latimer, E. T. . . .	25
____ R.	6		____ J. M.	9
Hutchinson, Wm.	6		Latimore, R.	7
Jacobs, Moses . .	22		Ledbetter, H. W. . . .	15
Johnson, Benjamn.	15		Lee, J. F.	23
____ Elbert	9		____ Stephen	24
____ J. W. H. . .	16		____ Thos.	10
____ Jas.	13		Leroy, P.	15
____ Jonathan . .	18		Lesley, Wm.	22
____ Jonathan . .	23		Leslie, Jas.	7
____ L.	6		Lesly, D.	8

____ R. H. . . .	22	McClenon, John	24
Liddell, B. . . .	8	McClmore, John . . .	13
Lifford, Terasa .	8	McCombs, H.	9
Light, A.	24	____ R.	10
Lindsay, James .	15	McCraven, Robert . . .	6
____ Jos.	8	McDowal, Patrick . .	13
Lipford, H. M. .	12	McDuffie, George . .	135
Livingston, Jonath. F.	18	McGee, M.	9
Lockhart, J. J. . .	8	McGehee, A. H. . .	9
Logan, Andrew . .	39	____ Charlett . . .	23
____ John	22	McKee, Elinor . . .	5
Lomax, Aaron . .	17	McKeller, David . .	22
____ Geo.	17	____ John	7
____ Lucy	13	____ Peter	15
____ Matilda . .	53	McKelvey, Jas. . . .	7
____ William . .	10	____ John	22
Lominac (?),M. W.	5	McKitrick, B.	24
Long, Franz . . .	8	McLaren, John . . .	12
____ Wm.	7	McMahan, Mary . .	5
Lucius, F.	9	McMillian, L. . . .	5
____ F. S. . . .	12	McNair, Robt. . . .	6
Lyddell, Jas. . .	8	McQuirns, Agnes . .	5
Lydell, Sarah . .	15	McWilliams, Robt. . .	13
Lynch, A. W. .	26	Maberry, Jas. L.	9
Lyon, Elijah . .	9	Mabery, R. L.	9
____ Elisha . . .	11	Maddox, Letice	6
Lyons, Jno. . . .	12	____ Richd.	35
____ Jos.	7	Mahone, John	5
____ T. J. . . .	9	Majors, Samuel B. .	5
Lysford, J. J. . .	8	Malden, A., Jr. . . .	5
McAdams, Charlote .	9	Malone, Jas.	7
McCalister, J. . . .	5	Man, R. M. . . .	5
____ Wm.	6	Mantz, A.	21
____ Wm.	9	Mantze, C. W. . .	21
McCalla, S.	27	Marion, Jane . . .	11
McCants, David W.	10	Marshal, Geo. . . .	31
____ Nat	31	____ Joseph	11
McCarter, M. . . .	7	Marshall, Saml. . .	81
McCaslan, Jas. . .	14	Martin, Edmund . .	5
____ M. O.	14	____ J. C.	11
____ Robt.	7	____ Jacob	21
____ Wm.	5	____ Jas.	6
McCaw, W. H. . .	41	____ John A.	33

____ John R. . . .	5	Murray, J.	26
____ Nancy	13	Nelson, Enoch	11
____ P.	21	Noble, Andrew . . .	12
____ R. H.	9	____ E. P.	43
____ S.	22	____ Mary	20
Mathews, John . .	7	____ Wm. P. . . .	16
____ Jos. C. . . .	7	Norrell, Joseph . .	10
Matison, Geo. . .	11	North, Jane	31
____ Liza	13	Norwood, Jas. . .	28
Mauldin, A., Sr. .	13	____ John	11
Mays, Mathew . .	17	____ W.	106
____ Medy	8	____ W.	11
Means, Wm. . .	8	Oliver, A.	11
Miller, Allen R.	16	____ J.	40
____ G. A.	37	Osborn, H.	5
____ H.	5	Owen, T. E.	21
____ Jacob . . .	14	Palmer, R. M. . . .	51
____ John . . .	9	Parker, Elizabeth . .	22
____ N. H. . .	7	____ J.	6
____ Sam . .	15	____ T.	38
Mills, W. L. .	8	Partlow, J. Y. L. .	38
Moore, Robert .	11	____ John	29
____ Thomas .	11	____ John A.	25
____ Thos . . .	8	____ Wm. D.	22
____ William .	16	Pascal, Sarah	17
Moragne, Isaac .	29	____ Wm. M. . . .	16
____ M. G. . .	7	Patterson, J.	12
____ P. B. . .	2	____ M. L.	63
____ Peter . .	20	Patton, Jane	23
Morgan, Malone .	6	Pearson, J. L.	36
Morison, Wm. .	7	Peart, James	6
Morris, J. A. . . .	16	Pelot, C. M.	7
____ Saml. . .	11	Pennal, H. F.	24
Morrow, James L.	7	Perrey, Lucy	5
____ Samuel . .	10	Perrin, E.	20
Morton, Thos. W.	7	____ T. C.	7
Mosely, E. B. . .	5	____ T. C.	15
____ Henry . . .	20	Peryman, Sarah . . .	14
____ J.	13	Petigru, R.	8
____ Jurdin . . .	12	____ T.	16
____ M.	14	____ Thos., USN .	32
____ Wm.	6	Porter, John	30
Murphy, M. . .	5	Posey, B. L.	13

Power, H. F....	22	Riley, Andrew	9
_____ J., Jr. .. .	10	Riley, Andrew....	18
Prater, J.S. N. ..	27	_____ Jas........	5
Pratt, Elihu	12	_____ Thos......	7
_____ John ...	6	Roberson, N.....	8
_____ Robert ..	21	_____ John......	12
_____ W. ...	8	_____ Wm......	5
Presley, E. E. .	10	Roberts, Thos. J....	5
Pressley, G. .	25	Robertson, J.....	18
Price, Jos., Jr. .	10	_____ Jas.	9
Prince, H. M. .	10	_____ M........	11
_____ Hudson ..	33	Robinson, Hugh ...	9
Pruit, Daniel..	8	_____ N.........	32
Puckett, Rhos. R. .	7	_____ Reubin	37
Pulliam, Rhoda ..	15	_____ Wm....	7
_____ Wiley....	8	Rodgers, Lewis	14
Pursley,Jas. ...	8	Rogers, D. M.......	17
Pyles, E. H. ..	7	_____ P..........	9
Raiford, Wm. P. .	24	Roof, Christian	15
Ramey, Johnson .	6	Roomans, John	8
Ramsay, D.	18	Ross, Stephen.....	6
Rasor, Christopher	31	_____ Thos.......	11
_____ E.....	19	Roterrick, John	13
_____ John	16	Rowland, Nat.	18
Ravinel, A.....	9	Ruff, Jno	11
Ray, Silas	5	Russel, John	13
Read, J. S. ...	28	Rykard, Jacob	5
Red, Geo.....	11	_____ Mary	10
_____ John C. ..	12	Sadler, William...	8
Reed, Saml...	18	Sanders, W. R.....	5
Reuff, G. A. ..	13	Scott, A........	9
Reynolds, Bennett .	22	_____ A.........	14
_____ Larkin	37	_____ J. D.......	6
_____ Vincent ...	9	_____ M........	31
Richardson, John .	9	_____ Wm. B.......	5
Rice, James H. ..	12	Seawright, J.......	14
Richey, J.....	7	Selby, Owen	5
_____ J. W.....	8	Sharp, Henry	12
_____ Jas. B. ...	20	_____ R. C.......	16
_____ Joseph ...	14	Sheppard, George ...	5
_____ Margaret ..	15	Shettesworth, Wade .	7
_____ R. Jr.....	8	Shirley, Nat	9
_____ R, Sr. ...	21	_____ Thos. L.....	15

Abbeville District Slaveholders

Sibert, G.	14	____ Robert R. . .	15
Sims, Thos. . .	7	Talbot, B.	6
Simmons,E. . .	11	Tallman, T. W. . .	8
____ M.	14	Tarbrough, L. . . .	25
Simpson, W. H..	6	Tarrant, John R. . .	25
Smith, Benjn. . .	5	Tatum, C. S.	32
____ Benjn. N. .	9	Tennent, W.	53
____ Charles. . .	28	Thacker, J. F. . . .	35
____ G. S.	23	Thomas, F. G. . .	31
____ James. . . .	16	____ T. W.	42
____ Joel	54	____ Wm.	5
____ Lewis . . .	9	Tilman, Edward . .	37
____ Peter . .	8	____ Nancy	29
____ Robert . .	6	Tinch, Margaret . . .	9
____ Robert . .	11	Tittle, A.	26
____ Robert . .	33	Todd, Elizabeth . . .	11
____ William .	7	Townes, H. H. . . .	15
____ William .	15	Tribble, E.	8
____ Wm. M. .	5	____ L. W.	11
Spear, J.	19	Tucker, B.	13
____ Wm.	20	Turner, Albert	11
Spearin,T. P. . .	6	____ Alexander . . .	5
Speed, M. . . .	21	____ John	8
____ Wm. . . .	8	____ Robert	12
Spence, H. . . .	9	____ Samuel	9
Sproull, Rebeco	50	Tusten, Jno. H.	5
Stark, K.	11	Vance, John	16
Starke, A. B.	24	Vanderver, J. M.	5
Stewart, L. G. . . .	6	Vernon, R.	6
Stuart, John	15	Wakefield, John	6
Studdard, Saml. .	8	Walker, S.	9
Sulvant, T. O. . .	21	Waller, Albert	11
Sumgin (?), A. .	13	____ Nancy	11
Swain, An	12	Wallis, Jane	6
____ Robert . . .	8	Wansley, W.	15
____ Wm. R. . .	6	Wardlaw, D. L. . .	4
Swilling, John .	9	____ D. M.	6
Taggart, Jas, Sr. . .	23	____ Jas.	60
____ Moses .	9	____ Jas.	8
____ Oliver . . .	9	____ Joseph	68
Talbert, Danl. . .	16	____ Margaret. . . .	6
____ Jas.	8	____ R. H.	10
____ Robert, Sr. .	15	Ware, A. N..	7

____ Jas. H. . . .	8
____ John	16
____ N. M. . . .	8
____ William . .	33
Waters, John C. .	16
____ Robert . . .	5
Watson, Elihu . . .	10
____ J. F.	65
____ Leroy	35
____ Mary P. . .	5
____ Richard . . .	21
Weatherall, Eliza .	8
____ Joseph . . .	5
Weed, Daniel A. .	8
Wharton, William .	14
White, E.	23
____ John	12
____ L. G. . . .	8
____ T.	5
Whitley, Wm. .	12
Wideman, A. . .	12
____ A.	6
____ E.	5
____ J.	5
____ Jno. . . .	26
____ L.	48
____ S.	19
Wier, Thos. .	17
Wilks, Thos. L.	17
Willard, J. C. . .	6
Williams, A. . .	5
____ J.	28
____ Jas.	8
____ John	13
____ L.	8
____ N. I.	9
____ Starling . .	27
____ Thos. W. .	50
Williamson, Sanders	29
Willy, David . .	8
Wilson, E. . . .	7
____ J.	10
____ J. R. . . .	5

____ James	12
____ Jas. L.	15
____ John C.	13
____ Martha	5
Wimbish, F. W. . . .	9
Wimms, Agnes. . . .	13
Words, M.	6
Wright, J. L.	5
____ James	7
Yarborough, H. . .	11
Young, Issack. . . .	7
____ M.	13
____ Mary	7
____ Wm.	21
Zimmerman, John.	6

1850 Census
(Owners of 5 or more)

Adams, Elizabeth . .	6
____ Jesse S.	19
____ John	6
____ John	25
____ John T.	7
Adamson, Jonathan B.	12
Adkins, David	19
____ Francis	23
Agnew, Enoch . . .	27
____ James	28
____ Joseph	13
____ Malinda	23
____ Malinda Jane .	5
____ Samuel	23
____ Samuel	9
____ Samuel W. .	12
____ William . . .	10
Aiken, Joseph . . .	11
Allen, Banister . . .	64
____ Charles P. . .	12
____ Enoch	13
____ James C. . .	16
____ Jane T. . . .	16
____ Lafayette W. .	8

Abbeville District Slaveholders

Name	Count	Name	Count
____ Samuel . . .	7	Beachum, Daniel	13
____ Sophronia .	22	Beard, Henry	9
Alston, James . .	89	____ Samuel	12
Anderson, David W. .	8	Beasley, Nancy . . .	7
____ George	16	Belcher, Robert E. . .	140
____ James	5	____ William W. . .	79
____ John	7	Bell, James E. G. . .	7
____ Lewis	8	____ Joseph F. . . .	16
____ Richard L. .	5	____ Lemuel	8
____ Robert . . .	27	____ William M. . .	10
____ U. U. . . .	6	Bentley, Henry . . .	5
____ William . . .	17	Bigby, George . . .	29
Andrews, James A. .	9	Billysly (?), Andrew	8
Ansley, Augustus Y.		Bird, Thomas B. . . .	61
& Nancy J. . . .	7	Birdy (?), Leroy . .	7
Archer, Robert A. . .	12	Black, Elizabeth . .	15
____ Sarah A. . . .	6	____ Elizabeth . . .	5
Armstrong, William .	12	____ William	7
Arnold, Alexander B. .	15	Blain, James	11
____ Francis	15	Blake, John's Est. .	21
____ Hart P.	21	____ William N. . .	28
____ Thomas	17	Bonner, John I. . .	5
Ashley, Joshua . .	7	Bonny, Franklin . .	6
Austin, Alexander .	7	Bowen, Serling . . .	9
Bailey, James . . .	7	Bowie, Quincy (?) .	9
Baker, Henrietta A.	8	Boyd, Frances . . .	9
____ Joseph T. . . .	20	Bradley, Archy . . .	12
____ Samuel . . .	44	____ John	10
____ Samuel S. .	6	____ William H. . .	23
Banks, James . .	7	Brady, Robert . . .	31
Barksdale, Sherard .	5	Branch, Isaac . . .	5
Barmore, Enoch . .	17	Branson, Levi . .	7
____ Larkin.	23	____ Eli	9
Barnes, Christian V.	5	Britt, Jacob B. . . .	14
Barnett, John J. . . .	23	____ James	7
Barr, Margaaret . .	6	____ Mary	5
Barrett, John P. . .	54	Brooks, Frances M. .	13
Baskin, James . . .	12	____ Henry	12
____ James H. . .	25	____ L. S.	39
____ James T. . .	5	____ Nancy	15
____ Jane	8	____ Stanmore B. . .	49
____ John	23	____ Susannah . . .	11
____ William S. .	10	____ William B. . .	58

____ William H. . .	5
Brough, Thomas . .	8
Brown, George M. .	5
____ Joseph	10
Brownlee, Ann . . .	8
____ George H. . .	11
____ John	36
____ Robert . . .	9
Buchanan, Elizabeth .	7
____ Elizabeth	7
____ Francis A. . . .	9
____ Robert	7
____ William	19
____ William	8
Bull, John B.	78
Burnet,John	18
____ Littleberry . .	5
Burt, Armistead . .	23
Burtin, Caleb . . .	17
____ Elizabeth . .	7
____ Josiah . . .	9
____ Peter L. . .	6
Bushellon, Joseph . .	5
Butler, William . . .	10
Cain, Sampson V. .	50
Calaham, John . . .	24
Caldwell, Edna . . .	22
____ James Y &	
Wm. H.'s Est. . . .	15
____ William H. . .	9
Calhoun, Agnes . .	7
____ Downs	64
____ Edward	45
____ Eliza	8
____ Elizabeth W.	7
____ Ephraim R. .	32
____ Frances J. . .	8
____ George M. .	21
____ James Edward .	183
____ John A. . . .	103
____ John J. . . .	12
____ Nathan . . .	45
____ Sarah	16

____ William D. . .	6
Callaham, Basil . . .	9
____ Elihu	7
Calvert, Jane M. . .	8
Cameron, Jane . . .	8
Campbell, William .	7
Cannon, Mary	23
Carlisle, Isaac	7
Carson, James . . .	33
____ Martin H. . .	10
Cary, Jane A. . . .	5
Cason, James . . .	5
Carter, Larkin J. .	28
Cater, Richard B. .	8
Chandler, Clarice (?)	5
Chaney, Simeon .	8
Chatham, Thomas .	69
Cheatham, Bartlett M.	34
____ Martha	8
____ Talbert	7
Chevis, Martha	5
Child, James W. . . .	29
____ Sarah's Est. . . .	15
Chiles, Elizabeth . . .	50
____ James M.	51
____ Jane E.	16
____ Thomas	39
Clark, Hardy	24
____ Major B.	114
Clay, John	7
Cleckley, David D. .	24
Clinkscales, Albert .	29
____ Francis	34
____ George B. . . .	25
____ James W. . . .	13
____ John	33
____ John B.	20
____ John F.	12
____ William . . .	7
Cobb, Andrew . . .	8
____ Charles A. . .	16
____ Edmond	10
____ James	23

____ Middleton . . .	5
____ Nathaniel . . .	8
Cochran, James N. .	11
____ John	23
____ Nancy	7
Coleman, Thomas L.	28
Collins, Charles . . .	7
Conner, Alexander P.	22
____ Francis A. . . .	33
____ Frederick	6
____ James	9
Cook, Frederick . . .	5
Cosby, William C.	16
Cothran, John . . .	76
Covin, Lewis . . .	20
Cowan, James . .	25
____ John	28
____ Samuel . .	24
____ Shepard G. .	14
____ Wade	7
Cox, Augustus M.	8
____ Gabriel	31
Crawford, James B.	6
____ Robert	11
____ Thomas . . .	21
Crews, Stanly . . .	27
Criswell, Henry H. .	39
____ James	7
Cromer, Philip . . .	26
Crozier, William A.	13
Cunningham, Benjamin F .	7
____ John	21
____ John	47
____ Nathaniel . . .	9
____ Sarah	5
____ Stephen W. .	5
____ Thomas	13
____ Thomas R. . .	7
Daracott, Herbert . . .	18
Davis, Ephraim . . .	6
____ John	14
____ John	10
____ Joshua	15

____ Nathaniel J.	23
____ Robert M.	34
____ Sarah M.	7
____ Thomas	7
____ Winston H.	15
Day, Edmund	8
DeBruhl, Stephen . . .	18
Dendy, Charles	67
____ Thomas B.	18
Devlin, James J. . . .	14
____ John, Jr.	10
____ John L.	17
____ Robert	23
Dickson, Joseph . . .	60
Donald, David (?) . .	11
____ David L.	5
____ John	26
____ John, Jr.	8
____ John H.	5
____ William	7
Donnelly, James . .	13
Dorn, William B. of	
Edgefield	5
Douglas, Thomas J.	12
Dowtin, John L. .	5
____ Thomas . . .	42
Drennan, Robert .	7
____ William T. .	18
Drennon, James . .	5
Dubose, Joshua . .	35
Dunn, Andrew . . .	6
____ William, Jr. .	13
____ William, Jr. .	8
____ William, Sr. .	8
Dunwoody, Samuel .	11
Eakin, Benjamin . . .	11
____ Sarah	5
____ Thomas	31
Edmonds, James A.	5
____ Samuel C. . .	19
Edwards, Andrew . .	6
Ellis, James C. . . .	14
____ John E.	8

1850 Census

____ John L. . . .	29		____ Harris Y. . . .	8
____ Robert	23		____ James	67
____ Robert	8		____ Robert C. . . .	7
English, Daniel . .	8		Gilmer, James J. . .	9
Fair, James	40		Givens, John	5
Faulkner, John . .	6		Gordon, Robert C. .	78
Ferguson, Thomas E. .	17		____ Thomas	7
Filpot, Joseph	9		Gracy, Minor W. .	18
Finley, Thos & Jane Est.	7		Graham, William .	5
Floyd, Jefferson	32		Graves, George . .	42
Foshee, Charles W. .	7		____ James P. . .	36
____ Joel	14		Gray, Absolom .	5
____ John	17		____ John	26
____ William C. .	15		____ John	12
Foster, John	30		____ John H. . .	11
____ John E. . . .	26		Grier, Robert C. .	7
____ Joseph	23		Griffin, Coleman . .	16
Franklin, Susan .	21		____ J. Coleman . .	26
____ William W.	9		____ Larkin	13
Fraser, A.	17		____ Richard A. . .	22
____ Mary	37		____ Vincent's Est. .	34
Frazier, Charity . .	20		Groves, Joseph . . .	17
____ James W. . .	45		Guillebeau, Peter . .	13
Fuller, Jones . . .	6		____ Peter L.	5
Fulton, Jane . . .	6		Gunison, Nathan . .	6
____ Thomas . .	7		Hacket, Elijah C. .	9
Gains, Elizabeth. .	15		____ Martin	45
____ William H. . .	5		____ William C. .	6
Gant, Thomas W. .	14		____ William L. .	14
Gardner, Jeremiah .	6		Haddon, Abram . . .	8
Gary, Thomas R. .	45		____ Abram W. . . .	15
Gassaway, James S.	5		____ James H.	8
Gaulden, Charles B	7		____ John T.	8
____ John	7		Hagan, Edward	10
Gibert, Benjamin E.	12		Hall, Robert H. . . .	5
____ Eliza H.	18		Hanvey, Matilda . .	11
____ James G. . . .	17		Harden, Isabella G. .	8
____ John A.	11		Hardy, Miles' Est . .	9
____ Stephen F. . .	17		Harkness, Robert C.	11
Giles, Andrew	26		Harper, James C. . .	14
____ Josiah P. . . .	5		____ Lindsay's Est.	18
____ Robert	14		Harris, Elizabeth . .	38
Gillam, Elizabeth . .	5		____ Nathaniel . . .	18

____ William . . .	11		____ Maximilian . . .	24
____ William H. .	7		Hutchison, Maximilian	17
Haskell, Charles T. .	138		____ Robert	17
____ William E. . .	43		Irvin, E. S.	24
Hawthorn, Andrew C.	27		____ John	6
____ D. O.	18		Irwin, Samuel	15
____ John M.	6		Jackson, Thomas . . .	5
____ Joseph	5		Jay, Tyra	9
____ Thomas	11		Jervis, Nancy	7
Haynie, Patrick C. .	16		Johnson, Albert . . .	17
Hays, John C. . . .	8		____ Frances	6
Hearst, John's Est.	46		____ James	23
____ John W. . . .	76		____ Jonathan	27
Heirston, Jane . . .	6		____ Leroy J.	14
Henry, Peter	5		____ Sugar	33
Herd, An	6		____ Thomas	7
Herndon, Benjamin .	44		____ Walter G. . . .	10
Hester, Louisa	16		Jones, Edward	21
____ Samuel	10		____ Elizabeth . . .	9
Hill, Elizabeth S. .	13		____ Henry A. . . .	19
____ Joshua	17		____ Joshua W. . .	30
____ Samuel L. .	17		____ Pinckney . . .	7
____ Thomas J. .	7		____ Rignal N. . .	18
____ William C. .	9		____ Robert Y. . .	62
____ William L. .	5		____ Sarah B. . . .	9
Hodges, Gabriel . .	17		____ Susan	13
____ George W. .	70		____ William T. . .	26
____ William . .	8		Jordan, Bartlett . . .	40
Holeman, Richard (?) J.	13		____ Jonathan . . .	46
Holland, John	47		____ Samuel	33
Holloman, Edward P.	18		Kay, Francis L. . .	11
Houston, Alexander .	35		____ Isabella	10
Huckebee, Green W.	26		____ James	28
Huger, Benjamin . .	75		____ James B. . . .	9
Hughes, Benjamin P.	10		____ John	11
Hughey, James . . .	9		____ Stephen (?). . .	11
____ Martha	5		Keller, David	34
____ Vachel	8		____ John	32
____ William M. .	5		____ Walter G. . .	5
Hunter, Alexander .	22		Kirkpatrick, Robert A.	7
____ John	6		Klugh, Pascal D. .	38
____ Mary A. . .	22		____ Wesley C. . .	12
Hutchinson, Irvin .	5		Laramore, Alexander	5

Latimer, Clement . . .	34
_____ Clement T. . . .	8
_____ James M., Sr. .	26
_____ Stephen	9
_____ ------ B.	7
Ledbettor, Henry W. .	43
Legard, Peter	7
Lee, Joseph F. . . .	32
_____ Stephen . . .	31
Leland, Horace W. .	14
LeRoy, James H. .	6
_____ John	6
_____ Philip	17
_____ Susan	14
Lesley, David . . .	15
_____ James L. . .	17
_____ John W. . .	5
_____ Joseph . . .	11
_____ William . .	24
_____ William (?) A.	9
Liddell, James T. . . .	27
Ligon, Joseph . . .	7
_____ Theresa . . .	10
Lindsay, James . .	36
Link, Aron	47
Lippford, Joel I. .	17
Lipscomb, James W.	11
_____ John	16
_____ Nathan L. . .	8
_____ Thomas C. .	25
Lites, Abraham . .	45
_____ Robert W. .	11
Little, Pairee . . .	6
Livingston, John, Sr. .	33
Lockhart, Joel . . .	26
Logan, Andrew's Est.	8
_____ Andrew . . .	47
_____ Frederick B. .	5
_____ Isaac	8
_____ John, Sr. . .	33
_____ John H. . . .	5
_____ William W.	10
Lomax, Barland (?) H.	5

_____ Elizabeth . . .	8
_____ George W. . .	21
_____ George W. . .	32
_____ John	11
_____ Lucian H. . .	33
_____ Lucy	25
_____ Samuel R. . .	9
_____ W. James . . .	58
_____ William	16
_____ William J. . .	26
_____ William W. .	10
Long, William, Jr. . .	9
Lyon, Elizabeth . . .	8
_____ John	7
_____ Thomas J. . . .	19
_____ William	6
McAdams, Charlotte .	9
_____ Johnson (?). . .	6
McBride, Thomas L. .	6
_____ William T.. . .	6
McCalla, George R. .	27
_____ Isaac	20
McCants, David W. . .	19
_____ Nathaniel	21
McCaslin, James. .	23
_____ Oliver	23
_____ Patric C. . . .	6
McCaw, William H.	75
McCelvey, James. . .	6
_____ Vincent	5
_____ William . .	7
McClain, David . . .	7
McClellan, John . .	30
McClinton, Samuel B.	20
McComb, Hannah . .	9
_____ John F.	10
McCord, Archibald . .	6
_____ James A.	6
_____ John	11
_____ John H	10
McCracken, James . .	11
_____ Thomas J. . .	7
McCurry, John . .	6

McDowal, Agatha C. . .	8
___ Nancy	5
McDuffie, George . .	202
McIlwain, James . .	6
McKee, Jackson . .	9
McKellar, John . .	10
___ Mary	6
___ Peter	32
McKelvey, James L. .	27
McKitric, Benjamin .	39
McLaren, John . . .	18
McLennan, John . .	25
McMahan, Fergus .	5
___ Mary	6
McMillin, Lavinia.	5
McNair, Robert . .	13
McNary, William .	7
McQuerns, Elizabeth .	5
Mabry, Mathias . . .	5
___ Reuben	19
Maddox, Richard . .	42
___ William . . .	7
Magee, Abner H. .	19
Magruder, ___ham .	5
Majors, Samuel B.	5
Mantz, Andrew . .	25
___ Stephen W.	21
Marion, Jane . . .	26
Mars, John A. . .	28
Marshall, George .	33
___ J. Foster . . .	38
___ Joseph	19
___ Joseph S. . .	26
___ Joseph W. W.	18
___ Samuel	89
___ Samuel S. . .	39
Martin, Benjamin Y.	27
___ Catharine . . .	7
___ Edward C. . .	10
___ Fares	30
___ George . . .	12
___ Jacob	20
___ James	10

___ James P.	5
___ John A.	39
___ John C.	132
___ Richard	23
___ Robert	6
___ William P.	6
Mathews, Isabella . . .	11
___ John	10
___ Joseph C.	6
___ Lewis	10
Mattison, Eliza . . .	19
___ George	25
Mauldin, Archibald, Jr.	5
___ John	5
___ John C.	10
___ William T.	6
Mays, Elizabeth . . .	7
___ Henry	5
___ Larkin	9
___ Meady	17
Means, William . . .	10
Merrimon, Lewis D.	8
Merriweather, Mary K.	19
___ Walter B.	6
Middleton, Hugh G. .	11
Miller, Allen T.	23
___ George A. . . .	42
___ Hamilton T. . . .	12
___ Jacob.	7
___ John	6
___ John T.	8
___ Nicholas H. . .	34
Moore, Augustus . .	7
___ Francis	13
___ John W.	44
___ Lucy	6
___ Margaret . . .	6
___ William A. . .	14
Moragne, Issac's Est.	41
___ Mary A. . . .	24
___ Peter B.	34
Morison, William . .	5
Morrah, David	17

____ Samuel R. . . .	25
Morris, Margaret . . .	10
Morrow, James L. . .	10
Morton, Augustus H.	22
____ Lucinda	83
Mosely, Benjamin F.	8
____ Charles R. . .	16
____ Henry	21
____ James A. . . .	7
____ John M. . . .	20
____ Mary	11
____ Tarleton P. .	7
____ Wesley	5
____ William . . .	9
Mundy, John . . .	7
Murphy, Mary . .	7
Nelson, Enoch . .	42
____ Henry H. . .	20
New, Daniel . . .	21
Nicholls, Thomas .	21
Nickles, George . .	18
Noble, Andrew A. .	21
____ Edward	14
____ William P. .	19
North, Jane G. . .	35
Norwood, James .	113
____ Mary	18
Oliver, Alexander .	21
____ John (Turst Est.)	47
Owen, Thomas E. . .	23
Pace, Sarah	14
Palmer, Champion D.	11
____ Hiram	5
____ Robert M. .	92
Parker, Ellen F. .	62
Parks, John . . .	5
Partlow, James Y. .	51
____ John A.	29
____ William D. .	48
Pascal, Jesse D. . .	5
____ Sarah P. . . .	13
Patterson, Cary . .	10
____ George S. .	9

____ James	25
____ Josiah	14
____ Josiah	9
____ Lewis J. . . .	72
____ Oney	5
Patton, John F. . . .	9
Pealor, Joseph . .	11
Pennel, William. .	6
Penny,Henry	5
Perrin, James M.. . .	7
____ Samuel	18
____ Thomas C. .	90
Pettigrew, George P.	8
____ Mary C.	11
Pettigrue, Elizabeth A.	6
____ Thomas	5
Pierman, Weldon . .	6
Piles, Lewis	7
Pool, Abram P. . . .	29
Porter, Elizabeth . .	5
Posey, Adison A. .	11
____ Benjamin . .	9
____ Wesley . . .	7
Power, Henry F. .	26
____ John, Jr. . .	18
Prather, James W. .	47
Pratt, Elizabeth . . .	12
____ John	17
____ Robert	11
Presly, Ebenezer , .	11
____ George W. . .	47
Pressly, James P. .	10
____ William A. .	6
Prince, Hugh M. .	26
Pruit, Daniel	14
Pucket, William C. .	10
Pursley, James	12
Raford, Susan C. . .	28
Ramey, Jordan . . .	10
Rasor, Ezekiel . . .	40
____ James C. . . .	6
Ray, Benjamin D. .	7
____ Silas	13

Abbeville District Slaveholders

Rega (?), John . .	54		____ Mary	15
Reid, Henry	9		____ Peter	8
____ John S.	28		Sale, Almina . . .	6
____ Lemuel . . .	10		____ Benjamin . .	11
____ Samuel . . .	20		____ Johnson . . .	23
____ William R.	12		Sanders, William . .	8
Reynolds, Bennet . .	42		Scott, Alexander . . .	20
____ John V.	21		____ John C.	6
____ Larkin	60		____ John Clark . . .	16
Richey, Andrew . .	5		____ Joseph A. . . .	5
____ Isaac	6		____ Thomas B. . .	5
____ James B. . . .	22		____ William B. . .	7
____ James W. . .	10		____ William J. . .	7
____ John	7		Scurry, Jesse	16
____ Margaret . .	26		Seawright, James .	11
____ Matilda . . .	21		____ Robert R. . .	6
____ Robert C. .	5		Selby, Martha . . .	6
____ William . .	10		Sharp, Ede	5
Richardson, James W. .	6		____ Marshall . .	12
Riley, Andrew . .	29		____ Robert C. .	17
____ Thomas . .	8		____ Robert C. .	13
Roberts, Benjamin F.	5		Shirley, Nancy . .	6
____ Thomas J. . .	12		Sibert, George . .	31
Robinson, Alexander P.	6		Simmons, Enoch .	11
____ Anne & Jesse .	11		Sims, Newton . . .	13
____ Hugh	6		____ Thomas . . .	7
____ Jane B.	7		Sitton, James Y. .	10
____ John	14		Smith, Benjamin .	11
____ Nancy	6		____ Charles	88
____ Nancy	35		____ James	6
____ Reuben	50		____ James F. . . .	7
____ William . . .	21		____ Joel	100
Rogers, Dionysius M.	30		____ John	7
____ Paul	17		____ John	8
Romans, John . .	14		____ John	8
____ William B.	5		____ Kyle	10
Ross, Thomas . .	11		____ Lewis	13
Rountree, Andrew J.	5		____ Martha	13
Rudd, Daniel . . .	15		____ Peter	6
____ Joseph . . .	34		____ Robert	9
Ruff, Christian's Est.	16		____ Robert J. . . .	5
____ John	14		____ Willard . . .	11
Rykard, Levi H.	6		____ William . .	15

____ William . . .	49	Tilman, Edward	42
____ William M.	8	Tittle, Archy	8
____ Willis	5	Todd, Elizabeth	18
Speed, Ezekiel . . .	8	Tolbert, Nancy	6
____ Ezekiel P. . .	9	____ Robert R. . . .	42
____ Michael . . .	14	Townes, Henry's Est	14
Speer, James M. .	8	____ Lucretia A. . . .	9
____ John	34	Townsend, Joel W. .	17
____ John A. . . .	10	Tribble, ____ kad . .	12
____ William . . .	30	____ Esse	10
Sproull, Charles . .	15	____ Lemuel W. .	16
____ Elihu	5	____ Stephen M. .	6
____ James C. . .	36	Truit, William . . .	9
____ Rebecca . . .	27	Tucker, Bartlet . . .	23
____ William . . .	13	Tullis, Sabra H. . .	9
Stark, James S. . .	11	Turner, Alexander .	13
____ Keziah	8	____ D. McNeill .	6
Stephens, Samuel F.	10	____ Samuel	17
Stevenson, Harmon . .	5	Tusten, James W. . .	10
Stewart, John A. . .	15	Vance, Allen	64
____ Sheppard G.	20	____ Joe H.	6
____ Thomas . .	16	____ John	32
Stokes, Joseph H.	10	____ Kincaid	27
Suber, John W. .	19	Walker, Solomon .	10
Summers, Elizabeth	8	Wallace, Jane . . .	8
Swain, Anna	20	Waller, Albert . .	17
____ Robert	11	____ Lewis A. . .	24
Swaringum, Ansel .	26	____ Nancy	29
Swilling, John . . .	21	Wanslow, Dabney .	28
Taggart, James . .	32	Wardlaw, David L. .	88
Talbert, James . .	13	____ David M. .	6
Talbot, Benjamin .	13	____ Hugh W. . . .	41
Talman, Bailey	5	____ Joseph	66
____ Moses O. .	26	____ Joseph	32
Tarrant, John R. .	37	____ Robt. H. . . .	37
Taylor, Thomas .	11	____ William A. .	66
____ William . .	58	Ware, Nicholas . .	9
Templeton, William L.	19	____ William . . .	37
Tennent, William . . .	79	Waters, John C. .	14
Thomas, Frederick G.	24	Watson, Amelia C. .	5
____ Thomas W. . .	52	____ Biphemia H. . .	7
Thompson,Thomas . .	18	____ Caspar W. . . .	15
Thornton, John G. .	5	____ Edward's Est. .	26

_____ Elihu	14	Wimbish, Alexander F.	10
_____ James F. . .	109	Winn, Andrew	7
_____ John	6	Witherspoon, Frances E.	23
_____ Mary T. . .	6	Wright, Mary	5
_____ Richard . .	44	Yarborough, Littleton .	18
Weed, Andrew J. .	7	Young, James M. . . .	11
Weems, Andrew J. .	18	_____ James N.	6
Wells, Josiah . . .	7	_____ William C. . .	28
Wharton, William L.	22	Zimmerman, Catherine .	10
White, Celestia . . .	35	_____ John	12
_____ Elizabeth . . .	7		
_____ James M. . .	5	**1860 Census**	
_____ John	33	(Owners of 5 or more)	
_____ Joseph C. . .	6		
_____ Richard M. . .	11	Abbott, Charles	28
_____ William R. . .	5	Abney, Mrs. D.	6
Wideman, Adam . .	23	Adams, Jesse S.''s Est .	32
_____ Asberry T. . .	11	_____ John D.	15
_____ Columbus A. .	6	Adamson, John	8
_____ James H. . . .	23	Aiken, D. Wyatt . . .	41
_____ John	59	Agnew, Alexr. M. . .	13
_____ Joshua	15	_____ Andrew	13
_____ Margaret . . .	10	_____ L. White	14
_____ Sarah	32	_____ Saml.	23
_____ Uel	15	_____ Wm.	12
Wier, Thomas . .	26	Alewine, John D. . . .	29
Willard, James C. .	16	Allen, Bannister . . .	58
Williams, Arthur . .	8	_____ Chas	21
_____ Eliza I. . . .	21	_____ George A. . . .	30
_____ Jacky	11	_____ J. A.	18
_____ James . . .	10	_____ James F	34
_____ John C. . .	14	_____ Mrs. Jane. . .	15
_____ Sterling . .	11	_____ John C.	32
_____ William A. .	32	Anderson, George .	17
Williamson, Jane .	8	_____ John	10
_____ Thomas . . .	7	_____ L. P.	6
Willie, David . . .	15	_____ R. M.	10
Willis, Stephen W. .	7	_____ Dr. W. L. .	21
Willson, Leroy C. .	9	Archer, Dr. Robt. A. . .	10
Wilson, John R. . .	18	_____ Mrs. S. A. . . .	6
_____ Louisa	7	Armstrong, William.	16
_____ Martha	6	Arnold, Franny . . .	43
_____ William . . .	7	_____ Hart.	30

____ Wm.	5	____ Simeon. . . .	7
Atkins, Mrs. . . .	6	____ Wm.	7
Austin, Alexr . . .	8	Bouchillon, J. L. .	6
Bailey, James . . .	30	Bowen, Sterling . . .	14
Baker, Jane T. .	28	Bowie, Franklin . . .	5
____ Joseph O. .	20	____ W. B.	7
____ Samuel S. . .	17	Bowman, A. Z.	5
Banks, Elias . . .	9	Boyd, Wm. E. . . .	11
____ James . . .	12	Bozeman, John B. . .	55
Barmore, Larkin.	23	Bradley, Archd.	24
____ Miss Nancy .	7	____ John	10
____ Mrs. Sarah. . .	12	____ W. K.	49
Barnes, C. V. .	6	Brady, Sarah	12
____ James T. . .	6	____ Sarah, Trustee . .	9
Barnett, H. . . .	5	Branyon, Thos. W . .	6
Barr, Rebecca . .	11	Brazal, Louisa	6
Barrets, John G. .	57	Britt, J. H.	12
Baskins, James H.	30	____ Jacob	31
____ James T. . . .	6	____ S.'s Est.	6
____ Stewart . . .	18	Brooks, C. E.	19
Beacham, David L. .	12	____ Jason T.	14
Beard, Henry	17	____ John W.	12
Beasley, Wm. F. . .	12	____ Stanmore B. . .	51
Belcher, Wm. W. . .	30	____ Thomas L. . . .	17
Bell, Elizabeth	13	____ W. B.	62
____ James E. G. .	9	____ Wm. H.	24
____ Joseph F. . .	22	Brown, John	5
____ Lemuel . . .	8	____ John W.	7
____ William . .	10	Brownlee, John . . .	46
Bigby, Marshall . .	9	____ Robt.	13
Bird, Eldred	9	____ Saml. R.	11
Black, James R. .	26	Bruce, James	47
____ James W. .	26	Buchanan, F. A. . . .	19
____ W. N. . . .	47	____ Jas. T.	11
____ Wesley A.	6	____ Jas. W. . . .	7
Blackwell, Joseph P.	23	____ Mary & F. B. .	21
Blain, James W. .	17	____ Robert	10
Blake, Dr. T. S. .	12	____ Wm.	24
____ W. K.	22	Bullock, William . .	7
Blease, H J. . .	6	Burdishan, S. S. . .	7
Bonner, John I. .	9	Burkhead, J. D. . .	6
Boozer, John . .	7	Burnett, Jno.	
____ Mrs. Mary .	6	Burt, A.	54

Abbeville District Slaveholders

Burton, Mrs. C. A. .	10	Child, Mrs. C.	6
____ John A. . .	13	____ Mrs. Jane	16
____ Joseph	8	____ Jas. W.	9
Butler, William . . .	14	____ Sarah's Est. . . .	23
Byrd, Dudley . .	25	Chiles, Mrs. E.	76
Cabell, Henry . .	127	____ John H.	13
Cade, Guilford . .	30	____ Robt.' s minors	5
Cain, Mrs. E. C. .	12	____ Rufus' minors'	6
Caldwell, G. R. . .	17	____ Thos. W.	49
____ Wm. C. . .	10	Clary, David	15
____ Wm. H . . .	13	Cleland, David. . . .	5
Calhoun, Mrs. A. .	7	Clinkscales, Adison . .	5
____ Dr. E. R. . .	24	____ Albert.	59
____ Edward	58	____ Barbara	11
____ Eliza	9	____ Frank	8
____ F. A.	39	____ Geo. B.	48
____ Fanny	8	____ James	6
____ Dr. J. W. . .	22	____ John F.	25
____ James C. . .	6	____ Lewis	10
____ James E. . .	201	____ Reuben	6
____ John A. . .	155	____ William . .	20
____ John F. . .	9	____ William	15
____ Nathl.	65	____ W. T.	8
____ Mrs. Susan. .	9	Cliply (?),J. S. .	8
Callaham, Basil . .	19	Cobb, Mrs. C.	5
____ Nancy	7	____ Jas. H.	11
____ S. W.	5	____ Nathl.	8
Calvert, James M. .	13	____ Richmond L. . .	6
Campbell, James. .	5	Cochran, James N.	50
____ Wm.	7	____ Jas. W.	7
Carlisle, Isaac. .	6	Coleman, H. . . .	17
Carter, Larkin J. . .	27	____ T. L.	34
____ Thornton. . . .	12	Colwell, Isaac.	6
____ William . .	7	Connor, A. P. . . .	77
Cason, Henry .	8	____ F. A.	42
Cater, T. A. . . .	13	Cook, Frederick. . .	14
Chaney, Simeon	12	____ Saml	15
Charles, Mariah. . .	11	Cooper, J. J. . . .	9
Cheatam (?), Wm . . .	18	Corley, C.	13
Cheatham, Caroline A.	8	Cosby, William . .	16
____ Sarah . . .	21	Cothran, Jas. S. . .	19
____ Thomas	72	____ John	94
____ Wm. J. . .	7	Covin, Lewis	35

Cowan, C. W. . . .	10	____ W. B.	42
____ Edmund	14	Douglas, Thos. A. . .	7
____ James	26	Dowtin, Emelie	9
____ John	41	____ James	12
____ Shepherd G. .	21	Dozier, A. P.	8
Cox, Agnes	12	Drenan, Wm. T. . .	26
Crawford, J. B. . .	8	Drennan, James . . .	7
____ Jno. A. . . .	5	____ Robert	17
____ Robert . . .	20	Dubose, James R. .	7
____ Thomas . .	35	____ Joshua	25
Cresswell, H. H. . .	54	Dunn, Mrs. Allie . .	7
Crews, Stanley . .	29	____ Dr. Andrew . .	17
Criswell, James . .	18	____ John	8
Cromer, A. F . . .	9	____ Mrs. Margaret .	8
____ Mrs. D. M. . .	20	____ William	11
____ Geo Wesley . .	32	Dunwoody, Lavinia	38
____ John P. . . .	5	Eakin, Benjamin H.	12
Cunningham, James A.	10	____ Sarah	14
____ Joel J. . . .	33	____ Thomas . . .	34
____ Josh	19	Edmunds, F. H. .	12
____ Nathl. . . .	5	____ J. A.	8
____ Thos. . . .	10	____ John	8
Dantzler, L. R. .	29	Edwards, Andrew . .	12
Davis, Edmund . . .	8	____ James M. . . .	6
____ John	21	Elgin, Hezekiah . .	5
____ N. J.	36	Elkins, Jack, Jr. . .	5
____ Robert M. .	50	Ellis, Christopher .	10
____ Thomas . .	10	____ James A. . . .	10
____ Dr. W. H. . .	27	____ James C. . . .	14
Dawson, Flora . .	8	____ Jessie	6
Dendy, Mrs. C. . .	17	____ John L. . . .	32
____ Mrs. M. J. .	11	____ Joseph	19
Devlin, James J. .	25	____ Robert	34
____ John	34	____ Thomas . . .	6
____ Dr. Robt. .	35	____ Mrs. Wm. . .	5
Dillashaw, J. . .	5	Elmore, Miss Ann E.	6
Dodson, Asberry .	5	____ Stephen	10
Donald, Col. Saml. M.	17	Etheridge, D.	6
____ Dr. James F. . . .	12	Fair, James	22
Donnald, John	7	____ S.	40
____ William	11	Fennel, Jno. L. . .	8
Donnelly, Rev. S. .	13	Ferguson, A. J. . .	6
Dorn, James	24	Fisher, Charles . .	8

Abbeville Slaveholders

_____ K. M.	9	_____ Matt.	6
Floyd, Jefferson . .	42	Gready (?),James W.	7
Fooshe, James W. . .	22	Grier, Robt. C. . . .	10
_____ Joel	17	Griffin, B. A.	39
_____ John W.	26	_____ J. W.	7
_____ Malcolm . . .	21	_____ Mrs. Mary . .	16
Foster, John	59	_____ T. C.	17
Franklin, Mrs. Susan .	31	_____ Thos. J.	9
_____ Wm.	12	_____ Wm. N. . . .	24
Frazier, J. W.	41	_____ W. W.	7
_____ Jane A.	19	Groves, Rignal . . .	16
Fuller, Jones	9	Guffin, C. B.	9
Gailes, Wm. A. . .	5	Hackett, Martin . .	70
Gains, Robt. C. . .	8	_____ W. F.	15
Galloway, Jonathan .	11	Haddon, Abraham. . .	7
Gardiner, Wm. . . .	13	_____ James H.	12
Gary, Dr. F. F. . .	12	_____ John T.	11
_____ Martin W. .	21	_____ Robt W.	20
_____ Mary A. . .	30	_____ Z.	5
Gaulden, John . .	19	Hagan, John . .	5
Gibert, J. A. . . .	35	Hall, Robert. . .	9
_____ Rev. J. F. .	28	Hamblin, A. B. .	7
_____ Stephen F. .	31	Hammond, W. J.. .	9
Gibson, William . .	9	Handon (?) Isabella.	9
Gilebeau, L. B. .	7	_____ Ralph	5
Giles, Andrew . .	15	Harkness, Robt. C.	10
Gillam, Harris .	5	Harmon, John . . .	7
_____ James D. .	37	_____ Mrs. M. . . .	13
_____ R. C. . . .	23	Harris, Mrs. Elizabeth .	45
Gillebeau, Andra . .	7	_____ Jeperiah	8
_____ Peter L. . .	14	_____ Jno. P.	5
_____ Susan . . .	12	_____ Milly	9
Gillespie, Andrew . .	14	_____ Nathl.	12
Gilman, Saml. . .	12	_____ T. A.	7
Gilmer, James J. .	11	_____ Wm.	20
Goodwin, P. W. .	8	_____ Wm. S. . . .	9
Gordon, James . .	26	Hart, Dr. Brantley C. .	13
_____ Robert T. .	62	Haskell, Charles T. .	160
Graham, Saml. . .	7	Hatton, Wm. R. . .	10
Graves, George . .	60	Hawthorn, Andrew C.	33
Gray, A. L.	20	_____ David O.	26
_____ Mrs. E. . . .	5	_____ Jno. M.	6
_____ John Harris .	36	_____ Mrs. Mary . .	5

____ Thomas	14	Jackson, Thomas . . .	9
Hay, John C.	12	Jay, Tyra	17
Hearst, Joseph L. . . .	8	Jennings, J. C.	5
____ Thos. J.	9	Johnson, Albert . . .	22
Henderson, Mason . .	6	____ Gideon (?) . .	15
Henry, Peter	6	____ Green	20
Herndon, Benjamin Z.	51	____ John B.	9
Hester, Louisa	18	____ Jonathan	31
____ Samuel J. . . .	18	____ Leroy	21
____ Thomas	17	____ M & A.	5
Hicks, William . .	59	____ Sugar	30
Higgins, Frances .	5	Johnston, John T. .	16
Hill, J. M.	8	Jones, H. A.	47
____ Mrs. S. J. . .	6	____ Israel	6
____ Thos. S. . .	18	____ Joshua W. . . .	35
____ W. W. . . .	8	____ Robt. Y.	93
____ William . .	12	____ S. H.	9
Hinton, John . .	13	____ Samuel	7
Hodges, G. W. .	60	____ Sarah A.	14
____ Gabriel . .	17	____ Dr. Wm. T. . .	27
____ Robt. . .	23	Jordan, Bartholomew .	47
____ Saml. A.	6	____ David J.	13
____ Wm. . . .	5	____ J. Turner. . . .	7
Holland, Dr. John .	65	____ Johnathon . . .	50
____ Dr. Jno. . . .	9	____ Samuel	40
Hollingsworth, James	11	____ Seth	6
Honney, Chas H. . .	7	Kay, Benjamin	11
Houston, A. R. . . .	15	____ Elias	10
Hoyt, Rev. T. A. . .	11	____ Mrs. Isabella . .	12
Huckaby, Caroline .	25	____ James B.	16
____ Jas. W.	5	____ Mary	8
Hughes, B. P. . . .	18	Keller, David	35
Hughey, James B. .	16	____ Mrs. E.	8
____ Vachel	11	____ W. G.	12
____ Wm. M. . .	10	Kennedy, A. B. . . .	8
Hunter, Alexr. . .	75	____ E. G.	9
____ Samuel . . .	19	____ Isaac	26
____ Wm. C. . .	48	____ J. P.	18
Hutchinson, John .	12	____ Joseph	20
____ Mrs. L.	6	____ Mitchel	5
____ Robt.	16	____ W. P.	7
Ingram, Nathan . .	5	Klugh, Henry G. .	25
Isham, John W. .	5	____ Pascal D. . .	38

____ Wesley C. . . .	17
Latimer, Benjamin M.	11
____ Dr. Benjamin M.	16
____ James M.	7
____ Micajah B. . . .	28
____ Stephen	16
Latimore, Clem . . .	17
Lattimore, Harrison .	7
____ James M. . . .	46
Law, James W. . . .	11
Lawson, H. W. . . .	12
Lawton, Rev. W. H.	64
Lee, Jane	11
____ Joseph F., Jr.	14
____ Joseph F., Sr.	5
____ Stephen . . .	33
Legard, P. E. . . .	6
Leland, Dr. H. W. .	31
LeRoy, John	5
____ Philip	15
____ Susan	17
Lesley, James L. .	30
____ John W. . . .	9
____ Mrs. L. . . .	15
____ Thomas . . .	8
____ William . . .	25
____ Wm. A. . . .	12
Lethe Farm School .	5
Level (?), Robt. G. .	8
Liddell, James T. . .	45
Lindsay, J. C.	10
____ J. O.	15
____ Poinsett . . .	5
____ Mrs. Polly A.	14
Link, John	15
____ Saml.	10
____ William . . .	6
Lipford, Joel J. . .	23
____ Wm. T. . . .	16
Lipscomb, J. W. .	22
____ M. B.	53
____ Thos. C. . .	40
____ Thos. J. . .	16

Lites, Joel	5
____ R. W.	38
Livingston, J. F. .	19
____ Dr. J. F. . . .	33
Lockhart, Joel . . .	28
Logan, F. B.	22
____ Isaac	11
____ Dr. J. H. . . .	6
____ Dr. Jno.	36
____ Mrs. L. C. W. .	11
Lomax, George . . .	12
____ James W. . . .	63
____ John H.	19
____ Lucian	12
____ Matilda V. . . .	35
____ Saml. R. . . .	19
____ Dr. Warren G. .	77
____ Wm. A.	16
____ Wm. J.	32
Long, William . . .	10
Lynch, Aaron W. . . .	57
Lyon, H. T.	24
____ John C. . . .	6
____ John T. . . .	10
____ Mrs. M. C. .	8
____ William . . .	16
Lythgoe, A. J. . . .	8
McAdams, Robert . .	13
McAuley, George. . .	83
McBride, Wm. S. . . .	11
McCants, David . . .	12
____ Nathl.	17
McCaslan, A. L. . .	13
____ M. O.	37
____ Robt. A. . . .	9
____ Robt. F. . . .	9
____ Wm.	17
McCaslin, James .	31
____ P. C.	9
McCaw, Elizabeth .	10
____ Wm.	9
McCelvy, Hugh . .	5
____ James	16

____ Willy	9	Maddox, William . . .	42
____ Wm.	16	Malone, James	8
McClean, Donald G. .	6	Mann, M. L.	9
McClellan, John . . .	34	____ Wm.	6
McClinton, S. D. .	19	Marion, Mrs. Jane . . .	23
____ Wm.	6	Mars, John A.	45
McCombs, Hanah . .	5	____ Wm. D.	12
____ J. F.	9	Marshall, Geo.	15
____ Wm.	9	____ Hon. J. F.	76
McCord, James . . .	6	____ J. H.	20
____ John	11	____ Dr. J. W. W. . .	42
____ John R.	13	____ Dr. Jas. S. . . .	51
McCracken, Mrs. S. .	7	____ Dr. S.	75
____ T. J.	20	____ Dr. S. S.	49
McCurry, Jno.	13	Martin, B. Y.	30
____ John	7	____ Cothran	9
McDill, James	5	____ Jacob	14
____ Wm. W.	7	____ James	5
McDonald, Matthew .	7	____ Jno. A.	15
McGaw, Mrs. Martha	6	____ Mrs. M.	69
____ S. S. C.	5	____ Phares	18
McGee, Abner H., Jr. .	11	____ Robert	9
____ Abner H., Sr. . .	20	____ Samuel	5
____ Mical	12	Mathis, Mrs. Frances .	16
____ Michael B. . . .	7	Mattison, Mrs. Eliza	9
____ Wm. J.	7	____ Gabriel	5
McGowan, Saml. . .	12	____ Urich (?) J. . . .	5
McGrandor (?), Baskin	14	Mauldin, Wm. T. . .	8
____ Mary	6	Mays, Larking . . .	7
McIlwain, James . . .	11	Meriwether, Mrs. Mary	22
McKee, Adam	9	____ W. B.	17
McKeller, John	15	Merrimon, L. D.	20
____ Miss Mary . . .	9	Middleton (?), H. J. .	22
____ Peter	41	Miller, Geo. W. . .	15
McKettrick, Jas. B. .	7	____ Isabella	10
McKinion (?), Jane .	11	____ Jacob	13
McKittrick, Benjn. .	33	____ James L. . . .	13
McLain, David . . .	9	____ Jno. T.	15
McLaren, John . . .	34	____ John	7
McLees, Rev. Jno. .	5	____ Mrs. M. C. .	43
McMacon, Fergus .	8	Milliford, Thos. B. .	6
McMullin, Mrs. L.	10	Monday, John	11
McNary, Wm. . .	17	Moore, Augustus W.	10

____ David	8	Parker, Edward F. . . .	5
____ Jonathan C.	5	____ Mrs. Ellen L. . .	74
____ John W. . .	5	Parks, Dr. F. G. . . .	6
____ Joseph T. .	9	____ John T.	20
____ Mrs. Lucy . .	8	____ L. C.	11
____ Margaret . . .	14	Partlow, Jas. Y. R. .	53
____ Wm	30	____ John A.	86
Moragne, Peter B. .	38	____ Wm. D.	47
Morrah, David . . .	27	Patterson, G. S. . .	23
____ Saml. R. . .	32	____ John	14
Morris, James H. .	17	____ Joshua (?) . . .	12
____ Mrs. M. . . .	13	____ L. J.	75
Morrison, A.	6	Patton, Edmund L. .	8
Morrow, J. L. . .	10	Pearman, William .	6
Morton, A. H. .	170	Pennel, Mrs. Ellen .	7
Mosely, Benjamin F.	14	Perrin, James	57
____ Dr. C. R. . . .	22	____ Samuel	25
____ Henry	13	____ Thos. C. . . .	130
____ John M. . . .	20	____ Wardlaw . . .	13
Murchison, B. R. .	13	Perryman, W. W. .	28
Naughton (?), James	6	____ W. W. for Watson	
Neel, W. G.	23	minors	43
Nelson, Enoch . .	78	Petigru, Miss	11
New, Daniel . . .	41	____ James L.	18
Newby, James . .	5	Pettigrew, George . .	17
Nichols, Mrs. E. B.	11	Pinson, H. M.	5
Nickles, George . . .	19	____ Thos. J.	9
Nicols, H. B.	6	Poole, A. P.	34
____ Wm. P. . . .	6	Porcher, Octavius T.	39
Noble, Andrew A. .	21	Porter, James W. . . .	5
____ Edward	19	Power, William J. . .	24
____ Wm. P. . . .	24	Powers, John	13
North, Mrs. Jane C.	25	Prather, W. H.	8
Norwood, James A.	195	Pratt, Elizabeth. . . .	12
Ogilvie, Rebecca . .	5	____ James	7
Oliver, Alexr. . . .	33	____ John	18
O'Neal, G. P. . . .	6	____ Nancy	10
____ J. B.	7	____ Robt.	20
Owens, Mrs. A. .	32	____ William	6
____ W. T.	14	Presley, J. W.	64
Paisley, William A. .	17	Pressly, Dr. E. E. . .	22
Palmer, Hiram . .	7	____ James P.	10
____ Robt. M. . .	107	____ Joseph	29

Prince, Hugh M., Jr. .	7
_____ Hugh M., Sr. .	26
_____ Washington . .	5
_____ Washington L.	5
Proffitt (?),Rev. J. R.	8
Pruit, Mrs. Alley . .	12
_____ Saml.	9
Puckett, Thos. R., Sr.	10
_____ William	10
Purcely, James . . .	7
_____ Wm. O.	6
Purdy, LeRoy	6
Pursley, J. C.	5
Quarles, Wm.	13
Radcliff, Vincent . .	5
Ramey, Edward . . .	8
Rasor, Ezekiel	51
Ray, Silas	12
Reid, Elizabeth A. . .	10
_____ Dr. John S. . . .	52
_____ Samuel	21
_____ Wm. H.	18
Reynolds, Bennet . .	33
_____ Larkin	80
Richardson, Walter .	35
Richey, Andrew . . .	7
_____ Eliza	8
_____ Mrs. Elizabeth .	10
_____ Geo. B.	18
_____ James W. . . .	18
_____ Isaac	6
Rigby, Mrs. Mary A.	12
Riley, Bert	6
_____ Green B. . . .	6
_____ Henry	11
_____ Mrs. Mary . .	12
_____ Thomas	8
Roberts, Benjamin F.	17
_____ Elizabeth	13
_____ Thos. J.	18
Robertson, David . .	9
_____ Hugh	11
Mrs. Nancy . .	17

_____ Thomas	10
_____ Wesley	48
_____ Wm.	29
Robinson, Ann . . .	5
_____ Mrs. C.	7
_____ Mrs. S. R. . .	5
_____ Mrs. Sarah . .	20
Rogers, D. M.	43
_____ Paul	13
_____ T.	12
Romans, E.	7
_____ Wm. B. . . .	6
Ross, Gains F. . .	5
Rothrock, John . .	6
Ruff, Mrs. M.	27
Russell, W. W. . . .	7
Rutledge, P. S. . . .	8
Rykard, L. H. . . .	6
_____ Peter	18
Sadler, John	13
Sale, Johnson . . .	26
_____ Mrs. Martha .	5
Salley, Dr. H. S. . . .	19
Sample, John B. . . .	11
Scott, John C.	28
_____ Wm. C.	8
Searles, E.	34
_____ P.'s Est. . .	13
Seawright, James .	8
_____ Robt. R.	9
_____ William . . .	6
Selby, Mrs. M. . . .	9
Self, Pressly	7
Sharp, Marshall . .	22
_____ Robt. C.	29
_____ Robt. C., Jr.	21
Shaw, James H. . . .	22
Sibert, George . . .	42
Simpson, John F. . .	9
Sims, Mrs. M. H. .	37
_____ Dr. Newton .	20
Sitton, James Y. . .	13

Abbeville District Slaveholders

Smith, Augustus M. .	135
_____ Benjamin	12
_____ Charles	60
_____ Christopher . .	17
_____ Rev. James F. .	17
_____ Margaret	5
_____ Peter	10
_____ Robt. J.	8
_____ Thos. W.	18
_____ W. Joel	87
_____ William	16
_____ Willis	14
_____ Wm.	8
_____ Wm.	58
_____ Wm. C. . . .	27
_____ Wm. W. . .	11
Sondley, A. R. .	7
Speed, Ezekiel . .	14
_____ Samuel . . .	24
Speer, Elizabeth . .	7
_____ John	38
_____ John C.	15
_____ William	22
Spikes, H. M. . . .	14
Sproul, C. W. . .	38
Stark, James . . .	7
Stevenson, Andrew .	7
Stewart,Dr. John A.	33
_____ N. W.	6
_____ Thomas	23
Sturkey, M. B. . . .	5
Sullivan, W. P. . .	23
Swain, Jane A. . .	9
Sweringin, Ansel .	40
Taggart, Capt. J. .	24
_____ James, Jr. . .	17
_____ Dr. M. C. .	24
_____ W. H. . . .	17
Talbert, B.	13
_____ Benjan. . .	7
Talbot, ----------	7
Talman, M. O. .	31
Tarrant, J. R. . .	57

_____ Morison	5
Taylor, C. J.	5
_____ Elizabeth . . .	8
_____ James	30
Tennent, Eliza . . .	18
_____ Patrick C. . .	8
_____ William . . .	66
_____ Wm.	14
Thomas, J. W.'s Est.	48
Thomson, Thomas . .	51
Thornton, John J. . .	10
_____ Mrs. Lucinda .	7
Tilman, Kitty	13
_____ Sally	14
Tolbert, G. W. . . .	11
_____ John	25
_____ Robert R. . . .	60
Townsend, Rev. Joel W.	17
Traylor, Mrs. Louisa . .	11
Tribble, Lemuel	21
_____ Stephen M. . . .	14
Tucker, Bartley S. . .	6
_____ Bentley	18
_____ Thomas	5
Turner, Alexr.	20
_____ Joshua	5
_____ Samuel	25
Vance, Allen	16
_____ James K.	34
_____ John	45
Vandiver, James M. .	5
Venning, W. C. . . .	29
Waddel, Dr. J. A. . .	14
Wakefield, Conrad . .	14
Walker, E. J.	10
_____ Martha A. . . .	5
_____ Sanders	10
_____ W. Y.	5
Wallace, Mrs. Jane .	11
Waller, Mrs. J. E. . .	22
_____ Mrs. Nancy . . .	11
_____ P. A.	41

Wardlaw, D. J...	8
____ Hon. D. L. .	91
____ D. M.	11
____ Dr. J. J. ...	45
____ M.	6
____ R. H.	39
____ Walter	55
Ware, Elizabeth ...	8
Waters, John C. ..	14
Watkins, William .	5
Watson minors (9) .	59
____ Catherine ...	34
____ Eliza	12
____ Mrs. Eliza H.	14
____ Geo. McD. ..	28
____ James F. ...	16
____ Mrs. Permelia .	9
____ Dr. W. H. ...	11
Weatherspoon, F.'s Est.	37
Weed, Andrew J. ...	16
Wells, Josiah	11
Wharton, William ..	20
White, James L. ..	14
____ James M. ..	16
____ John	39
____ R. M.	29
____ Wm. R. ..	12
Whitley, Wm. ..	5
Wickliffe, Wm. .	8
Wideman, A. T. ...	35
____ Allen	44
____ John	65
____ John H. ...	8
____ Joshem (?) .	21

____ Mary	14
____ Mrs. Mary ...	8
____ Sarah	37
Wier, John A.	11
Wilkinson, Henry ..	5
Willard, James	19
____ Dr. S. J.	6
Williams, Benjamin W. .	6
____ Mrs. Dasilla ...	13
____ Mrs. Eliza Z. ..	25
____ Mrs. F.	11
____ James	15
____ Rev. John C. ..	28
____ Roger	14
Wills, Laphin (?) ...	10
Wilson, John H. ...	23
____ LeRoy	13
____ Mrs. N & J ...	6
____ Saml. A.	12
____ William	10
____ Wm. A.	13
Wimbush, Alexr. P. .	14
Winn, Henry M. ...	21
____ Robt. N.	7
Yarborough, Littleton ..	20
Young, James	16
____ James M.	18
____ John N.	14
____ Valentine	6
____ William	44
Zeigler, M. Goodwin .	14
Zimmerman, Mrs. C. .	7

Part II. Largest Property Holders in Abbeville District
1860 Census

(age) Name	Real Estate	Personal	Total
(62) James E. Calhoun	650, 000	276, 243	926, 243
(32) Aug. M. Smith	200, 000	250, 000	450, 000
also in same household			
Geo. M. Smith		75, 000	75, 000
Mrs. Ann Owens	4, 000	26, 000	30, 000
(42) Aug. H. Morton	292, 240	134, 000	426, 240
(38) J. H. Marshall	175, 000	150, 000	325, 000
(43) J. F. Marshall	128, 700	188, 000	316, 000
(72) Samuel Marshall	31, 000	226, 470	257, 470
(49) James A. Norwood	45, 000	175, 380	218, 380
also in same household, three students: (21) W. H. Belcher, (20)			
Jno. H. Belcher & (16) Mary Belcher - each 12, 000			
(60) Chas. T. Haskell	54, 000	146, 555	200, 555
(57) Allen Vance	73, 000	125, 000	198, 000
(53 John A. Calhoun	50, 000	138, 000	188, 000
(56) Thomas C. Perrin	57, 000	127, 256	184, 256
(71) Bannister Allen	17, 270	165, 979	183, 249
(46) John W. Hearst	48, 000	125, 000	173, 240
(52) Jas. Y. R. Partlow	57, 000	90, 000	47, 000
(40) Saml. S. Marshall	24, 000	117, 000	131, 000
also in above household, Catherine Watson (15)			44, 000
(44) John A. Partlow	40, 000	80, 000	120, 000
(60) Geo.W. Pressly	24, 500	95, 000	119, 500
(52) Thos. Cheatham	27, 600	90, 760	118, 360
(54) R. M. Palmer	22, 005	96, 300	118, 305
(60) Jas. H. Cothran	40, 000	75, 000	115, 000
(40) Henry A. Jones	40, 000	75, 000	115, 000
(49) Elizh. Thomas	12, 148	102, 210	114, 358
(50) Mrs. Mary Martin	18, 000	95, 000	113, 000
(39) Geo. McCalla	36, 000	76, 400	112, 400
(29) W. W. Perryman	20, 000	89, 000	109, 000
also, four others in above household held total of			80, 000
(38) Andrew Simonds	9, 000	100, 000	109, 000
(38) James R. Cochran	21, 000	84, 110	105, 110
(54) James Creswell	34, 000	70, 000	104, 000
(43) Alex P. Connor	20, 000	83, 231	103, 231
(60) William Smith	15, 600	86, 132	101, 732
(51) George Graves	30, 000	67, 631	97, 631
(45) John McLaren	60, 000	33, 000	93, 000
(57) Wm. D. Partlow	16, 000	75, 000	91, 000
(65) John Wideman	7, 600	83, 000	90, 600
(52) Francis Arnold	15, 000	75, 000	90, 000
(53) John White	15, 000	75, 000	90, 000
(60) William Tennent	20, 000	70, 000	90, 000
(28) John G. Barrett	18, 000	68, 000	86, 000
(57) Stanmore B. Brooks	27, 300	58, 000	85, 300
(73) Phares Martin	43, 000	40, 870	83, 870
(30) Jno. Holland	18, 000	65, 000	83,000

Census of 1860

(59) Jonathan Jordan	12, 000	70, 504	82, 504
(73) Martin Hackett	12, 000	70, 260	82, 260
(45) Thomas Thomson	22, 250	60, 000	82, 250
(46) Albert J. Clinkscales	12, 500	69, 688	82, 188
(54) W. Butler Brooks	21, 450	60, 090	81, 540
(47) David O. Hawthorn	12, 000	69, 400	81, 400
(35) G. Warren Lomax	7, 500	71, 500	79, 000
(45) W. K. Bradley	15, 000	62, 000	77, 000
(38) W. H. Lawton	19, 000	57, 000	76, 000
(65) Ellen L. Parker	21, 000	55, 000	76, 000
(50) Dionysius M Rogers	28, 000	48, 000	76, 000
(48) Henry H. Creswell	25, 000	50, 875	75, 875
(37) Jno. H. Wideman	13, 000	62, 600	75, 600
also in same household, three minors:			
(20) Alfred Watson		21, 066	21, 066
(16) Jas. B. Watson		23, 666	23, 666
(18 ---- Watson		27, 762	27, 762
(59) Andrew C. Hawthorn	23, 000	51, 800	74, 800
(66) Thos. W. Chiles	5, 005	59, 520	74, 525
(34) Jno. B. Bozeman	13, 700	60, 800	74, 500
(38) Benjamin Z. Herndon	17, 000	56, 200	73, 200
(62) Samuel Jordan	36, 000	37, 000	73, 000
(63) Ezekiel Rasor	15, 000	57, 875	72, 875
(46) Enoch Nelson	12, 000	60, 000	72, 000
(45) James M. Latimer	20, 000	51, 994	71, 994
(85) Alex Hunter	13, 000	58, 545	71, 545
(58) Mrs. Eliza Chiles	11, 520	60, 000	71, 000
(52) Robt. R. Tolbert	13, 000	57, 726	70, 726
(57) Armistead Burt	20, 000	50, 000	70, 000
(67) Geo. W. Hodges	10, 000	60, 000	70, 000
(34) Jos. S. Marshall	16, 200	52, 732	68, 932
(34) P.A. Waller	8, 000	68, 000	68, 000
(46) Pat H. Bradley	20, 000	47, 725	67, 725
(70) Nathan Calhoun	19, 000	48, 630	67, 630
(37) William Hix	14, 480	51, 480	65, 960
(38) James Lomax	8, 000	57, 492	65, 492
(47) L. D. Merrimon	13, 000	52, 300	65, 300
(40) Wesley Robertson	12, 360	52, 900	65, 260
(65) John S. Reid	20, 000	45, 000	65, 000
(52) Charlie Smith	15, 000	50, 000	65, 000
(60) Robert Ellis	18, 000	45, 800	63, 800
(63) Elizh. Harris	12, 500	41, 000	63, 500
(56) John Cowan	16, 000	47, 480	63, 480
(50) Jas. W. Frazier	20, 000	43, 000	63, 000
(55) John Vance	17, 000	45, 400	62, 400
(34) Jefferson Floyd	15, 168	47, 122	62, 290
(38) James Perrin	27, 000	35, 000	62, 000
(49) Jno. Tarrant	7, 000	54, 280	61, 280
(58) John A. Mars	22, 000	38, 250	60, 250

Census of 1860

(47) George B. Clinkscales	10, 000	50, 000	60, 000
(57) Aaron W. Lynch	10, 000	50, 000	60, 000
(48) Robert M. Davis	14, 640	44, 845	59, 485
(39) Dr. Jas. A. Stuart	20, 000	39, 315	59, 315
(50) John Foster	10, 000	49, 190	59, 190
(41) Robt. H. Lites	9, 000	50, 000	59, 000
(54) John Brownlee	11, 200	46, 926	58, 126
(72) Bartholomew Jordan	15, 000	43, 000	58, 000
(42) Joseph K. Vance	18, 000	39, 700	57, 700
also, in above household Bigie Watson (female)			21, 500
(35) A. Tatum Wideman	14, 000	43, 360	57, 360
(45) William Maddox	8, 000	49, 000	57, 000
(60) Jas. M. Chiles	18, 730	37, 234	56, 964
(52) Edwin Calhoun	8, 984	47, 832	56, 816
(54) N. Jeff Davis	24, 000	32, 390	56, 390
(60) Geo. Sibert	8, 060	48, 205	56, 265
(23) Milledge R. Lipscomb	21, 000	35, 000	56, 000
45) James Bailey	9, 000	46, 000	55, 000
(40) C. W. Sproull	14, 400	40, 376	54, 776
(76) Andrew Giles	8, 000	46, 506	54, 506
(67) Dr. John Logan	15, 000	39, 400	54, 400
(50) John W. Moore	12, 000	42, 300	54, 300
(45) Jas. H. Shaw	23, 000	31, 200	54, 200
(31) H. H. Harper	21, 000	33, 058	54, 058
(43) Jos. J. Wardlaw	9, 000	45, 000	54, 000
(26) W. Joel Smith	4, 000	50, 000	54, 000
(34) Samuel McGowan	8, 400	45, 000	53, 400
(35) J. W. Clinkscales	1, 200	52, 000	53, 200
(40) Thos. C. Lipscomb	16, 000	37, 000	53, 000
(56) John F. Livingston	12, 400	40, 420	52, 820
(48) Wesley Cromer	5, 700	47, 000	52, 700
(41) Jno. C. Williams	14, 000	28, 600	52, 600
(73) David Kellar	8, 450	44, 055	52, 505
(44) Robert Pratt	12, 000	40, 000	52, 000
(56) Hugh M. Wardlaw	10, 000	42, 000	52,000
(67) Pascal D. Klugh	12, 000	42, 000	52,000
(68) Joel Lockhart	7, 680	43, 256	50, 936
(30) W. C. Hunter	12, 000	38, 262	50, 262
(40) Robt. C. Gillam	20, 000	30, 000	50, 000
(55) Robt. H. Wardllaw	20, 000	30, 000	50, 000
(42) Francis A. Connor	10, 000	40, 000	50, 000
(39) R. A. Griffin	9, 000	40, 000	49, 000
(65) John L. Ellis	8, 300	40, 000	48, 300
(47) Adam Wideman	10, 000	37, 200	47, 200
(58) Larkin Barmore	10, 000	37, 100	47, 100
(21) Walter Richmond	16, 360	30, 600	46, 960
(47) James T. Liddell	9, 000	37, 702	46, 702
(45) James Bruce	7, 860	38, 681	46, 451
(43) James Taylor	15, 500	30, 160	45, 660
(39) Joel J. Clinkscales	10, 000	35, 570	45, 570

Census of 1860

(69) Jas. G. Gillam	5, 000	40, 000	45, 000
(40) H. W. Leland	10, 000	35, 000	45, 000
(34) Jno. L. Parks	4, 000	40, 777	44, 777
(66) Robert M. White	12, 000	32, 600	44, 600
(40) W. H. Davis	13, 000	31, 232	44, 232
(56) Jacob Britt	11, 000	33, 000	44, 000
(32) James W. Foster	10, 000	33,955	43, 955
(43) Samuel Perrin	5, 000	38, 860	43, 860
(57) Bennett Reynolds	14, 000	29, 000	43, 000
(43) William Carter	7, 000	36, 000	43, 000
(53) Daniel New	8, 000	35, 000	43, 000
(53) John R. Wilson	15, 000	27, 000	42, 000
(74) John Speer	8, 896	32, 474	41, 370
(46) Joshua Jones	10, 000	30, 600	40, 600
(60) Robt. Devlin	5, 000	35, 420	40, 420
(29) John C. Scott	10, 000	30, 225	40, 225
(36) Isaac Kennedy	7, 000	33, 000	40, 000
(48) Jane T. Baker	10, 000	30, 000	40, 000
(54) Mary A. Gary	10, 000	30, 000	40, 000
also, with above 4 children with $5,000 each 20, 000			
(39) Wm. A. Moore	7, 000	33, 000	40, 000
(57) Abner H. McGee	8, 000	31, 965	39, 965
(66) H. B. Poole	8, 400	31, 282	39, 682
(49) John Harris Gray	9, 093	30, 510	39, 603
(52) John Pratt	4, 500	35, 000	39, 500
(40) Thos. L. Coleman	2, 500	36, 900	39, 400
(56) Ansel Sweargin	4, 270	35, 116	39, 386
(29) Joseph Pressly	9, 000	30, 000	39, 000
(37) D.Wyatt Aiken	9, 000	30, 000	39, 000
(44) Jno. Wright Fooshe	9, 150	29, 800	38, 950
(60) Ann H. Sims	6, 500	32, 000	38, 500
(51) Ebenezer E. Pressly	15, 000	23, 500	38, 500
(60) Thomas Eakin	9, 700	28, 742	38, 442
(54) James Gordon	11, 400	26, 769	38, 169
(43) George A. Allen	15, 000	23, 102	38, 102
(64) Miss Sarah Wideman	4, 300	33, 560	37, 860
(52) Jas. F. Gibert	9, 500	28, 327	37, 827
(47) William Caldwell	21, 000	16, 700	37, 700
(42) Nimrod W. Stewart	7, 500	30, 000	37, 500
(37) Jas. L. Allen	7, 000	30, 000	37, 000
(61) Louis Covin	13, 000	24, 000	37, 000
(25) Jno. Tolbert	10, 000	26, 860	36, 860
(58) Ephraim R. Calhoun	7, 500	29, 000	36, 500
(49) Jas. H. Britt	6, 000	30, 350	36, 350
(33) John H. Wilson	8, 000	28, 000	36, 000
(37(Edw. Parker	6, 000	3-. 000	36.000
(56) William Truitt	20, 000	16, 000	36, 000
(50) Conrad Wakefield	20, 000	16, 000	36, 000
(54) George Nichols	17, 000	19, 000	36, 000
(52) James Dorn		35, 600	35, 600

(67) Alex Oliver	8, 500	26, 959	35, 459
(24) William W. Belcher	6, 450	28, 989	35, 439
(28) William J. Power	8, 392	26, 833	35, 225
(23) R. M. Perryman		35, 000	35, 000
(48) Benj. P. Hughes	9, 000	26, 000	35, 000
(49) Marshall Sharp	10, 000	24, 830	34, 830
(45) Caroline A. Huckabee	14, 300	20, 384	34, 684
(73) Robt. C. Sharp	6, 400	27, 800	34, 200
(84) Henry Moseley	12, 904	21, 199	34, 103
(52) Joel J. Lipsford	4, 000	30, 000	34, 000
(42) James T. Allen	7, 032	26, 836	33, 868
(55) Johnson Lake	5, 000	28, 775	33, 775
(57) Sam. Donald	5, 000	28, 400	33, 400
(61) James Cowan	9, 000	24, 300	33, 300
(39) T. Yancey Martin	8, 000	25, 275	33, 275
(30) W. C. Henning	10, 000	23, 200	33, 200
(35) Henry H. Clamp	8, 000	25, 000	33, 000
(45) William Robertson	5, 500	27, 235	32, 735
(43) Wm. J. Lomax	4, 640	28, 000	32, 640
(26) Benj. M. Winstock	4, 400	28, 000	32, 400
(30) Absolom Gray	10, 000	22, 390	32, 390
(65) James Taggart	10, 000	22, 300	32, 300
(75) Jonathan Johnson	3, 170	29, 105	32, 275
(46) Hugh G. Middleton	5, 860	26, 305	32, 165
(43) John F. Clinkscales	8, 160	24, 000	32, 160
(33) Jno. A. Allen	8, 500	23, 600	32, 100
(73) WilliamSpeer	10, 000	22, 049	32, 049
(47) William Clinkscales	12, 000	20, 000	32, 000
(47) James L. Lesley	6, 000	26, 000	32, 000
(56) Robert Hutchinson	12, 000	19, 957	31, 957
(52) James Pressly	2, 500	29, 200	31, 700
(38) Sarah E. Cheatham	11, 235	20, 400	31, 635
(44) Saml. D. McClinton	6, 000	25, 580	31, 580
(40) Lemuel Reid	7, 836	23, 390	31, 226
(44) Samuel D. Speed	6, 000	25, 098	31, 098
(75) Samuel W. Tribble	6, 000	25, 000	31, 000
(43) Moses Winstock	5, 000	26, 000	31, 000
(58) Stanley Crews	3, 000	28, 000	31, 000
(39) J. Albert Gibert	8, 000	22, 930	30, 930
(63) Benjamin M. Gibert	9, 592	21, 249	30, 841
(26) John C. Allen	1, 500	29, 340	30, 840
(39) Martha Ruff	5, 500	25, 000	30, 500
(40) R. H. Eakin	5, 500	24, 955	30, 455
(73) Hart Arnold	4, 300	26, 030	30, 330
(43) Joseph S. Britt	7, 320	23, 000	30, 320
(55) Jane North	4, 500	25, 740	30, 240
(60) Jas. W. Blain	4, 200	26, 000	30, 200
(34) Jas. W. Calhoun	5, 000	25, 000	30, 000
(41) David Clary		30, 000	30, 000
(40) Wm. McCelvey	10, 240	19, 690	29, 930

Census of 1860

(44) Dr. Newton Sims	8, 000	21, 875	29, 875
(59) Mrs. Susan Franklin	4, 500	25, 188	29, 688
(63) William T. Jones	5, 500	24, 150	29, 650
(56) Jas. L. Devlin	10, 000	19, 626	29, 626
(40) W. H. Taggart	5, 500	24, 000	29, 500
(50) Jonathan Galloway	6, 200	23, 300	29, 300
(61) W. N. Blake	13, 500	15, 780	29, 280
(37) Joseph R. Black	6, 700	22, 511	29, 211
(40) Martha C. Lyon	6, 200	23, 000	29, 200
(67) Wm. Lesley	7, 000	22, 125	29, 125
(30) Tyre Jay	6, 000	23, 000	29, 000
(36) Edw. Noble	9, 000	20, 000	29, 000
(63) Hugh M. Prince, Sr.	5, 250	23, 690	28, 940
(46) Robt. Sharp	4, 000	24, 700	28, 700
(43) Micajah B. Latimer	6, 000	22, 640	28, 640
(30) Jas. S. Cothran	6, 500	22, 000	28, 500
(32) William M. Griffin	6, 500	21,860	28, 360
(72) James H. Baskin	6, 000	22, 263	28, 263
(47) Henry Beard	10, 460	17, 733	28,193
(44) J. Fooshe	6, 000	22, 000	28, 000
(50) James Ellis	7, 000	21, 000	28, 000
(63) William Armstrong	8, 000	20, 000	28, 000
(55) Jane E. Waller	10, 000	17, 950	27, 950
(35) Jas. F. Donald	3, 000	24, 850	27, 850
(44) Saml. Cook	13, 200	14, 500	27, 700
(66) Robt. Y. Jones	13, 160	14, 530	27, 690
(45) James W. Black	7, 000	20, 550	27, 550
(33) W. G. Neel	6, 500	21, 000	27, 500
(36) James Y. Sitton	12, 500	15, 000	27, 500
(32) J. Benson Black	2, 500	25, 000	27, 500
(38) Dr. H. T. Lyon	4, 000	23, 400	27, 400
(51) James Seawright	12, 000	15, 400	27, 400
(23) Hag (?) M. Speed	8, 450	18, 881	27,331
(58) Saml. Agnew	7, 000	20, 260	27, 260
(33) Elizabeth McCaw	4, 600	22, 542	27, 142
(35) Francis M. Brooks	4, 500	22, 518	27, 018
(31) Jno. N. Lipscomb	7, 000	20, 000	27, 000
(43) John A. Wier	7, 000	20, 000	27, 000
(78) Alexr. Houston	10, 000	17, 000	27, 000
(24) William T. Tatom	8, 000	19, 000	27, 000
(57) H. C. Smith	5, 000	22, 000	27, 000
(49) Chas. R. Moseley	7, 000	20, 000	27, 000
(30) Jos. P. Blackwell	4, 000	22, 925	26, 925
(38) Eliza A. Brown	2, 000	24, 800	26, 800
(61) Mrs. Eliza Williams	2, 700	24, 100	26, 800
(55) Samuel Turner	4, 000	22, 772	26, 772
(31) Geo. R. Caldwell	8, 800	17, 962	26, 762
(50) Peter Rykard	4, 500	22, 237	26, 737
(39) Dr. W. L. Anderson	6, 000	20, 702	26, 702

Census of 1860

(51) David G. Jordan	8, 700	18, 000	26, 700
(63) Isabella Kay	4, 000	22, 500	26, 500
also 3 others in household with total of			11, 000
(37) Wm. H. Brooks	3, 000	23, 500	26, 500
(50) D. Littleton Yarborough	6, 000	20, 442	26, 442
(44) LeRoy J. Johnson	7, 680	18, 724	26, 404
(24) C. Elisha Books	9, 000	17, 000	26, 000
(59) Benjn. Smith	9, 000	17, 000	26, 000
(43) Maurice Strauss	6, 000	20, 000	26, 000
(60) Archd. Bradley	6, 000	20, 000	26, 000
(72) Lovenna Dunwoody	1, 000	25, 000	26, 000
(44) Wm. McCelvey	6, 240	19, 690	25, 930
(54) Jas. Willard	6, 500	19, 340	25, 840
(70) Nancy Robertson	2, 000	23, 700	25, 750
(29) Julius F. DuPree	2, 000	23, 555	25, 555
(50) Sarah Brady	1, 500	23, 930	25, 430
(49) Sheppard G. Cowan	2, 000	23, 400	25, 400
(34) Dr. Henry G. Klugh		25, 000	25, 000
(50) Mrs. E. Lipford	7, 000	18, 000	25, 000
(29) Geo H. Waddell	8, 000	17, 000	25, 000
(34) Moses T. Owen	6, 000	19, 000	25, 000
(30) Dr. A. P. Boozer	7, 600	17, 300	24, 900
(77) William Young	10, 000	14, 629	24, 629
(45) W. B. Merriwether	8, 000	16, 600	24, 600
(40) William F. Sullivan	4, 000	20, 522	24, 522
(32) Thomas S. Blake	5, 000	19, 500	24, 500
(30) Thos. L. Lipscomb	6, 000	18, 500	24, 500
(34) James L. Miller	7, 200	17, 200	24, 400
(47) Robt. W. Hodges	5, 600	18, 769	24, 369
(87) Bartley Tucker	8, 550	15, 811	24, 361
(45) Ezekiel Speed	12, 000	12, 210	24, 210
(30) John J. Johnston	5, 000	19, 175	24, 175
(56) William C. Cosby	9, 160	15, 000	24, 160
(54) William P. Noble	6, 000	18, 000	24, 000
(63) Joseph T. Baker	3, 600	20, 163	23, 763
(56) Mary A. Lindsay	5, 400	18, 300	23, 700
also in same household 3 minors with a total of			15, 900
(56) Stephen F. Latimer	10, 000	13, 700	23, 700
(68) James W. Richey	4, 000	19, 700	23, 700
(46) Thos. J. Roberts	6, 000	17, 570	23, 570
(45) Sugar Johnson	3, 832	19, 710	23, 542
(49) Wesley C. Klugh	4, 200	19, 315	23, 515
(61) Silas Kay	9, 000	14, 500	23, 500
(48) James B. Kay	3, 500	20, 000	23, 500
(43) S. White Agnew	6, 200	17, 300	23, 500
(49) L. Green (?) Johnson	6, 750	16, 700	23, 450
(25) William V. Clinkscales	8, 400	14, 944	23, 344
also same household Barbara Clinkscales (54) with			7, 200

(57) Kittie Tillman	7, 000	16, 319	23, 319
also in same household Sallie Tillman (17) with			14, 000
(68) Jos. F. Bell	6, 600	16, 560	23, 160
(44) W. M. Hughey	4, 000	19, 125	23, 125
(24) Jas. F. Watson	8, 000	15, 000	23, 000
(74) John (?) Bradley	3, 000	20, 000	23, 000
(28) Dr. F. F. Gary	5, 000	18, 000	23, 000
(28) Wm. D. Mars	3, 000	20, 000	23, 000
(59) Isaac Branch	3, 000	20, 000	23, 000
(60) Mrs. M. Morris	8, 000	15, 000	23, 000
(51) John M. Moseley	3, 800	19, 175	22, 975
(22) Geo. Marshall	10, 000	12, 960	22, 960
(41) Mrs. D. R. Cromer	4, 920	18, 000	22, 920
(50) Wm. H. Caldwell	12, 500	10, 326	22, 826
(50) James A. Fraser	4, 000	18, 792	22, 792
(36) Christopher Smith	6, 100	16, 610	22, 710
(59) Joel W. Townsend	6, 000	16, 518	22, 518
(39) Geo. S. Patterson	2, 500	20, 000	22, 500
(78) Jacob Martin	6, 900	15, 433	22, 353
(46) Jno. N. Young	5, 000	17, 350	22, 350
(33) John T. Lyon	4, 500	17, 810	22, 310
(37) Edward Cowan	2, 300	20, 000	22, 300
(29) Thos. L. Brooks	7, 000	15, 300	22, 300
(26) Jas. L. White	6, 000	16, 266	22, 266
(51) Jno. Gaulden	5, 856	16, 300	22, 156
(57) William Buchanan	2, 800	19, 243	22, 043
(44) Philip A. Rutledge	4, 000	18, 000	22, 000
(54) Basil Callahan	4, 500	17, 492	21, 992
(44) Henry M. Winn	3, 000	18, 969	21, 969
(46) Francis A. Buchanan	4, 440	17, 500	21, 940
(40) Benj. F. Moseley	6, 000	15, 850	21, 850
(22) John A. Burton	6, 846	15, 000	21, 846
(40) Thos. L. McCracken	3, 000	18, 713	21, 713
(43) Stewart W. Baskin	6, 000	15, 692	21, 692
(46) Chas. P. Allen	6, 492	15, 155	21, 647
(62) Thomas Jackson	6, 000	15, 600	21, 600
(32) Roger L. Williams	6, 000	15, 496	21, 496
(50) John W. Lomax	4, 448	17, 000	21, 448
(44) Wm. A. Pressly	4, 000	17, 445	21, 445
(37) Henry S. Cason	1, 700	19, 702	21, 402
(32) James M. White	3, 800	17, 491	21, 291
(35) Jas. Cunningham	3, 200	18, 082	21, 282
(53) Reginald N. Graves	2, 000	19, 195	21, 195
(41) Hugh Robertson	4, 780	16, 300	21, 080
(48) William McNary	4, 270	16, 810	21, 080
(60) Mrs. Jane Allen	4, 000	17, 000	21, 000
(30) J. Fraser Livingston	5, 000	16, 000	21, 000
(57) Green B. Riley	4, 000	17, 000	21, 000
(55) Robt. Drennan	4, 800	16, 135	20, 935

Census of 1860

(44) Fred B. Logan	3, 500	17, 412	20, 912
(43) Robert McAdams	7, 500	13, 274	20, 774
(45) Andrew Dunn	3, 000	17, 700	20, 700
(55) Albert Johnson	3, 500	17, 166	20, 666
(80) Jane H. Marion	1, 200	19, 400	20, 600
(45) Mrs. Alley Pruitt	8, 000	12, 600	20, 600
(66) Gabriel Hodges	5, 500	15, 075	20, 575
(27) Benj M. Lattimore	5, 000	15, 470	20, 470
(35) Andrew Agnew	5, 000	15, 450	20, 450
(58) Phobie B. Brown	6, 600	13, 765	20, 365
(22) Dr. W. H. Watson	6, 400	13, 954	20, 354
(41) James M. Young	6, 975	13, 353	20, 328
(80) Joshua DuBose	2, 200	18, 000	20, 200
(64) Robert Crawford	4, 000	16, 200	20, 200
(66) Alex Turner	2, 714	17, 400	20, 114
(70) Sarah Robertson		20, 000	20, 000
(31) William H. Parker	6, 000	14, 000	20, 000
(46) William Gardner		20, 000	20, 000
(45) W. F. Hackett		20, 000	20, 000
(38) Jno. I. Bonner	5, 000	15, 000	20, 000
(53) Geo. H. Round		20, 000	20, 000
(43) Isaac Logan	10, 000	10, 000	20, 000
(44) George P. Pettigrew	4, 000	15, 840	19, 840
(47) Wm. A. Crozier	4, 000	15, 745	19, 745
(60) Martha Wilson	1, 500	18, 000	19, 500
(46) John Davis	4, 000	15, 472	19, 472
(41) James Clinkscales	10, 000	9, 410	19, 410
(25) W. Y. Quarles	3, 800	15, 600	19, 400
(57) William Lyon	5, 500	13, 823	19, 323
(67) Andrew Edwards	8, 800	10, 500	19, 300
(33) Geo. B. Richey	7, 000	12, 300	19, 300
(39) Benjn M. Latimer	1, 500	17, 700	19, 200
(80) Mary Hearmon	5, 000	14, 200	19, 200
(38) Jos. F. Lee	3, 000	16, 200	19, 200
(44) Edward Davis	10, 000	9, 200	19, 200
(37) Saml. s. Baker	2, 000	17, 154	19, 154
(56) James H. McCelvey	4, 000	15, 150	19, 150
(42) Jacob Miller	6, 000	13, 000	19, 000
(57) Andw. J. Weed	4, 000	15, 000	19, 000
(30) Alison Clinkscales	6, 000	13, 000	19, 000
(93) Elizabeth Pratt	4, 000	15, 000	19, 000
(33) Geo. W. Lomax	4, 000	15, 000	19, 000
(38) James F. Lomax	4, 000	15, 000	19, 000
(36) Jos. L. Hearst	8, 740	10, 252	18, 992
(37) Wm. A. Lomax	4, 750	14, 240	18, 990
(30) Jno. H. Chiles	4, 000	14, 930	18, 930
(52) Robert H. Hall	6, 000	12, 905	18, 905
(38) Jno. H. Wideman	870	18, 000	18, 870
(33) Christopher Ellis	4, 000	14, 750	18, 750

Census of 1860

(52) John Link	3, 500	15, 250	18, 750
(42) Clem T. Latimer	3, 400	15, 236	18, 636
(49) Robert Brownlee	5, 600	13, 000	18, 600
(58) Susan LeRoy	4, 272	14, 265	18, 537
(49) James H. Cobb	5, 000	13, 500	18, 500
(56) James B. Hughey	3, 984	14, 485	18, 469
(66) John Burnet	2, 500	15, 950	18, 450
(49) Thos. J. Hill	4, 500	13, 944	18, 444
(63) Samuel Gilmer	2, 400	16, 000	18, 400
(59) A. L. Morrow	4, 962	13, 296	18, 258
(42) William Donald	5, 000	13, 200	18, 200
(66) Rebecca Barr	3, 000	15, 150	18, 150
(55) Jno. McKellar	5, 080	13, 053	18, 053
(47) --- L. McCaslin	6, 000	12, 000	18, 000
(53) Wm. McCaslan	3, 000	15, 000	18, 000
(45) D. M. Wardlaw	4, 000	14, 000	18, 000
(25) Robt. H. White	16, 000	2, 000	18, 000
(36) Joseph T. Moore	10, 000	8, 000	18, 000
(30) John P. Kennedy		18, 000	18, 000
(40) Felix G. Parks	5, 000	13, 000	18, 000
(41) William Agnew	4, 000	14, 000	18, 000
(30) Thomas W. Smith		18, 000	18, 000
(30) M. G. Zeigler	4, 000	14, 000	18, 000
(73) Mary Meriwether		18, 000	18, 000
(68) Dr. Jos. F. Lee		18, 000	18, 000
(70) James C. Ellis	4, 000	14, 000	18, 000
(45) John R. McCord	3, 000	15, 000	18, 000
(36) William McComb	11, 000	6, 864	17, 864
(38) Saml. A. Wilson	3, 280	14, 460	17, 740
(50) Mrs. Jane Chiles	6, 240	11, 500	17, 740
(44) Peter S. Guillebeau	5, 000	12, 716	17, 716
(46) John Sadler	5, 000	12, 600	17, 600
(73) Lou Hester	1, 500	16, 088	17, 588
(37) Abner H. McGee, Jr.	6, 000	11, 575	17, 575
(42) Robert G. Lord	3, 000	14, 565	17, 565
(27) Wardlaw Perrin	4, 500	13, 000	17, 500
(29) Jas. C. Calhoun	6, 000	11, 500	17, 500
(42) John Enright	10, 000	7, 500	17, 500
(41) Elizabeth Bell	4, 800	12, 682	17, 482
(62) Sarah B. Jones	5, 300	12, 135	17, 435
(54) Thomas Crawford	7, 000	10, 425	17, 425
(56) Louisa Lesley	4, 000	13, 400	17, 400
(56) Mary Riley	3, 752	13, 500	17, 252
(39) John T. Miller	3, 000	14, 140	17, 140
(51) Thos. Hawthorn	3, 000	14, 100	17, 100
(27) Saml. R. Brownlee	3, 000	14, 100	17, 100
(38) A. M. Blake	5, 000	12, 000	17, 000
(26) M. Israel		17, 000	17, 000
(50) Elizabeth A. Reid	5, 000	12, 000	17, 000

Census of 1860

(42) William Smith	3,000	14,000	17,000
(42) Robert A. Archer	3,000	4,000	17,000
(29) John R. Sample	3,000	14,000	17,000
(48) Fred Cook	2,965	14,000	16,965
(53) James Haddon	2,500	14,420	16,920
(47) Robert McAdams	10,000	6,900	16,900
(51) Elias Kay	4,860	12,027	16,887
(59) Sterling Bowen	6,000	10,822	16,822
(28) James Taggart	6,000	10,800	16,800
(36) Stephen M. Tribble	4,000	12,800	16,800
(69) David S. Beacham	5,000	11,790	16,790
(27) William Tennent	4,000	12,785	16,785
(42) Charles A. Cobb	2,500	14,235	16,735
\(44) Samuel R. Lomax	2,000	14,600	16,600
(45) Jno. S. Chipley	4,800	11,700	16,500
(40) Benjamin D. Kay	4,850	11,625	16,475
(49) Chas. Fooshe	5,352	11,102	16,454
(65) John C. Waters	3,600	12,800	16,400
(27) Thomas Ellis	3,200	13,200	16,400
(38) William Coleman		16,250	16,250
(63) Simeon Chaney	5,000	11,192	16,192
(52) Jno. A. Martin	1,000	15,188	16,188
(57) John C. Hays	3,900	12,260	16,160
(64) Eliza Mattison	2,600	13,500	16,100
(27) James Brooks	2,000	14,000	16,000
(35) Brantley C. Hart	4,000	12,000	16,000
(50) Wm. M. Bell	2,000	14,000	16,000
(52) Wade (?) G. Keller	3,000	13,000	16,000
(43) John W. Brooks	4,000	12,000	16,000
(39) William Puckett	3,360	12,600	15,960
(33) Joseph Young	2,200	13,747	15,947
(50) Robert Martin	6,500	9,400	15,900
(43) C. Corley	2,500	13,240	15,740
(30) Geo. McD. Miller	3,000	12,730	15,730
(38) Hiram W. Lawson	3,600	12,000	15,600
(61) Eliza Byrd	3,500	12,000	15,500
(55) Nancy Waller	3,500	12,000	15,500
(73) Andrew Gillespie	4,000	11,469	15,469
(59) James Drennan	4,000	11,390	15,390
(72) James Williams	2,500	12,875	15,375
(42) Thornton Carter	1,960	13,360	15,320
(73) Paul Rogers	1,010	14,300	15,310
(39) Stephen Elmore	650	14,650	15,300
(46) Margt. Moore	3,000	12,220	15,220
(44) James M. Calvert	3,000	12,200	15,200
(42) Jno. Patterson	3,200	12,000	15,200
(42) William Franklin	3,360	11,786	15,146
(38) Wm. O. Pursley	1,800	13,328	15,128
(66) Vachel Hughey	3,000	12,000	15,000

Census of 1860

-(51) Joshua Wideman	5, 000	10, 000	15, 000
(48) Jno. McCreary	3, 000	12, 000	15, 000
(65) Jno. D. Adams		15, 000	15, 000
(31) Robert Buchanan	4, 000	11, 000	15, 000
(38) John F. Simpson	3, 000	12, 000	15, 000
(34) Alexr. M. Agnew	3, 500	11, 415	14, 915
(20) John C. Alewine	3, 000	11, 800	14, 800
(49) Capt. Pat McCaslan	4, 800	10, 000	14, 800
(65) Philip LeRoy	2, 500	12, 226	14, 726
(29) Benj. W.Williams	7, 950	6, 766	14, 716
(37) Henry B. Nickles	7, 500	7, 135	14, 635
(42) R. A. Lesley	1, 500	13, 045	14, 545
(52) John T. Haddon	3, 000	11, 494	14, 494
(43) John C. Speer	2, 505	11, 945	14, 450
(36) Wm. T. Clinkscales	6, 300	8, 136	14, 436
(62) Thomas Davis	5, 000	9, 385	14, 385
(34) John Elkins	7, 500	6, 860	14, 360
(42) Adam J. McKee	3, 300	11, 000	14, 300
(42) Louisa Logan	1, 600	12, 700	14, 300
(48) William Dunn	4, 000	10, 200	14, 200
(30) Augustus T. Lythgoe	4, 000	10, 200	14, 200
(44) Robert Dunn	6, 800	7, 390	14, 190
(39) Wm. Clark Scott	5, 000	9, 172	14, 172
(38) Lewis Clinkscales	3, 000	11, 095	14, 095
(23) Thomas Mahon		14, 000	14, 000
(17) Sallie Tillman		14, 000	14, 000
(40) William McGaw	6, 000	8, 000	14, 000
(50) William Butler	2, 000	12, 000	14, 000
(66) Jno. B. Adamson	3, 700	10, 250	13, 950
(38) John F. McComb	4, 825	9, 050	13, 875
(52) William Ellis	1, 800	12, 000	13, 800
(78) Isabella Harden	5, 625	8, 123	13, 738
(31) James Stack	5, 950	7, 700	13, 650
(43) W. T. Hammond	3, 000	10, 543	13, 543
(35) Dr. Thomas Hester		13, 500	13, 500
(40) John Hermon	1, 500	12, 000	13, 500
(48) Saml. Link	3, 480	10, 000	13, 480
(30) Octavius T. Porcher	6, 000	7, 390	13, 390
(58) Nancy Beasley	2, 400	10, 869	13, 269
(62) Jas. L. Gilmer	3, 000	10, 265	13, 265
(38) Jno. Donald	4, 200	9, 065	13, 265
(49) Robt. Seawright	3, 000	10, 250	13, 250
(29) John Boozer	2, 600	10, 600	13, 200
(49) James Killingsworth	4, 000	9, 155	13, 155
(32) Jos. H. Lites	3, 792	9, 290	13, 082
(67) Milly Harris	5, 000	8, 000	13, 000
(59) David W. McCants		13, 000	13, 000
(32) Wm. McClinton	3, 000	10, 000	13, 000
(50) David Moore	5, 000	8, 000	13, 000

(36) T. A. Cater	3, 000	9, 906	12, 906
(33) David J. Wardlaw	3, 000	9, 870	12, 870
(45) James E. G. Bell	4, 800	8, 054	12, 854
(43) Thos. J. Cunningham	2, 500	10, 333	12, 833
(70) Dousilla Williams	2, 000	10, 825	12, 825
(43) Sanders Walker	2, 800	10, 000	12, 800
(49) Jno. G. Thornton	3, 000	9, 800	12, 800
(68) Nathaniel Cobb	2, 800	10, 000	12, 800
(56) Wilson (?) Wilson	1, 200	11, 555	12, 755
(54) Thomas A. Douglas	4, 800	7, 932	12, 732
(28) James Pratt	4, 000	8, 700	12, 700
(52) William S. Harris	4, 000	8, 600	12, 600
(51) Rev. Wm. H. Davis	2, 000	10, 600	12, 600
(51) Thos. W. Branyon	4, 500	8, 000	12, 500
(66) James Pursley	3, 500	9, 000	12, 500
(53) Samuel Donelly	3, 500	9, 000	12, 500
(54) Eliz Robinson	3, 500	9, 000	12, 500
(36) Gibson Johnson	2, 500	9, 852	12, 352
(26) T. A. Harris	2, 660	9, 655	12, 315
(28) Wm. R. White		12, 250	12, 250
(70) Jane Wallace	1, 800	10, 320	12, 120
(52) Elizabeth Taylor	3, 000	9, 109	12, 109
(52) Agnes Cox	2, 800	9, 236	12, 036
(52) James Banks	1, 560	10, 500	12, 060
(20) James T. Buchanan	2, 176	9, 834	12, 010
(69) Josiah Wells	6, 000	6, 000	12, 000
( ) Theo. R. Rogers		12, 000	12, 000
(23) W. F. Maxwell		12, 000	12, 000
(35) Edmund L. Patton	2, 000	10, 000	12, 000
(41) J. Jenkins Lee		12, 000	12, 000
(29) William A. Gaines	4, 000	8, 000	12, 000
(14) Virginia Hayward		12, 000	12, 000
(40) John W. Lesley	3, 000	8, 965	11, 965
(27) James D. Chalmers	250	11, 700	11, 950
(49) David McLain	2, 800	9, 000	11, 800
(26) Franklin Clinkscales	5, 400	6, 400	11, 800
(56) Wm. L. Campbell	4, 000	7, 795	11, 795
(64) John McCord	3, 724	8, 000	11, 724
(50) Susan Guillebeau	1, 150	10, 480	11, 630
(34) M. Mary Scott	5, 000	6, 630	11, 630
(50) Mary Norwood	1, 500	10, 115	11, 615
(55) Permelia Watson	2, 600	9, 000	11, 600
in same household 5 minors with total of			16, 075
(42) Wm. B. Romans	5, 000	6, 600	11, 600
(41) Andrew Stevenson	2, 000	9, 550	11, 550
(46) Jas. A. McCord	4, 000	7, 526	11, 726
(54) Jno. B. Johnson	2, 664	8, 902	11, 564
(49) Matthew McDonald	1, 200	10, 300	11, 500
(24) John F. Calhoun	3, 000	8, 447	11, 447

(67) C. V. Barnes	6, 000	5, 433	11, 533
(40) Andrew Richey	2, 000	9, 350	11, 350
(44) Jos. J. Cooper	2, 000	9, 350	11, 350
(37) James Jones	4, 300	7, 000	11, 300
(70) Alex Austin	3, 500	7, 765	11, 265
(34) Washington L. Prince	3, 500	7, 780	11, 280
(42) Saml. E. Pruitt	3, 500	7, 700	11, 200
(42) James McIlwain	2, 000	9, 155	11, 155
(38) Wm. W. McDill	3, 300	7, 800	11, 100
(36) Robert C. Harkness	3, 549	7, 538	11, 087
(21) William Pratt	800	10, 280	11, 080
(41) Mary A. Bigby	2, 000	9, 065	11, 065
(31) Thomas Lesley	3, 000	8, 052	11, 052
(65) Isabella Miller	3, 000	8, 050	11, 050
(60) William Smith	3, 000	8, 025	11, 025
(28) James Barnes		11, 015	11, 015
(50) LeRoy Purdy	3, 000	8, 000	11, 000
(37) Allen T. Bell	2, 000	9, 000	11, 000
(64) William Long	3, 000	8, 000	11, 000
(21) Jane Robertson		11, 000	11, 000
(42) James A. Swaine	2, 000	9, 000	11, 000
(38) James R. Cunningham	2, 000	9, 000	11, 000
(45) William Gibson	2, 500	8, 475	10, 975
(65) Fergus McMahan	3, 600	7, 254	10, 854
(46) Wiley Newby	3, 000	7, 838	10, 838
(66) Eliza Kellam	4, 000	6, 800	10, 800
(40) Samuel Jones	4, 200	6, 592	10, 792
(57) William Gordon	3, 316	7, 464	10, 780
(40) James Burton	4, 000	6, 759	10, 759
(30) Edmond Kennedy	2, 000	8, 712	10, 712
(52) Henry Riley	2, 000	8, 707	10, 707
(31) James J. Tolbert	600	10, 000	10, 600
(28) John R. Clinkscales	600	10, 000	10, 600
(52) Mary McGruder	3, 700	6, 840	10, 540
(64) Wm. Hodges	5, 500	5, 015	10, 515
(30) Rev. J.R. Proffit	1, 896	8, 752	10, 648
(34) Washington Prince	3, 900	6, 605	10, 505
(40) Samuel J. Hester		10, 500	10, 500
(30) James A. Ellis	2, 500	8, 000	10, 500
(75) Jas. A. Bailey	3, 500	7, 000	10, 500
(26) Richmond Cobb	1, 500	9, 000	10, 500
(75) Hannah McComb	3, 000	7, 497	10, 497
(40) Jno. A. Seawright	2, 000	8, 450	10, 450
(60) Joseph Bouchillon	2, 800	7, 620	10, 420
(41) Peter Henry	2, 400	8, 000	10, 400
(58) Robert J. Smith	2, 000	8, 380	10, 380
(54) Mason Henderson	2, 000	8, 365	10, 365
(29) Saml. J. Willard	1, 760	8, 600	10, 360
(40) Frances E. Moseley	4, 000	6, 300	10, 300

Census of 1860

(45) Samuel Graham	2, 500	7, 745	10,245
(61) Eliz. Richey	2, 000	8, 230	10, 230
(42) Andrew Morrison	3, 900	6, 300	10, 200
(57) Jas. Malone	3, 522	6, 615	10, 137
(38) Eliz B. Nichols	1, 870	8, 212	10, 082
(27) Saml. Hunter		10, 077	10, 077
(45) Wm. T. Mauldin	2, 500	7, 526	10, 026
(32) James M. Lattimore	2, 560	7, 460	10, 020
(33) James Shirley	4, 000	6, 000	10, 000
(50) Josh Ashley	4, 000	6, 000	10, 000
(70) Catherine Hamilton	2, 000	8, 000	10, 000
(31) Jno. D. Johnson	4, 000	6, 000	10, 000
(55) Sarah E. McCracken	3, 000	7, 000	10, 000
(48) L. Oliver Shoemaker	9, 500	500	10, 000
(31) Owen J. Ferguson		10, 000	10, 000
(62) Josiah Patterson	2, 000	8, 000	10, 000

Creative Journalism in the 1850s: the *New York Times* and the Brooks Dinner at Ninety Six, October, 1856

The New York Times, December 16, 1897, carried an obituary notice of Patrick H. Carey whom it characterized as "one of the first court stenographers in this country and a noted newspaperman in ante-bellum days." It reported that he was born in County Antrim, Ireland on March 13, 1834. He early chose stenography as his profession, and in his late teens he was first employed on the *Dublin Telegraph*. He came to the United States in 1853 and was first employed on the New York *Evening Express*. The obituary said "he soon became intimate with many of the noted lawyers and newspaper men of that day, among them Henry J. Raymond, James T. Brady, David Dudley Field and Charles O'Connor. Under Mr. Raymond he was employed on the staff of the *New York Times*. In the days of the "Bleeding Kansas" trouble he went to that State as secretary of Gov. Robert J. Walker, and also as correspondent of the *Times*. His letters to the paper attracted wide attention. He afterward acted for a while as Washington correspondent of *The Times*.

The *New York Times* in its ninth year (on October 8, 1856) chose to devote its entire front page and most of page 2 to an account of an appreciation dinner staged by the constituents of South Carolina Congressman Preston Brooks at Ninety Six near his home. The occasion was set to show popular support for Brooks' conduct some weeks earlier when he had entered the chamber of the United States Senate and unmercifully beat the Senator from Massachusetts, Charles Sumner, with his cane. Henry Raymond, the founder and editor of the *New York Times* and one of the founding fathers for the new Republican Party, sent Patrick H. Carey who was designated as a "special reporter" to the Ninety Six event, and he played this story for its relation to the presidential contest of 1856.

Banner headlines proclaimed "South Carolina on the Presidential Question. Brooks at Home. Grand Festival at Ninety Six. More Canes and Goblets. Blood and Murder-- Thunder and Lightning. Fire and Fury--Slavery or Death-- Dissolution, Secession, or Eternal Smash! The 'Union' in Articulo Mortis. The Great Southern Republic That Is To Be. All the Preliminaries Settled. Speeches of Preston Brooks, Maj. Gen. McGowan, Senator Butler, Senator Toombs, Dr. S. V. Caine, Major Griffin, Mr. Prestly [sic], etc." The byline read "From the Special Reporter of the *New York Daily Times*.

There was no identification of the *Times*' "Special Reporter," but four days earlier on the 4th when the *Times* had carried a long featured article from Charleston on the Taber-Magrath duel, its author was indicated as "our own reporter, " and he appended the initials P. H. C. at the bottom of the column. He represented himself in South Carolina as a reporter for Thomas Francis

Patrick H. Carey, the *New York Times* and the Brooks Dinner, 1856

Meagher's *Irish News*, a journal which had a more favorable reputation in the South. The *Times* obituary which was written four decades later declared that Carey was intimate with the Irish patriots in American, and particularly with Meagher. Although neither paper noted this fact, he wrote accounts of his trip South and the Brooks celebration for both papers.

In 1856, the *Times* was strongly promoting the John C. Fremont candidacy for president, and it had quickly seized upon the Brooks-Sumner Affair as quite helpful in the campaign. On May 24, it commented editorially, as follows: "A New York dogkiller has notions of honor that would make it impossible for him to commit such an outrage. It has been reserved for Preston S. Brooks of South Carolina -- Member of Congress from a State which prides herself upon the chivalry of her sons -- to perpetrate the act." On October 8, it carried the following notice on the editorial page: "We publish this morning a very full report of a very remarkable banquet given at Ninety Six, in South Carolina to Col. Preston S. Brooks, in approbation of his murderous assault on Senator Sumner. It was a fitting climax to the honor which the Slave interest has showered on his head for that disgraceful act."

The article began, as follows: "I arrived at Ninety Six on Wednesday afternoon about 2 o'clock, but finding no tolerable house of entertainment in the neighborhood, I made my way to a little wayside hotel some ten miles further up the road at a village named Greenwood. I had been furnished in Charleston with letters of recommendation to the proprietor, on presenting which I was received with great cordiality, and provided with every accommodation that the place could supply."

Carey then reported on a conversation which he had with a fellow traveler, a South Carolinian (from nearby Anderson) who had been to Kansas, a subject which was apparently of great interest to Editor Raymond. Earlier in 1856, the *New York Times* had carried a four page supplement with Senator Sumner's speech on the Kansas Question , the only instance in its history when it had given more space to one story than it now gave to the Brooks' celebration. Carey wrote, "On my journey thither I met in the cars one Major Wilkes, a very smart and intelligent fellow who was just on his way home from Kansas. He was accompanied by two men, who had formed a part of a troop of thirty which he raised in South Carolina to aid the Missourians in their efforts to expel the Free-State settlers. His baggage, at least all that I could see, consisted of a bowie knife, a gun, and -- strange accompaniment - - a fiddle. His companions were similarly provided, minus the music." Wilkes was disillusioned with his two experiences in Kansas and "firmly determined never to set foot in Kansas again." Carey added, "I commended his resolution and praised his judgment."

Carey and the *New York Times* at Brooks Dinner, 1856

Carey was quite pleased with "the little village of Greenwood, where I stayed till Friday morning, . . . one of the pleasantest spots I know of; embedded in groves of oak and persimmon, surrounded by a beautiful undulating country excellently cultivated, inhabited by planters of respectable means, and quiet as a Sunday morning, it was to me a very picture of rural peace and happiness. Nor were the people so primitive in their notions as one fresh from the North would be likely to expect. The village contains four schools and two or three houses of worship. I found everybody with whom I conversed thoroughly familiar with the politics of the country and not at all ignorant of public affairs generally."

He then balanced this praise with some critical observations: "In some respects, it is true, they are lamentably behind the age. There is an obvious lack among them of public enterprise, though individually there is a sharp lookout for the main chance. Railroad travel is tantalizingly slow. Half the time is spent on stopping on the road, and when the trains get fairly in motion the speed rarely exceeds a moderate horse-trot. I spent precisely seventeen hours and a half in going from Charleston to Greenwood--a distance of two hundred and fifteen miles, and that too, in continuous travel. It should be borne in mind, however, as a sort of offset to this tardiness, that accidents on these roads are almost unknown."

Carey commented humorously on a local newspaper which reported that Major General McGowan (the scheduled keynote speaker for the Brooks' celebration) at a muster ground "in the neighborhood of Columbia" had made "a brief but pathetic speech" which he called "appropriate to anyone who had seen such a muster."

In another example, he wrote "of the ignorance which pervades at the South on subjects outside of politics, an amusing instance was afforded me the morning I left Greenwood. A gentleman, otherwise very well informed, indeed, asked me with the greatest sincerity imaginable, whether Meagher's *Irish News* was published in English." Carey failed to note here that the subject likely came up because he represented himself in South Carolina as a reporter for the *Irish News*. While he was impressed unfavorably with his meals on the trip, he was willing to praise the temperance of the citizens, as follows: "In the matter of domestic economy, our Southern friends do not seem to excel. Their cooking is simply execrable. They give you cold fowl, and cold beefsteak, and cold coffee, and cold potatoes, and (which must be regarded as rather a relieving feature, it is seldom that you can get anything to drink at country inns but cold water. I was much struck by the temperate habits of the people generally."

Aside from the speakers at the festival, Carey's attention focused mostly upon Dr. Ephraim Calhoun of Greenwood who owned the hotel where Carey spent the two evenings before the festival. He continued, "The Doctor, as my host was styled, for he had once practiced physic, and the title stuck to him (N. B. -- Every man above thirty in South Carolina has a professional title.) The Doctor, I repeat, was an old gentleman of great native shrewdness, considerable information, and much experience, but like everybody else I met, he was laboring under secession mania. We frequently got into conversation about Slavery and the "impending crisis." He did not seem to "keer" much, as he said himself, who was elected President, because he thought that even Buchanan's success would only protract the "crisis" for four years more. 'I'll tell you what it is,' said he to me one evening. 'We believe Fremont will be elected and we want to see him elected, for that will bring on the 'crisis.' We have nothing to gain by the Union. It is a positive loss to us, for it is a partnership to which we supply more than two-thirds of the capital and from which we receive less than one third of the profits. We don't 'keer a d-n' for your Northern manufactures. The moment of the announcement of the separation of the Southern States from the confederacy reaches England, a British ambassador will be dispatched to Charleston to make a treaty providing for reciprocal free trade between us and Great Britain, and to assure us that a heavy import will be laid on all goods exported to England from the Northern States. Then, Sir, we shall buy better goods than yours at a cheaper rate, and the North will go to the devil. That's all. Why, Sir, if England doesn't do that, she will go to the devil, too. She is governed by capital, and without our cotton, her capitalists would have nothing to work on, her laborers and mechanics would have nothing to do, and civil war would follow as sure as my hat is on my head.'

I ventured to suggest that as England had never been necessarily in love with the Union, she might seize the opportunity to embroil the two sections in war, and then, when they had mutually exhausted their energies, cooly step in and seize the cotton growing country for herself. He pooh-pooh'd at this, declared such a thing was impossible, and expressed a fervent hope that the issue between the North and South should now be settled. He just wanted to let the North feel how powerless she would be alone. He just wanted the experiment of a separation to be tried, were it only for four years, and then have the confederacy renewed again, if both sections desired it. Of that he had no doubt, however, and he was perfectly satisfied that the South in renewing the compact could dictate her own terms.

Occasionally the discourse turned on the Slavery question. After nightfall, it was customary for some of the neighbors to drop in on us, as the weather was quite cool, we usually seated ourselves round a roaring log fire in the sitting room. Here the matter was discussed right and left, up and down, in all its

Carey, the *New York Times*, Brooks Dinner, 1856

possible bearings, moral, social, and political. The Negro, according to the Southern idea, is the happiest man alive--at least if he isn't he ought to be. 'Just look at my Negroes,' said the Doctor, 'Wheer can you find a more contented set of people? They want for nothing, they have no responsibility; they are not overwrought, they are substantially fed, and I'm sure I never abuse them. Of course, theer are some masters who treat their Negroes harshly, but that is not the fault of the system.

Your laborers North are often treated as brutally, for if they are not beaten, now and then they are starved. That's all the difference. Why don't your philanthrophists expend theer superflous charity at home? Why don't they mind theer own business and let us alone, G--d d--n them. I suppose that they think that we have no other object in view than to make money off our Negroes. Now, look at my house servants. Sir, I never make a cent on them. Theer's our housekeeper; I would not sell her for any amount of money. She is invaluable. She never was beaten in my house but once, and that was for grossly mistreating her own child. I was sick in bed at the time and could not get up, so I called my wife to whip her. I have had but few field hands, and the few I have are not profitable to me. I have a fellow out theer who is a carpenter, and another a blacksmith, and that other fellow that pumps into the cistern at the railroad--they make me something, but it is not much.' 'It is true,' he added, with charming *naivete*, 'I generally keep a good many breeding women about my house, and reer up a considerable number of little niggers, and in that way, I realize as much, I believe, as people who have more laborers.'

His article next dealt with the trip to Ninety Six and especially with his visit to Star Fort which led to a recapitulation of the Revolutionary campaign there. "The private vehicle" in which he rode to Star Fort had been graciously loaned him by Dr. Calhoun, but in the *Times*, he wrote "our conveyance was very rickety, and the road was rough as a washboard. We were always either dragging up a hill or backing down one, but fortunately succeeded in reaching our destination without accident." Carey said that he went to the Fort partly for "intrinsic interest," but also because of his "notion that it may have been chosen as the theatre of the Brooks demonstration upon other grounds than mere convenience." This allusion fit the *Times* assumption that South Carolina was ready for another "revolution."

In Abbeville's *Independent Press*, October 24, 1856, editor W. A. Lee wrote, "We have just finished reading an amusing and rather graphic account of the Brooks' demonstration at Ninety Six, occupying two closely printed pages in the *New York Times*. The paper is edited by Raymond, the yoke-fellow of Bennett and Greeley, and is a *rara avis* in these parts. We are indebted for our

Carey, the *New York Times*, Brooks Dinner, 1856

copy to a friend to whom it was sent. Being a single copy, it has been well thumbed in passing from hand to hand, and is now pretty well reduced to the state to which our Northern brethren think we wish to consign the Union; and presents those marks of rupture and dismemberment from which Daniel Webster was accustomed to avert the eyes of his imagination. . .our reporter, by the way, seems to be quite an able one; but contrary to the maxims of Horace, aspires to be something more than a retailer of other men's thoughts, and has a mind of his own, which he expresses freely on all occasions.

As introductory to the dinner, and the report of the speeches, he gives an account of his wayside experiences. His estimate of Southern society and manners is upon the whole favorable, though his detailed account of certain conversations in Greenwood, is, we are told, grossly incorrect. We can afford to be amused at his extravagances, and where he blunders upon the truth, to accept it, according to the well known maxim, even from an enemy."

Lee was rather more pleased with Carey's coverage of the speeches at the Brooks affair and said he thought the reporter "has done justice to his [Gen McGowan, the chief speaker] clear and logical statements, his rounded periods, his apt quotations, and fervid style, though much is lost, in the absence of that easy elocution, and impassioned utterance, which lend a charm to the spoken word."

The *Independent Press*, October 31, 1856, carried lengthy excerpts and summaries from P H. Carey's "Glimpses of the South," in Meagher's *Irish News*. Its contrasting tone is indicated by its opening impressionistic picture:

"Charleston, as everybody knows who knows anything, is the commercial capital of South Carolina, and what is more, one of the finest cities in the Union. Its situation is rather low, and the country behind it, is too flat to warrant us in claiming for it much of the picturesque. The approach from the harbor, however, is beautiful. On the right lies Sullivan's Island, with its low tropical-looking houses, its magnificent hotel, and Fort Moultrie, great in revolutionary annals, on its further extremity. On the left, a pretty undulating friend of shore, green as emerald, stretches away as far as the eye can reach, until lost in the blue haze of the horizon. In front rise the tall spires and white towers of the city, bathed in a flood of golden light, and springing, as it were, from the very bosom of the bay.

'I saw from out the wave her structure rise,
As from the stroke of an enchanter's wand,'

The city viewed internally, is clean; the streets spacious; the buildings, generally handsome; the stores elegant; and its business aspect indicates wealth, prosperity, and progress. The greatest drawback is its unhealthiness during the

Carey, the *New York Times*, Brooks Dinner, 1856

warm months. . . .[as evidence for his warm feelings for its citizens whom he met] I can hardly describe the pleasure I experienced in meeting some old friends in Charleston, whom I had not seen for several years before, and who, with a hospitality that used only to be Irish, and with a warmth of friendship and nobility of kindness that are seldom found anywhere out of the State, did their best to make my stay agreeable. I am bound to say that they succeeded to perfection. To one fresh from the North and to one habituated to Northern feelings and character, the quick sensibilities, overflowing nature, chivalric tone and convival temper that form the prominent traits of our Southern brethren, cannot fail at first sight to appear somewhat extravagant. This impression soon wears away, however; and even if it did not, it is an extravagance with which nobody can be displeased. Certainly I, for one, regreted my inability to enjoy more of it."

While describing the Taber-Magrath duel which was chief topic of conversation in Charleston at the time, his tone is quite conciliatory: "This duello code is a marked feature of the Southern society, and has always been in vogue among races characterised by strong sensibilities and excitability of temper. It is not my business here to enter into a disquisition of the ethics of it, but I cannot refrain from expressing the opinion that it is a very absurd manner of settling quarrels. Something, it is true, may be said in its favor. But what of that? I do not doubt that something might be said in favor of the devil, and I am sure there never was a bad thing in existence in regard to which something good, or tending to good, might not be advanced. I can readily conceive of circumstances in which one man would not only be justified, but bound to kill another, but no strength of fancy could devise circumstances under which the obligation to kill would be mutual--unless, it be in war--and I question even that."

In the article on the Taber-Magrath duel which the *New York Times* had carried on October 4, Carey told the following story: "The first thing I heard at the breakfast table this morning, was addressed by an old gentleman, in a white choker, to his opposite neighbor.

"Well," said he, "that was a brotherly act of young Magrath's."

"Yes," said the other, "but I am afraid it is not ended yet."

"Why, it cannot be that it is going further."

"Yes, Sir; what protection would there be for a gentleman if every scoundrel were at liberty to insult him, were it not for the *code of honor?*"

"But will not the force of public opinion put an end both to such caviling and to such results?"

"No," replied the other, "such events are inevitable here. Just consider what you or I would do under such circumstances. By the way, did you hear anything of the conduct of the duelists when they were brought on the ground?"

"No, Sir, not a word," said White choker.

"Well, I have been informed, on good authority, that Magrath did not know how to take his position, for he actually presented his left side to his antagonist. They were then arranged properly; Taber, who was a practised duelist, lined Magrath every time, but withal Connor [Taber's second] refused to take the advantage therein offered in favor of his principles. You know what happened. It seems to have been an intervention of Providence."

"Oh, Lord," said our venerable friend, as he dropped his knife and fork and raised his eyes to the ceiling.

I left the table before the old gentleman recovered his equanimity enough to resume his breakfast."

In his *Times* article, he commented on the length of time which the railroad trip took from Charleston to Greenwood and on the monotony of the landscape in the low country, but in his *Irish News* account, he emphasized how as his journey neared its end, "the prospects improves. Well cultivated fields stretch down to the road. Pleasant farm houses, embedded in oak and magnolia, with the smoke of the Negroes' huts rising up out of the dense groves, here and there meet the view, and gladden both eye and heart. The whole face of nature is changed. Even the very steam engine (to my surprise I found it named after that venerable warrior, *Brian Bonhoime*) seems to derive new vigor from the altered circumstances and rattles away with acclerated speed."

In the *Irish News*, he displayed a more tolerant view of slavery. For example, he wrote, "It is a strange fact,' observed a Southern gentleman to me one day, 'that the harshest, most exacting, and most abusive slave owners among us are Northern men. They have no sympathy with the slave, no consideration for his inferior capacity, and no confidence in his integrity. Even the Northern women, who sometimes come down here to teach our schools, exhibit a repugnance to the slave that is strangely at variance with their professions of love for them at the North, and with what we would expect from the tender heart of the sex. We, on the contrary, look upon the slave as part of our family. They grow up among us, their children mix with ours from their earliest childhood, and affections are formed in that way which the growth of years only serves to strengthen.'"

His "Glimpses of the South" led Editor W. A. Lee of the *Independent Press* to describe Carey as "a very intelligent eye witness. . . [with] a real Irish imagination, a good fund of Irish humor, and a style which throws a rich coloring upon the most common incidents." Lee happily relays to his Abbeville readers the friendly contrast which Carey makes between the South and the North, as follows:

"I found the people [of the South] sober, intelligent, high-minded, patriotic, and kind hearted. One thing I mused, to-wit -- the squalid misery of the laboring classes of the North. I saw no poverty. And you may depend upon it, the absence of poverty is a very superior feature in a community.

Another interesting trait, or class of traits, in Northern society never shows its face among our Southern friends. The people have no penchant for *isms*; and, let me tell you, they manage to get on wonderfully well without them. There are no cadaverous, sapless, man-forsaken females, turning politics into a burlesque, philosophy into farce, and religion into a reproach. There are no long-headed fanatics preaching a millennium of free-love. There are no Hiss Committees, no convent-burners, no addle-patted ranters, no Know-Nothings. There are no "minister of the Gospel" -- Save the mark! --sermonizing from the text -- "Go ye into the world and shoot at every creature," turning the church into the play-house, and making rowdyism of religion. But it may be urged, "Slavery is there." "Well, Sir, what of it? You are not responsible for it. You have no business with it.   Look around you, and you will see Slavery everywhere -- aye, under your nose! Slavery ten thousand times worse than any involuntary servitude."

The *Independent Press*, November 7, 1856, carried the following from the New York *Day Book*: "The Celebration at Ninety Six, S. C. The *New York Times*, in hopes of getting some capital to prop up the expiring fortunes of Fremont, sent a reporter down to South Carolina to report the proceedings of the festival given to Col. Brooks. The reporter, who was sent, gave a doleful account of the ignorance of the people, and among others whom he abused was Mr. E. R. Calhoun, the landlord of the Hotel at Greenwood, where he stopped. Mr. C. has, it appears, seen a copy of the *Times*, and writes to us to say that no such ridiculous conversation, as he reported, took place. In his own language, he says, 'I unequivocally pronounce it absolutely false and without even the semblance of a foundation. In fact, everything that he said about the South was a misrepresentation and a gross caricature.' Mr. C. says that he treated the fellow with more than ordinary courtesy, and he is astonished he could be so ungrateful. He represented himself, while there, as connected with the *Irish News* of this city, but we learn that no man by the name of Carey, the one he sailed under at the South, belongs to that paper. He was an Irishman, and professed to hate the abolitionists, though reporting for the *Times*. He is, doubtless, some renegade Irishman who disgraces the name."

The *Independent Press*, November 14, 1856, contained the following in

Carey, the *New York Times*, Brooks Dinner, 1856

relation to Carey & Calhoun:

"Greenwood, Nov. 11, 1856

Dear Sir: Enclosed is a letter, which I have just received from P. H. Carey, who reported for the *New York Times* on the proceedings of the Brooks' dinner. Although marked 'private,' I think that I have the right of using so much of it as is necessary to exonerate me from the charge of a ridiculous and profane conversation, contained in the preface to his report as published in the *Times*. If you think it not dishonorable in me, I will thank you to publish the first two pages in your next issue. E. R. Calhoun.

Boston, Mass. Nov. 4, 1856

Dear Sir: A few days ago, before I left New York, a friend handed me a copy of the *Day Book*, in which allusion was made to a certain letter you had written to the editor of that paper, denying the accuracy of my report of the Brooks' Festival and charging me with base ingratitude. I have been so much employed since then that it is only now I could spare the leisure to write to you. I am very sorry that such a paragraph should ever have appeared, but especially sorry that you should have felt yourself warranted in writing such a letter as that referred to in it. Not, let me assure you, that I care a single straw so far as I am concerned, but merely for the sake of right and truth in the abstract.

In the first place, I beg you sincerely to believe that, in anything I said or wrote about you, I never for a moment meant the slightest disparagement of you. On the contrary, I believe (for I have not a copy by me) that when I did allude to you it was always in the spirit of kindness. And so it has ever been with me in referring to your unwavering hospitality and good nature to me whilst I was a guest with you. Nothing was farther from my intention than to cast a slur upon you or your friends.

Now, as to the reported conversation, my business South was not to report conversations, but to ascertain the direction of the current of Southern feeling, and to report the speeches of the banquet to your Congressional Representative. Both of these duties I claim to have faithfully discharged, and I am quite certain you would not be disposed to dispute the fact. I merely put the Southern argument in ordinary use into your mouth, in order to save the introduction of a variety of personages, and frequent dialogues into the introductory remarks. These arguments you, I feel certain, would not repudiate. P. H. Carey."

The Unusual Story of Mrs. Floride Bonneau Colhoun's Nephews

Mrs. Floride Bonneau Colhoun is best known in South Carolina history as the mother-in-law of John C. Calhoun. When the future Vice President began his association with his future mother-in-law, he was at Yale and was ill, and Mrs. Colhoun, the widow of his first cousin, John Ewing Colhoun, invited him to New Port, R. I. to recuperate. He was unable to accept her invitation until after commencement in September, 1804.

John Ewing Colhoun (he took the variant spelling, although his widow would later be addressed as "Mrs. Calhoun") was the son of Ezekiel Calhoun, a brother of John C. Calhoun's father Patrick. John Ewing was a graduate of Princeton who practiced law in Charleston and there he met Floride Bonneau, a member of a well to do Huguenot family who were planters in South Santee Parish. John E. Colhoun had plantations in the low country and near Pendleton where they had a summer residence. After a short service in the South Carolina General Assembly and the state senate, he was selected in 1801 as a U. S. Senator from South Carolina. After attendance of only one term, he died in Pendleton in 1802.

After his death, Floride Bonneau Colhoun with the three surviving children lived primarily at Bonneau's Ferry on the Cooper River approximately twenty miles above Charleston. Sometime they lived in Charleston or Pendleton. Often she spent months at her cottage at Newport, less than a hundred miles from New Haven. One year after Calhoun's first visit to Newport, an observer noted that Mrs. Colhoun arrived at Newport in her family coach, "drawn by four gray horses with the reins held by an English coachman in full livery." Two decades later (1823), her famous son-in-law wrote her older son, John Ewing, Jr. who looked out for her planting interest in South Caorlina, "You know that her habits are such as to require considerable expenditure, not on herself but others who have no claim on her." He added, "She, I think, is correcting this habit, but still she could not be contented were she restricted in her means."

She was notably generous to family members. A neighbor in Newport and a fellow Carolinian, Isaac Ball, noted that on September 13, 1806 he "call'd to see Mrs. Calhoun who lives very comfortably with her 3 children, Mr. Pickens' daughter and two of James Buseau [sic]'s children she *had* brought from Halifax."

That summer another guest was her cousin John with whom she had developed a close bond. After his first visit to Newport following his Yale graduation, he returned to South Carolina and studied law in Abbeville under George Bowie. In April, 1805, Mrs. Colhoun with her three children and her servants took him in her family carriage from South Carolina to Newport.

A tradition later recounted by James Edward Calhoun, Mrs. Colhoun's youngest son, was that at the request of her young cousin, Mrs. Colhoun assented to a side trip to Monticello where the future vice president met President Jefferson. Calhoun's biographers differ over whether to accept this tradition. Margaret Coit in her popular 1950 biography, *John C. Calhoun, An American Portrait*, (which won a Pulitzer for biography) argued for its truth. Miss Coit was often willing to value such traditions. Charles M. Wiltse rejected this tradition in the first volume of his biographical series on Calhoun. In *John C. Calhoun, Nationalist*, he noted that it was based exclusively on an account of Mrs. Colhoun's seven year old James Edward.

Calhoun went on to Litchfield from Newport, and be began to attend the law lectures of two nationally known legal scholars. In September 9, 1805 after he had received a letter from Mrs. Colhoun addressing him as "Dear John," he replied, "I thank you for your affectionate mode of address which, I assure you, is much more agreeable to my feeling than any other. Your whole actions in kindness and affection have been to me, like a mother's tenderness. I know not how I shall make sufficient return; unless it is by acting in a manner worthy of your friendship and esteem; which, with this assistance of him [God] who is the author of all good resolutions and actions, I hope to do so."

Her reply in a September 14th letter indicated her own strong religious feeling, as follows: "What unspeakable blessing, that I the most helpless of mortals have been brought to put my whole trust and confidence in Him who has enabled me to say His Will be done." She wrote that she was considering placing her two sons, John and James, in a school near Litchfield because "one great inducement for me to put them there is, that they will be near you, and you cou'd sometimes see them." John C. Calhoun replied, "I do not think Newport is a proper place for boys of John and James age."

An undercurrent in the correspondence between the two came to contain oblique references to his feelings for Mrs. Colhoun's young daughter, also named Floride. Another subject in the letters indicated that after his return to Abbeville, he was looking after Mrs. Colhoun's nephews at Moses Waddel's Willington Academy. In October, 1807, he wrote Mrs. Colhoun from Abbeville, "It gives me real pleasure to find simernaries [sic] of learning become so respectable and numerous. Mr. Waddel still continues to have a fine school. He is much pleased with the behavoir and progress of your Nephew. He bids fair to make an excellent scholar. Not long since, I attended an examination at Mr. Waddel's.

In October, 1809, from Abbeville he wrote Mrs. Colhoun in Newport and reported to her that "your friends here are all well, & except Wentworth have enjoyed good health this fall. He had an attack of fall fever; which I've no doubt he brought on by too much study and too little exercise. He is now well; and at Pend[eton."

His letters to Mrs. Colhoun indicated that his strong feeling for her continued to deepen. In July, 1809, he wrote, "so unlimited is my confidence in your prudence and friendship, that to you I make the full and entire disclosure of the most inward recesses of my thoughts; while to all the world, even to my brothers, I am silent."

On January 20th, 1810, he wrote Mrs. Colhoun, "I sent your letter to Wentworth the day after my arrival and expect to be at Dr. Waddel's myself in two or three days." In June, 1810, he wrote, "I left Dr. Wadell's two days ago. Mrs. Boisseau and your two nephews were then well. Wentworth still continues to apply himself too closely. His constitution is not sufficiently strong for the exertions he makes."

In the last paragraph of a letter to Newport in August, he wrote, "I wish I could conclude my letter as pleasantly as I have begun. I suppose by this time you have heard of the misconduct of Wentworth Boisseau. You, and I, and the world have been much deceived in him. O how strange it is! At first I could not believe it; but when I could no longer disbelieve, I was shocked beyond measure. Even now I cannot force it out of my mind. He is blasted forever in this country. A whole life of virtue could not restore his character. It is the first instance of that crime ever heard of in this part of the world. I cannot conceive how he contracted the odious habit, except while a sailor to the West Indies. I have not seen him; nor do I wish to do so. The last mail, I had a letter from him, in which he asked my advice. I freely gave him my opinion to leave the country, and fly to some remote part; to give up all ideas of happiness in this life, and, by a life of contrition, to make his peace with heaven. May God grant him sincere repentence..

I suppose you have heard particulars as Dr. Waddel told me he would write you. Do not mention anything of it to Floride. O how it would wound her tender and innocent heart to hear of it. His mother knows nothing of it. It must be almost her death."

On September 7th, 1810, he wrote in a postscript to a letter to Mrs. Colhoun: "I cannot omit saying a word of the wretched Wentworth. About a week ago he came privately to my office to get my aid and advice. As his character is blasted here and the crime punishable with death I advised him to fly immediately and furnished him with money. By this time he has fled to some foreign part. O what a reverse. I wish I could offer consolation to you. You have been kind and beneficent to him, but he proved wholly unworthy of it. He seemed penitential."

Mrs. Calhoun's Nephews

These Calhoun letters to Floride Bonneau Colhoun before his marriage to her daughter are all found in the first volume of *The Calhoun Papers*. A half century earlier in *The Correspondence of John C. Calhoun*, which was issued by the American Historical Association in 1899, the collection omitted the August 24, 1810 letter to Mrs. Colhoun entirely and the postscript to the September 7, 1810 letter. In his preface Editor J. Franklin Jameson explained that "the trustees of Clemson College enjoined the editor to print no passages that would give pain to the living. But there are few such passages."

What connection did Floride Bonneau have with the Boisseau family? Her mother first married David Boisseau and bore him a son and daughter before his death. In her second marriage to Samuel Bonneau she bore two daughters, Elizabeth who married Ezekiel Pickens and Floride who married John Ewing Colhoun. The son by her first marriage was James Boisseau and the daughter whose name seems to have been lost married Peter Sinkler. The Boisseau daughter who married Peter Sinkler had no issue, but her brother James thereby came to live at one of Peter Sinkler's plantations. ("Peyre Records" compiled by Martha B. Burns and Alice G. Burkette in *Transactions of the Huguenot Society*, 1974).

Samuel DuBose in an address before the Black Oak Agricultural Society in April, 1858 (reprinted in T. Gaillard Thomas, *A Contribution to the History of the Huguenots of South Carolina*, p. 74) related the following story of James Boisseau and Peter Sinkler. He described how Peter Sinkler grew up without property; and, with diligent efforts, at his death left "his children three valuable plantations and upwards of three hundred slaves." He continued, "He died in Charleston a prisoner to the British under the most cruel treatment. Before he was carried from his plantation, he was made to witness the destruction of the following property, *viz.*, twenty thousand pounds of indigo worth one dollar and fifty cents a pound, one hundred and thirty head of cattle, one hundred and fifty four head of sheep, two hundred head of hogs, three thousand bushells of grain, twenty thousand rails, household furniture valued at 2,500 pounds sterling, besides carrying off fifty-five negroes, sixteen blood horses."

When the American Revolution broke out, Sinkler took a leadership role with Francis Marion's brigade. When he was back home recruiting, "the enemy having ascertained this determined, if possible, to capture him. . . . His own brother-in-law James Boisseau, who had enjoyed no other home but his, was won over by bribery to betray him. He was captured in the following manner. His house was situated within fifty yards of the Santee swamp, and it was his habit, when necessary, to retire by the back way to his usual place of concealment. Boisseau with sufficient force below, threaded his way to a spot which he knew Mr. Sinkler would enter it. Soon after a force was seen descending the avenue. The victim took his hat and returning to this place of concealment found himself in the arms of his captors. . . . [He was] carried off a prisoner to the provost in Charleston, and there, without change of clothes, he was thrust into the southeast room of the post office cellar, among a crowd as unfortunate as himself, without bedding, or even straw to lie upon. Typhus fever soon terminated their sufferings. As his reward Boisseau enjoyed for life a commission in the British army and a civil station in Nova Scotia." Samuel DuBose was a grandson of Peter Sinkler.

James Boisseau in the *Loyalist Transcripts*, (LIII, 155 microfilm in SCDAH) told a quite different story. He said that the rest of his family were Whigs, even his mother (also the mother of Floride Bonneau), and they tried unsuccessfully to change his loyalty. He was even offered a pardon by Governor John Rutledge, but he maintained his loyalty to the British government, and thereby lost his property.

Wallace Brown in his *The Kings's Friends, The Composition and Motives of the American Loyalist Claimants* (1965), a friendly treatment of the American Loyalists, accepted Boisseau's version as taken from the Loyalist records and stresses his loss of valuable property because of his convictions. In 1788 on the death of Samuel Bonneau, his will listed among the beneficiaries, James Edward Boisseau if "he returns to this State and has restored to him his property which is now under forfeiture to the State." (Caroline T. Moore, *Abstracts of Wills of Charleston District, South Carolina, 1783-1800.* 162.)

In Murtie June Clark's *Loyalists in the Southern Campaign*, (1981, Vol. I, 6, 17, 19, 90, 91, 91, 92, 184) the pay rolls for Loyalist troops in Charleston from 1781 to 1783 and in Country Harbour, Nova Scotia in 1784, list him as an officer in several South Carolina loyalist companies. He was designated variously as a cornet, Lieutenant, 1st Sergeant and Ensign. In Nova Scotia he was assigned four servants, Nelly, Ned, Charles and Cato.

Apparently, Wentworth Boisseau took John C. Calhoun's advice and disappeared. His younger brother, who bore his father's name, must have returned to Nova Scotia. As early as 1828, he was found in Charleston. In July, 1830, James E. Boisseau was naturalized at Charleston. He was listed as 36 years old, from the Island of Cape Breton, and as a hardware merchant residing in Charleston. "A Citizen," in a memoir in the Abbeville *Medium* (March 27, 1872) recalled that Andrew Giles in the 1830s had a store in Lowndesville in partnership with "a Mr. Boisseau." When James Edward Boisseau died in New York in 1850, two of the executors named in his will were Langdon Bowie, a merchant from Charleston, and James McCarter, a bookseller of Charleston. Bowie was a native of Abbeville, and he had been a merchant there as well. Among the beneficiaries to James Edward Boisseau's estate were the Orphans' House "lately established" in Charleston and the Ladies Benevolent Society there.

The *Calhoun Papers* give evidence of his close relation to his aunt and her family. In 1836, he was in New York when he sent two boxes to his cousin John Ewing Bonneau in Charleston to be given to Floride Colhoun Calhoun and her brother James Edward Colhoun. In 1837, John C. Calhoun wrote his son Patrick, then a cadet at West Point, to contact Mr. Ingoldsby "who will advance you the funds you may need until the return of Mr. Boisseau to New York who will then furnish you with what you may need."

In 1838, after James Edward Boisseau had been asked to help secure a loan for John C. Calhoun's son Andrew Pickens Calhoun, Boisseau wrote Mr. Calhoun (April 23) to say that "for the present" Andrew had decided not to purchase the land as he had planned. However, Edward Boisseau (as he now was called by the Calhoun family) wrote, "Allow me to say, at any time you may require a loan, my name and my exertions, will be at your service to aid you in the same." He reported that he had advanced Patrick about $230, and he assured Patrick's father, "I shall be glad to extend to him any further indulgence he may require."

On August 7, 1838, Boisseau reported that he had settled a bill for Mr. Calhoun and promised, "Any further services I can render yourself or family you have only to notify me; they will be most cheerfully executed." He congratulated "little John" [C. Calhoun, Jr.] for his success in shooting squirrels. He asked that the boy's mother, Floride, be informed that "I have some very choice sweetmeats in store for her, only awaiting the arrival of some Pendleton merchant to forward them." He thanked Calhoun "for the invitation you tender me; should I visit the South this winter, I will avail myself of your kindness." He also said that Patrick (then at West Point) "is well."

On January 20, 1839, Calhoun wrote his daughter, Anna Clemson, that Mr. Boisseau was being asked to aid her husband to secure a "conditional arrangement" to assure him against "failure." On February 1, 1839, Floride Calhoun wrote her son Patrick that "I received a long letter from Cousin Edward Boisseau. He is quite well, and in the letter he asks my acceptance of a silver coffee urn, and all he says he wishes in return from me, is a good cup of coffee when he comes to see me which he hopes to do this summer. Is he not a good kind hearted man, as ever was. I am sure that I have reason to speak well of his kindness and liberality. I hope you write him often."

Mrs. Calhoun's Nephews

On June 9, 1841, when Cadet Patrick Calhoun had finished West Point, his father again directed him to secure "advances" from Edward Boisseau "and you must not fail to express to him the great obligation which I am under, as well as yourself for his kindness toward you. He has been a good friend."

On February 15, 1842, Floride Calhoun wrote her husband that " I received a long and affectionate letter from Edward Boisseau, in which he mentions having sent me a pair of rocking chairs for my drawing room as a present." August 18, 1842, Calhoun wrote James Edward] Colhoun to express his distress at "the embarassed condition of your brother [John Ewing Calhoun] and added, "I know not what resources Edward Boisseau can command, but I think it not improbable that if you were to write to him and state all the facts, he might be induced, if he has means, to make some arrangements."

On November 12, 1842, Calhoun wrote his son-in-law Thomas G. Clemson that if he visited New York, "do not fail to call on Mr. Boisseau. He is of the House of Ingesby [Ingoldsby] & Co. and will be very glad to see you." December 19, 1842, Floride wrote Lt. Patrick Calhoun, then in the Choctaw Nation, that "I received a long letter from Edward Boisseau a few days since; he has sent me two hundred dollars worth at least of presents, such as caps, lace of all sorts, silk stockings, beautiful pocket handkerchiefs, dresses, beautiful Mosaic breastpins."

On July 19, 1843, Calhoun wrote Francis Pickens in Edgefield that he was going "to the North," and he added, "If you direct a letter to New York enclosed to J. Edward Boisseau , I will get it.

In a letter of October 20, 1844, Thomas G. Clemson, who was at that time a U. S. Consul in Belgium, described the clothes he was sending Calhoun from Europe as "the very highest priced articles that can be had." He said that "the box containing the clothes was sent to Mr. Beaseley. our Consul at Harve to be forwarded to Mr. Boisseau." On December 3, 1845, Floride Calhoun wrote Margaret M. Calhoun in Alabama that " I have just received a long and affectionate letter from Edward [Boisseau] in answer to mine written just before I left home, in it he says he wishes me to get what I wish in Washington, and he will pay for it, and that I must write him for anything I wish in New York, and he will take pleasure in getting it. The gold pencil which he sent to Mr. Calhoun is superb. Cornelia's dress is beautiful, he says he would not send mine until I arrived in Washington. Is he not the kindest person in the world?"

On April 5th, 1847, Patrick Calhoun wrote his father from New York that he was contemplating marriage to a young lady whose father was a former Representative from Kentucky. He continued, "my funds have run very low and some additional means will be necessary to me." If Mr. Calhoun could advance him such means, he wrote, "I can manage it through Cousin Edward Boisseau." On June 27, 1847, Anna Clemson in a letter to her father wrote, "tell mother my trunk has not yet arrived & I wish she would write to ask cousin Edward if it has been shipped for Antwerp."

Edward Boisseau served as the middleman in the Calhoun family communication with Anna and Thomas G. Clemson in Belgium. When the Clemsons returned from Belgium, Anna wrote her father from New York on May 22, 1849, as follows: "We arrived here three day ago, & as usual, Cousin Edward Boisseau, with his constant kindness, has kept us going from morning till night. Even now, he has taken the others to Hoboken, but I begged off, in order to have a few moments to devote to you." By unusual coincidence, both Anna's father and Cousin Edward died about a year later.

Edward Boisseau's role in the 1840s was to follow in the role which his Aunt Floride had earlier played in the Calhouns' fortunes. Charles M. Wiltse in his *John C. Calhoun, Nationalist* gives a sympathetic appraisal of "old Mrs. Calhoun" in the 1820s as follows: "In the late summer of 1822 the dreaded cholera threatened to sweep down upon the Capitol, and all who could leave the city did so. The stout Huguenot soul of old Mrs. Calhoun saw no terror in the epidemic, but a God-given instrument of salvation; and she gave all her energy to a religious revival which made its appearance, not altogether without her assistance, in the fall. Despite the remonstrances of her daughter and son-in-law, she would visit the public houses, whence she almost literally dragged the unregenerate off to be saved. . . . She spent money recklessly, mostly on others, without concerning herself seriously as to where it was coming from."

In the fall of 1822 she bought a beautiful home on the heights above Georgetown which she deeded to her son James Edward who was not even in Washington at the time. Calhoun worried that "she will in the long run find it dear." In the summer of 1823, Calhoun himself moved to this spacious house which had been built in 1800 and was surrounded by twenty acres of woods. The Calhouns called it "Oakly," and it later became famous as Dumbarton Oaks, the site in 1944 of a conference in which the United States, Britain, China and the U. S. S. R. came to an agreement to create the United Nations.

James Edward Boisseau's will, which was filed in New York in January, 1851, shows a generous disposition worthy of his Aunt Floride's. Among his beneficiaries were Floride Colhoun Calhoun, her daughter Anna Clemson, the sons of John Ewing Colhoun, Jr. (one of whom bore his name). His bequests included the Fire Department of New York City and St. Peter's Church and St. Thomas's Church (in each instance for "the poor,") the overseers of the poor house in Abbeville District, the overseers of the poor house nearest to "old

Pendleton," the Orphans' Home "lately established in Charleston," and the Ladies Benevolent Society of that city.

The Boisseau bequest to the Commissioners of the Poor in Abbeville District created what came to be known as the Boisseau Fund which was noted in their annual reports. By the later 1850s, income from this source was used to build a structure at the poor farm which was known as "the Boisseau Chapel" and to pay a stipend to Rev. Gibert to have services there. The Boisseau Fund somehow "disappeared" during the turmoil of the Reconstruction politics, but the chapel still attracted public attention. In 1872, the grand jury presentment reported that without the authorization of the county commissioners, "Boisseau Chapel is used for a school house. . .This chapel, as is well known, was built for the Poor of this county, by a bequest of the benevolent gentleman whose name it bears."

In 1880, the grand jury reported that "the church house" at the poor farm was being used as the residence of the white paupers. In 1885, the grand jury again in its report on the poor farm noted that "one of the houses now occupied was donated as a house of worship; we recommend that other houses be built suitable for dwellings, and the chapel be used as a place of worship."

This is the last public reference to the Boisseau Chapel," and perhaps the last reference to the Boisseau name in the county in which the Willington Academy was located where Wentworth and James Edward Boisseau were in attendance earlier in the 19th Century.

Harold Lawrence's Poem, "Hominy Pot" and the Mt. Carmel Incidents on Which It Was Based

Among the most intriguing poems in Harold Lawrence's fine collection of poems, *Southland*, was "Hominy Pot." "Hominy Pot" was based upon an oral tradition told by "an aged descendant of Tut Danford who was bound and thrown into this whirlpool at the mouth of Russell Creek, McCormick County, S. C." [t happened in 1889 when this was still a part of Abbeville County, twenty eight years before McCormick County was created] by confederates of the blacks who robbed and burned Baker's Store in the town of Mt. Carmel." Like many tales, this tradition was based upon an actual happening, in this case, two incidents; but in the telling and re-telling, it had undergone some obvious changes. Research into the newspaper accounts of the two incidents, as well as the legal records, indicate some of the changes. The extant records indicate that .the robbery involving Tutt Dansford was in1889 and took place at the W. N. Mercier & Co store. The Baker store robbery came in 1895, six years later. Neither robbery resulted in a store burning, although the 1889 case involved an attempted arson.

Lawrence's poem tells a fascinating story, as follows:

Hominy Pot

Whippoorwills were out that night
old man Fe Baker's store was robbed
singing their death threats in unison
condemning those miserable souls
stumbling like drunks over sacks and boxes
while poverty's other children slept.
Arms burdened and stinging with salt pork
pockets strangling on candy and chewing tobacco
they rose like pilfering crows
when a floor-board creaked
and left the place a shambles.
One braver than the rest came back
and burned the ledger pages
of his white creditor
leaving a smoking candle
to touch off its mischief in the cracks
of the leather binding
so that daylight broke on the old bald head
of Fe Baker weeping by the ruins
gazing down into them like he would
a smouldering hickory pit
And the whippoorwills stopped.

Hominy Pot

Tut Danford knew who did it
and they were out again that evening
like choristers appointed to the graveyard quiet
shrilling their emphasis from the woods
as he stood between two crowds
receiving more attention than a dead man
and swelling up with it
when the constable used Mister with his name.
The black folks whispered,
"Hush, Tut! Hush!"
while the white ones said,
"Talk on, Danford! Talk on!"
And he talked on in a natural pride
talking so fast he talked up the dust
in the middle of the road.
He talked on until someone broke and ran
and he talked on after an arrest was made.
As the darkness and the whippoorwills
and his tongue got thicker
Tut talked on
and talked himself right into
the hominy pot.
It was waiting for him
that next night as he walked along
looking up at the sky's deep velvet
and humming a tune.
The stars came out
just as the others did who grabbed him
and dragged him to the river
where he grasped a tree so tightly
the bark came off in his hands
as he was pulled begging and pleading
to the mouldered ground.
They tied his hands and feet
and gagged that talking mouth of his
and, sliding down the steep Savannah bank,
held him in the flatboat
while the rock was fastened to his chest
and then like ghosts in dreams
they poled out to that suck-hole
at the mouth of Russell Creek
and dropped him in.
It took a week to lay the talk to rest.

Hominy Pot

Some said he had run off
while others guessed the hominy pot
but all agreed that if a body knew
it would not tell
although such a body did.
On a day when the whippoorwills were shrieking
chiding those who had almost forgotten
up from the whirlpool's gullet
where the Confederate sea; was tossed
on that wild ride out of Abbeville
and from which no man's bones returned
Tut shot straight and true
swelled a little larger than in life
with at Igratic gas inside
and bringing the rock up with him.
It was sundown when he crested out
five days later than Jesus
but since those who did nit had not talked
and no one had the straight of things
he thought he would come back
one more time
and tell it for himself.

Mr. Carmel was one of the small towns which drew up along the Savannah Valley Railroad when it was completed from Augusta, Ga. to Anderson, S. C. ikn 1885-1886. It was located on the ridge between Little River and the Savannah River, and it came to replace Calhoun Mills as the trade center for Calhoun Township, settlement. Before the coming of the railroad, Mt. Carmel was little more than the location of Lewis Covin's store.

In the Summer of 1885, a news account noted that "A dpot on the SVRR [Savannah Valley Riilroad] has been located at Mt. Carmel. This was a wise choice. The locality is remarkable for its health. Two new stores in the place aare doing a remarkable business and one more is in the course of construction. A first class high school will be taught in the place." In February, the town chose its first officials: W. R. Powell, intendant, M. M. Tarrant, Theodore G. Baker, Mit. Paschal, and P. L. McKelvey, wardens (July 9, 1885).

The town continued to grow in 1886. In September, "Daniel," the local correspondent for the Abbeville *Medium* (Sept. 16, 1886) reported that it now had six stores and four new ones were under construction. Seventeen new buildings were under way. He noted that T. G. Baker, whose steam saw mill was running full time, needed some of his materials himself since he was operating the old store of Lewis Covin which dated from the 1830's.

The Abbeville *Press and Banner*, May 15, 1889, carried the following story: "A NEGRO IN HOMINY POT. Dead Men Give No Testimony Against Criminals. Tutt Dansford, the Negro who Turned States' Evidence, is Thrown in the Savannah 's Most Dangerous Whirlpool. Our wide awake and attentive correspondent at Mount Carmel sends the following account of the finding of the body of Tutt Dansford in the Savannah river.

The deceased lived about one mile from the river. He was called from his house at night, and went off with someone unknown to his family. Not coming back that night, his wife gave the alarm, fearing that he had been foully dealt with. Upon examination it is said that the place where he was seized could be plainly seen, and recognized by the evidence of a scuffle. At the precipice from which he was thrown into the river, there were unmistakable signs of a scuffle, and those in search for him, had no doubt that he had been thrown into the river at that place. Several tracks were plainly seen. It is said the tracks of Robert Partlow were recognized among the rest.

It is to be hoped that the Governor will offer a suitable reward for the apprehension of the perpetrators of so shocking a deed. The good name of the State demands that the Governor give this matter his attention.

Tutt Dansford is one of the parties of Negroes indicted for robbing a store at Mount Carmel. He turned States' evidence. Robert Partlow escaped after his arrest, and Tutt Dansford's death may be attributed to the desire on the part of the criminals to get rid of him as an evidence against them:

MOUNT CARMEL, S. C., May 13, 1889

At 9 o'clock this A. M. the body of Tutt Dansford, colored, who was foully murdered last Tuesday night, was found floating in Savannah river near this point. A jury of inquest was impaneled and found that he came to his death by being drowned by parties unknown. His remains were pulled ashore and buried on the bank of the river by his friends. About two hundred people were on the grounds and excitement ran high. Four Negroes were arrested on the spot and one or two since. Our citizens are determined to bring the perpetrators of this foul midnight murder to speedy justice. The body presents an awful spectacle to the eye of civilized man: The hands were tied securely behind his back with his suspenders and a hickory withe and his pants were tied tightly around his body and immediately in the center of his back with the same hickory withe was tied hard and fast a large flat rock which would weigh about 50 pounds. (A handkerchief was closely and tightly drawn across and tied around his neck used as a "gag," his drawers were drawn down over his feet and tied tightly around each ankle. In this manner he was cast into the "Hominy Pot" in Savannah river, and his body having been loosened the previous day by "drag hooks," had risen to the surface and floated down the Savannah river about two miles, and just opposite the Point, or the town of Lisbon."

JLC (Covin) in his Mt. Carmel news column in the Abbeville *Medium*, June 7, 1888, reported that "W. N. Mercier & Co. store was broken into last Saturday night and a lot of goods stolen. The thieves went through the transom above the back door. This was a bold burglary." Nearly ten months later, April 10, 1889, "M" in the Abbeville *Press and Banner*, reported a similar break-in in the same store, as follows: "Some unknown parties effected an entrance into the store of Messrs. W. N. Mercier & Co. this morning before day by boring out a hole in the back door and lifting the bar. They succeeded in making way with a large amount of goods such as bacon, flour, dress goods, velvets, tobacco, etc. To add to their crime they strewed kerosene over the floor and in the lard barrel and tried by setting fire to paper and dozens of boxes of matches to cover their guilt by fire -- but fortunately in this they did not succeed. Mr. H. P. Mercier opening the store this morning found the lard barrel on fire which he of course extinguished.

This is the second attempt to rob this store and we have a large number of men now on track of the 'midnight fiends' and we sincerely trust they will be found, when justice will be meted to them."

A week later (April 17, 1889), the *Press and Banner* carried a list of persons in jail with the crimes with which they were charged, and this list included Allen Partlow and Gilbert Huff who were charged with burglary and attempted arson. The following week, April 24, 1899, "M" in his column in the same paper praised the "untiring energy and zeal" of the Mt. Carmel citizens who helped seize "the parties who entered the store of N. W. Mercier & Co." Mercier was an Augusta firm which had put up a branch at Mt. Carmel.

Following the discovery of Tutt Dansford's body, the *Press and Banner*, May 22, 1889, published a report by "Citizen" from Mt. Carmel on May 20th that three men had been sent to jail for the murder of Tutt Dansford. The third man was Andrew Partlow, possibly a relative of Bob or Allen Partlow. The first trial in June dealt only with the store break in. The testimony showed that Bob Partlow, Gilbert Huff, Allen Partlow, Tutt Dansford. It further revealed that they stole goods therefrom to the amount of one hundred and sixty nine dollars. The jury found them guilty of house breaking and grand larceny.

In October, the State carried out the only trial which dealt with Tutt Dansford's murder in "The case against Charles McClendon , as accessory of [the murder of] Tutt Dansford. . . . Several jurors were challenged in this case. The defendant is charged with being an accessory before the fact to the murder of Tutt Dansford by throwing him in the Hominy Pot in the Savannah river. The rocks which were tied to Tutt Dansford's body were produced in court with the withe with which it was tied and his pantaloons. The rocks weigh about twenty two pounds. . . . After some further testimony the State seeing that it had failed to make out a case consented to a verdict of not guilty."

In April, 1893, the Abbeville *Medium* reported that Major DuBose, "a gentleman of color," caught a 23 1/2 lb. Catfish, "the King of Hominy Pot," which he brought to Abbeville and sold for $1.50. It commented, "after all . . . [perhaps] Major DuBose's action is a just retribution on the fishes of Hominy Pot, which in former years remorselessly feasted on human flesh and now men, in turn, devour their flesh."

The break-in at T. G. Baker's storehouse in Mt. Carmel which was referred to in Lawrence's poem occurred six years later in the Spring of 1895. Unlike the story in the poem, Baker's store was not burned. On the night of the 12th of April, 1895. "Doc" Sanders and Pink Ware plundered Baker's goods, but they made the mistake of employing one Nancy Calhoun to dispose of the stolen wares, and she confessed to the authorities. T. G. Baker secured a arrest warrant for Sanders from his brother-in-law, J. L. Covin who was the local magistrate Baker and the magistrate's constable, J. R. Tarrant, found Sanders plowing in his field. Sanders had his own weapon, and an exchange of gunfire led to his death by gunshots by Tarrant and Baker.

Sanders' death led to reported unrest in the black community in Mt. Carmel. As the story developed, the Abbeville *Medium* sent a special correspondent who filed stories which featured rumors of a "race riot." On the strength of these rumors, Governor John Gary Evans directed the Abbeville Rifles to go to Mt. Carmel to maintain order.

The Abbeville Rifles went from Abbeville to Calhoun Falls by special railroad car, and from that point they traveled to Mt. Carmel on two wagons "alternately riding and walking." Quickly, they rounded up the leaders who were reputed planing the uprising. Two were sentenced to thirty days on the county chain gang, and in only a little more than twenty four hours, the Abbeville Rifles were back home. The other Abbeville newspaper, the *Press and Banner*, praised the Abbeville Rifles, but its editor, Hugh Wilson commented that "our people regret that there has been such a hullabaloo about what seems to be as near nothing as possible."

Hominy Pot

The *Medium* was unwilling to give on the story.. In its July 4 issue, it carried a somewhat enigmatic communication from Edward Keiser. Ernest Lander in his recent *Tales of Calhoun Falls* noted Keiser's role in the transport of the Abbeville militia, as follows: "On one occasion in the late nineties, when a race riot threatened to break out in Mt. Carmel, and Abbeville militia was sent to the scene via Calhoun Falls, Mr. Keiser was called upon in the middle of the night to furnish transport for the militiamen from Calhoun Falls to Mt. Carmel. He complied with the request."

Under the headline, "A Tempest in the Teapot, or the Tea Totally Terrified," Kaiser's letter was printed, as follows:

"Editor of *Medium*,

I received a letter through the mail on June 28th of which the following is a copy.

'Mt. Carmel, June 28th, 1895

To Edward Keiser, Sir:

The people of this community have their eyes on you, and if we have any more trouble we will hold you responsible, we understand you charged 24 dollars for hauling Abbeville Rifles to Mt. Carmel, you want to bail out of jail the friends who would murder and burn our people and property, if anything happens you had better look out, take warning.   CITIZEN.'

I make it a point to answer all mail matter promptly. As 'Citizen' had not the courage to sign his own name, my only way to answer him is to go 'into print' (This is my maiden attempt). For the people of Mt. Carmel I have the greatest respect, and knowingly would not do an act to cause them discomfort. For 'Citizen' my respect is not unbound.

So far as transporting the troops to the Mt. Carmel war is concerned, I am only guilty of this. The troops came to my store about midnight. I was in bed I left my couch, opened my store, illuminated it and turned it over to the Soldiers, while I went out into the night, and about the neighborhood and helphed [sic] to hunt up conveyances, which took no little time and while I felt all the time I was engaged that I was an Aid [sic]de-camp in an unholy war still as the cry was going up from Mt. Carmel 'Come over into Macedonia and help us' I pushed with vigor on.   Others conveyed the troops, and not I. My mules speed the plow and speed the harrow and not mules of war. As for furnishing bail for 'the friends' (and while I am not the judge, there seems to be quite a difference of opinions as to whether they are friends or Martyrs) right now I am not over anxious about bailing them, or I should attend to the matter promptly.   I should not consult 'Citizen' in the premises. If 'citizen' feels called upon to write me again, will he kindly sign his own name, that may frighten me more than an anonymous epistle.

Respectfully, Edward Keiser."

Hominy Pot

Lander's work indicates why the people of Mt. Carmel may have been suspicious of Keiser's sympathies in the event of a racial conflict. He was closely associated with the black population on the Savannah side of Abbeville County, because as a manager of James Edward Calhoun's Millwood plantation he had dealt personally with many black tenants, as a pioneer Calhoun Falls merchant, he had continued that relationship, and he was "married" to a fair-skinned mulatto woman. (Lander, pp. 11, 47.) His letter indicated that he had sympathy for the blacks of Mt. Carmel, although he also showed an understanding as well of the feelings of the whites.

W. L. Miller in the *Medium*, June 27, 1895, attempted to answer Keiser, while at the same time he sarcastically declared that "the good people of Mt. Carmel" did not care whether or not they lost the "respect" of "Keiser and company." He revealed that when the warrants which were sworn out versus the "rioters" had proved to be "deficient," he and W. R. Powell [as well as presumably other Mt. Carmel whites" could have secured new warrants, but agreed not to do so when the black leaders "bound themselves to keep the peace."

The threat of a race riot was played largely in the columns of the *Medium* in contrast to Hugh Wilson's *Press and Banner's* coverage.

THE MISSING SHERIFF
(Abbeville *Medium*, September 4, 1878)

Sheriff Jones Mysteriously Disappears and Haunted by a Dread Secret Seeks Safety in Flight – The Safe Disclosures - His Anxious Bondsman.

For several weeks vague rumors have been in circulation in this community as to the official standing of Mr. Joshua Y. Jones, the widely-known, popular and efficient Sheriff of this county. No importance was attached to these reports, for it was generally believed that they had no foundation in fact and were simply the emanations of envious and ill-disposed persons. First it was said that the Sheriff was neglecting his office too much to take part in the primary political canvass then agitating the county in which he had no personal interest; then it was remarked that he aced very much unlike a sane person in many little things, and then that he was behind with the collections in his office. One tale followed another and the situation became so serious that an investigation of his affairs was proposed by his bondsman. The delay of few days, until certain important private collections could be made was asked for and granted and by special arrangement between the Sheriff and his bondsmen last Thursday week, August 26th, was designated as the day for making a thorough and complete investigation of his office and its effects. This arrangement was the best that could be made though not altogether satisfactory to the securities who daily became more solicitous about the matter. The week before the day fixed for the investigation, Thursday, 22nd ultimo Mr. Jones went down to Columbia in charge of Jeff David whose confinement in the State penitentiary had been ordered by Governor Hampton. This was the last seen of Sheriff Jones in Abbeville. He reached Columbia in safety, delivered his charge to the proper authorities, had the papers in the case all properly signed up and on Thursday night left the city, taking passage on the Charlotte, Columbia and Augusta railroad for the North. How far north he went and what his purpose was at that time we did not know. No information as to his movements was received until some four or five days after his leaving this place. No one suspected his designs and he sent no word home as to the reason for his absence, his place of destination or abode. The family became so much distressed by his continued absence that on Friday after his disappearance a dispatch was sent to Mr. Lowrance of the Wheeler House in Columbia asking him what he knew of the missing man. He answered that the Sheriff left Columbia Thursday night 22nd going up the Charlotte road, as he said in search of some escaped prisoners. It was then thought that perhaps the Sheriff was on the hunt for the negro Woods who committed the Cowan murder near Donnaldsville on the 15th of August and who was supposed to have fled in the direction of Virginia, having formerly lived in that section of country. For the apprehension of this man the Sheriff had offered a reward of twenty-five dollars and it was only thought that he wished to find the fugitive, and while saving the reward, enjoy the distinction of having run the murderer down. This was the view some took of the case but others were of the opinion that Jones had taken advantage of the special railroad rates and gone on a flying visit to the White Sulphur Springs in Virginia. But little apprehension was felt at his prolonged absence. And silence even by his own family and most intimate friends and the public were all unsuspecting of the real state of the case. Up to last Saturday it was confidently expected that the absent man would return and so much concerned in the matter were some of his friends and bondsmen that they awaited his arrival at the depot only to be disappointed. The mail on Saturday, however, brought a letter from the fugitive which partly explained the mystery only to leave it a greater mystery than ever.

This letter was addressed to "Mr. Robert Jones, jr., " and was postmarked Cincinnati, O., Aug, 28, 10 a. m." It was written on a sheet ofpaper, the letter head of some railroad company or mercantile office from which the printing had been torn. It was to his mother and was probably written on board an Ohio river steamer. The writer said that a whole boat load of people had died up the river from where he then was from yellow fever, that he was sick in body and in mind and thought he had the fever; that he would get off at Pittsburgh and go from there to Canada or England. The letter also contained a postal card containing the combination of the safe in the Sheriff's office and addressed to his brother Robert as follows:

Dear Brother: This is the safe combination which will explain all: Turn to the left 3 times or more stopping at 31, then turn back to 16, then around twice to 16, then back to 47, then back to 47, then around stopping at 47, then reverse until unlocked.   Josh.

Upon the reception of this news the bondsmen were surrounded and on Saturday night the Sheriff's safe was opened in their presence. The combination worked perfectly and inside the safe were found letters addressed to his mother, to his brother Robert, to S. C. Cason, Esq., and to the people of the county. These letters only succeeded in leaving the matter in greater mystery if possible than before and ever since the air has been full of the wildest speculations. The letter were generally of a private nature though containing no clue to the conduct of their writer. No other papers of importance were found in the safe and no money. The letter to the public reads like the product of a greatly goaded imagination and of the ordinary suicide literature of the day as follows:

To my once Friends of Abbeville County:
I say once for I suppose when they learn what I have to state they will throw scorn and contempt upon my name. By one hour of neglect, I have wrecked my own happiness, my future hopes of prosperity, my good name inherited from as good a man as ever lived upon the soil of Abbeville

county. It is my only consolation that his honored gray hairs will not be brought with sorrow to the grave, and God forbid that any negligence of mine should cause the honest and fair people of this county to think one iota less of the memory of my father.

Hell offers no more terrible punishment than I have suffered for the last few weeks. I have traveled, I have talked, I have read, I have drank, but no use – Conscience, like Banquo's Ghost, will not slumber at my bidding. I have sprung from my bed in the dead hours of night lashed by Consciencc for my negligence. I have been robbed , whether through negligence or not I am at a loss to say; but such is the fact.

I have told it to no living human being and the dread secret has haunted me night and day. I cannot meet my Bondsmen, I cannot meet my friends with suspicion written in their faces. But the time for concealment is out. Next Monday is set apart for my showing what money is on hand and by that time I shall be on the Ocean. You need not try to bring me back until I have the funds to replace what my negligence has lost. I would never have the courage to do so here, but if my Bondsman have this to pay, I will refund it if I have to live on bread and water and work my finger nails off. I have not time to make a statement but the books will show what has been stolen.

I ask my friends, if I have any, to let me go for I will never come to Abbeville county again only as a corpse. I will never be incarcerated in the walls of a jail. I have raised sufficient money from Devlin and Lawson to carry me safely and securely across the ocean. There I will stay until my reputation is made as bright as it was a few weeks since.

Yours with a heavy heart.

J. Y . JONES.

The office was turned over to the Clerk of the Court and on Sunday the Sheriff's securities met and made an examination of the condition of things. Investigation was far from satisfactory and the bondsmen expressed very serious concern as to the losses they would sustain in making good the accounts of the office. The street corner clubs held an extra meeting and rolled this sweet morsel under their tongues and the hotel lobbies were filled with excited throngs through the day trying to account for the mysterious disappearance and framing excuses or planning the criminality of the unfortunate fugitive according as their hearts were warm and sympathetic of as they believed in universal human depravity. No definite action was taken – nothing could be done but to await developments. The office would not balance by some eighteen hundred or two thousand dollars, which amount was short in the E. A. Mars matter and in the Cochran-Mackey suit. As a set off against these claims there were due bills in the office to the amount of $315 and the costs on cases not yet settled about $1000. . . . . . The bondsmen were Jacob Miller, B. F. Roberts (now in Texas- Thomas Jones, Hugh Wilson, Jacob Kurz, R. E. Hill, J. C. Douglass, J. R. F. Wilson, Edward Roche, and R. N. Pratt. . .

Joshua Y. Jones

.The whole matter has been a painful surprise to the public. . . He was the most popular young man in the county . . . lived in a community among a people who were life time admirers of his father. . . Mr. Jones was of a nervous temperament and did almost everything on the spur of the moment. He magnified his troubles into mountains, had a mania for knowing every man in the county and would travel days at a time to extend his acquaintances. He had hobbies and he rode them to death – several years ago he was a crack farmer, then he went at public speaking, then he took up the woman problem and so on down to his last folly: keeping a record of all the white voters. He was very careless at time about his office and on several occasions went out on the street leaving his safe unlocked and the door open with hundreds of dollars lying exposed. On one occasion while being shaved in the barber shop he sprang to his feet saying he had left his pocket book containing two hundred dollar on the table in his office, but he supposed nobody would touch it and fell back into the chair going through the shaving process. . . .

Another strange feature about the affair is that the Sheriff was to have been married about the middle of October and in making his flight he left not one line or a message to his betrothed. . . . The family of the fugitive are in great distress. Such another case never before occurred in all the history of Abbeville County. "

The *Press and Banner* reported that Governor Hampton appointed Robert E. Hill to fill out the term of the departed Jones. On October 23, 1878, it carried a notice of a Sheriff's Sale in a suit by W. A. Le vs. J. Y. Jones.. " 1 Sorrel horse "Bob, " a bridle and saddle, buggy and harness, a clock and a sofa lounge levied on as property of J. Y. Jones.". Hill bought these items. The next note about Jones (May 21, 1879) was "J. Y. Jones heard from. Will return when he earns enough money."

J. Y. Jones' father Robert was a well known merchant in Abbeville who had been a member of the town council in 1858-59, the county sheriff 1863-65, May (then called Intendant) from 1866 to 1869. In the federal census of 1860 when Jos. Y. was 7 years old, his father was listed as a 40 year old merchant in Abbeville.

The *Press and Banner*, Sept. 22, 1875 reported that "J. Y. Jones is engaged in making a complete map of every township in the county.... When completed this will be the first map of this kind that has ever been made of Abbeville County."

In 1876 (Aug. 9) it reported that 10 of the 20 County Democratic clubs put forward "our young Labor Reform leader Mr. Joshua Y Jones for Sheriff.. In Aug. 23, 1876 , the same paper reported the result of the primary election where Jones won with a vote of 1215 to the next candidate's 283. Capt. James Pratt of Due West, President Jimmy Carter's great-grandfather, ran fourth in that primary.

About a year after his disappearance, J. Y. Jones returned.. The Abbeville *Medium* , October 22, 1879. reported "At home again. Mr.

Joshua Y. Jones

Joshua Y. Jones , ex-sheriff of this county is at the residence of his mother in Fort Pickens. He is in very bad health and partly confined to bed by fever. He is prepared to straighten up the affairs of his office and settle all his indebtedness both private and   official. He is very much broken down and brown with exposure on the Plains where he has been herding cattle for the past year. He left Fort Worth Tex. ten or fifteen days ago, but was quarantined in New Mexico and compelled to take a back track and work his way to the creditors of ex-Sheriff Jones.through a more circuitous course.

Important Notice: I am now   prepared to settle in full all the indebtedness of brother Joshua Y. Jones, both private and official. All parties holding claims against him will present the same to me in my shop at the Abbeville Hotel. The official bondsmen of my brother will meet me at that place Friday night. A. W. Jones. He apparently recovered his health. The *Medium*, Jan 17, 1884 reported "J. Y. Jones is a most fast runner. The other day he was to take the train for Abbeville from Wardlaw's Crossing. He sat in Mr. Wardlaw's house and chatted quietly until the train had passed, Then he   leaped up, told his friends good bye and overtook the cars in a fair foot race. He made about ten feet every jump and although the engine had a heavy load of steam he made the trip of about half a mile to get on the track and stopped it. "

He took and active part in the Farmer's Alliance movement, and became a clerk at the S. C. Senate. In 1894, through the   aid of Senator Irby, he got a job in the U. S. Senate in Washington. The *Press and Banner*, June 13. 1890 announced: "To be Married. Church wedding June 13, 1894. No cards. Hon. J. Y. Jones to Miss Emma Tolbert in Smithville Baptist church . They will then leave for Washington, adopted home of Mr. Jones."   In July, *the Press and Banner's* editor Hugh Wilson while in Washington dropped by to see the Tolberts, and he wrote that J. Y. had "a good paying job with the Senate," and will stay till Senate adjourns.

On of the last times that J. Y. Jones attracted the attention of the *Press and Banner* which on March 13, 1907 by " his own bizarre account:

On last Saturday at his supper table, J. Y. Jones of Smithville had the misfortune to be shot. It seems his brother-in-law A. M. Tolbert boards with him. There is bad blood between them. Thy had not spoken since July last although eating at the same table. No words had passed between them for seven long months.

Last Sunday night at the supper table without a word he drew his pistol while sitting two feet of Jones' place to Jones' temple and just as Jones saw his intention he threw back his head. . . . The ball grazed the bone cutting the forntal artery. The only words Tolbert spoke were "get out of here and stay out." He as on the verge of shooting a second time when Jones said to him " don't think it necessary, you have killed me."

Jones walked down to Red Tolbert bareheaded, the blood streaming from the artery. R. R. Tolbert told him it was not fatal wound unless he bled to death. But Tolbert refused to stop the blood with a ligature. W. O. Cromer three miles from Tolbert's on the road to Abbeville tied a towel around the wound and Dr. Neuffer said it save the life of Jones.

Jones was on the street yesterday, but he remained in bed Monday weak from loss of blood. Jones tells us he has not suffered a moment with pain. He looks upon Dr. Neuffer as the ablest surgeon in South Carolina.

Abbeville Lynchings in Historical Perspective

Although the lynching of Anthony Crawford in Abbeville in October, 1916 was the only lynching in the area to command national attention, both at the time and in the years that followed, it was not entirely unique.

In September, 1891, at the regular meeting of the Abbeville Literary Club where members read essays on subjects of their choosing (religious and political topics excluded), Judge Frank B. Gary (he was a brother of Lieutenant Governor E. Gary) read his essay on "Lynch Law." In his view, "lynching is never justified." Judge Samuel McGowan led the discussion which followed, and he endorsed Gary's sentiments. In fact, he said that "the act of lynching was a blot on the good name and order of a community." McGowan was probably the most respected person in Abbeville at that time. Thomas P. Cothran, the lawyer son of a U. S. Congressman, took a different position. He held that for offenses against women, lynching was not only justifiable but was actually commendable. W. Christie Benet, the Scottish born lawyer who was Samuel McGowan's son-in-law concurred in the views expressed by Cothran. Benet said he would have no hesitation in joining a lynching party in defense of a woman. He thought that lynching was usually led by the counsel and encouragement of safe leaders. In the opinion of Hugh Wilson, the editor of the *Press and Banner* the consensus of the club members was in accord with Cothran and Benet.

Three years after Gary's essay, Judge Samuel McGowan presided over a case of a little publicized lynching in Due West Township in which a woman was involved although hardly in the way Cothran and Benet would have thought. A group of five armed men abducted a black man and a white woman from Peter Ricketts' house. They declared that they had a warrant from Governor Tillman for their arrest on a charge of adultery, and they carried Dennis Hutchinson into the night and beat him to death with clubs. Dr. John A. Robinson of Due West examined the body and certified as to the cause of death. Ultimately on the testimony of the woman's brother and son, five men were brought to trial in Abbeville. The grand jury indicted the men but the trial jury found them "not guilty."

The following month, April, 1894, a black man wrote a note to a white lady in Lowndesville. The newspaper account said the note was "handed to one of the most cultured and popular young ladies in this section by a Negro, Isaac Anderson. In handing the note, he said it was 'April fool.' When the lady read it she found its contents to be of an offensive character. It closed with 'Don't tell this, if you do, I will be a dead nigger before tomorrow night,' showing that he fully recognized the consequences which he was braving." A public meeting of 100 whites and 50 blacks decreed that he be whipped and his ear lobes be cut off, and he was escorted across the Savannah on Harper's Ferry. His goods were carried over and his family, which the news report described as "large," were told not to come back to Lowndesville.

Near Greenwood in the previous year, 1893 (Greenwood was in Abbeville County until 1897) a vagabond Negro, Jake , assaulted a 55-year old married white woman whose dog frightened him off. He was caught by a posse of white and black men who led him to an open field where he was bound to a limb of a tree and shot. The correspondent of the *Press and Banner* paid tribute to the colored women who identified him and to the Negroes who were among the armed party. The paper declared, "Too much praise cannot be given to the colored people who manifested such an intense desire to have the wretch caught and punished." The newspaper add that "The same man committed an assault on a white woman in this community a few years ago, but as her character was questionable he was allowed to go unpunished."

In the summer of 1903, a mob considered lynching a negro from Georgia who was captured after trying to break into a house because he said he was looking for "peaches,." And they voted not to hang him. The *Press and Banner*, August 19, 1903. Reported the following story: "A little more than a week ago a negro by the name of Charlie Stark appeared at the home of a gentleman in the Sharon neighborhood, and seeing the house in darkness, proceeded to the window of a room in which his daughter slept and at once proceeded to raise the sash which awakened the young lady, who seeing him at the window gave the alarm, but by the time the house hold was up, the negro had disappeared.

On last Saturday night he again made his appearance and as the window was fastened down he did not succeed in raising the sash, so went for one of the doors when the young lady heard the noise, and again called her father, but before he could get out the negro had left under cover of darkness, but this visit was just after a rain and his tracks were plainly to be seen, so in the morning (Sunday) a party set out to track him up and were soon up with him. Finding where he had stopped at a negro's house and changed his shoes for a larger number, they followed and came up with him at Turkey Hill about three or four miles distant. The news of his capture soon spread far and near and in a short time more than fifty well armed and determined men were gathered around the prisoner, when calls "lynch him," were heard from many throats, others wanted to burn him, and a fire was soon kindled. While some of the crowd wanted him drowned in the river. A jury was empanelled to dispose of his case, and after the wise counsel of older heads being given under mature deliberation. The jury stood three in favor of lynching him and seven not to take his life, so he was taken out into the public road and given a severe whipping, and turned loose with instructions never to be seen in that neighborhood again.

It seems from all that we could learn he was a Georgian negro, and was loafing about through the country. He worked part of last year for a farmer in the neighborhood and finally ran away, slipping his contract,

The negro confessed that he was the one they were looking for, and said he was trying to arouse someone to give him some peaches. If he had been in his Georgian home, his fate would most likely been very different."

Also, in 1893, John Palmer, a colored man of Promised Land who was known to have money, a watch, and a pistol on his person, was brutally murdered. The news paper report was that "he had many friends among his neighbors of both colors, and they are sparing no effort to track down the criminals." A local columnist for the *Press and Banner* reported that an eye witness said he saw the "negroes who killed John Palmer near Verdery chained together and surrounded by a crowd of armed Negroes who looked as if they would lynch them." This was not confirmed.

Three times a mob breached the Abbeville jail (now the Abbeville Museum) and carried a black man to be lynched. The first time was in 1883, when Dr. H. G. Klugh of Cokesbury was knocked out when he came up behind a robber who was stealing his cotton. Dave Roberts was arrested and carried to the Abbeville jail. On New Year's Eve, an armed crowd forced the sheriff's son, who was the jailer, to let them take Roberts out where he was strung up in a tree halfway between Abbeville and Greenwood and shot. Twenty years later, another Cokesbury black, Wince McNary, made a death bed confession that he was the person who knocked Dr. Klugh unconscious.

The *Press and Banner* Feb. 6, 1907) reported "Tree Destroyed – from limb of which a mob hanged an innocent man. Last Saturday was a week ago a rabbit pursued by hunters sought refugee n the hollow of an old oak on which Dave Roberts was hanged by lynchers about twenty years ago. The hunters in the effort to smoke the game out set fire to the tree, and after burning for several days it fell. The tree was on the side of the public road leading to Greenwood & nearly two miles east of Abbeville. It stood on the land now owned by W. A. Long of this city. Dave Roberts was a Negro who was found with seed cotton, Dr. Klugh interrupted him. The Doctor was knocked down. Roberts was charged with the cime and place in the jail at Abbeville. One Sunday night lynchers came and took him out. They marched him to the tree of which we have spoken and hanged him to a limb. "

The second time was in 1914 when John Thomas, a "light colored" Negro who was 23 years old frightened a 14 year old white girl along the railroad tracks near Honea Path and escaped a search party. He was located in Florida and brought back and lodged in the Abbeville jail. A mob of more than a hundred men in automobiles and buggies assembled near Groggy Springs and went to Abbeville where they stormed the jail, overpowering Sheriff Lyon. They took Thomas up the Due West road near the Long Cane cemetery. When it appeared they may kill him, the Sheriff asked them to honor their pledge to save his life. They emasculated him, and Lyon took him back to the jail in his automobile and secured Dr. Jack Pressly to dress his wounds.

A similar punishment was visited on Jake Davis in Greenwood in August, 1911. The daughter of a Greenwood merchant was on her way to his store when a shower made her take cover where she was approached by Davis in a threatening manner. She ran to a neighbor's house, and Davis was arrested and lodged in the Greenwood jail. The correspondent of the *Press and Banner* said that a crowd of several hundred men came to the jail where they used sledge hammers and axes to break the door open. The prisoner was emasculated and the lobes of his ears cut off. The paper noted that "After this he walked to the office of a physician who dressed his wounds and sent him to his home."

The third prisoner who was taken from the Abbeville jail by force and lynched was Anthony Crawford in October, 1916. Nineteen years later, a potential lynching was thwarted by the plans of Sheriff F. B. McLane. McLane had been the jailer who was forced to give Crawford up in 1916. In August, 1935, Jim Strickland, a white man, was reportedly badly beaten near Calhoun Falls by a mob of blacks, and nine were arrested and taken to Abbeville. When the sheriff learned that there was danger to the blacks, he had them sent to Greenwood. About a hundred armed whites from Calhoun Falls came in trucks to the jail. The sheriff also had secured an order from the state governor for the Abbeville National Guard to set up two machine guns to protect the jail. The mob leaders decided to get into their trucks and go back to Calhoun Falls.

Tom Norrell, a Methodist minister at Ware Shoals whose wife taught at Erskine, told me that his grandfather, Watson Norrell, was one of the men who manned the machine guns. One of his cousins was a member of the Calhoun Falls group, and later the cousin asked Tom's grand father, "Watson, would you have shot us?" His reply was that he would have obeyed his commanding officer.

Rev. Norrell's comment was that the prisoners probably suffered anyway. This led me to research what happened to them. I found that five of the nine were released without charges, and one plead guilty and was given a year's sentence. The other three were released when an all-white jury failed to convict them.

Abbeville Lynchings

Three years earlier (1932), the National Guard was instrumental in preventing another lynching. A. J. Ferguson, one of the two white men who were court appointed administrators of the Anthony Crawford's estate, was killed by one of his black tenant farmers in April, 1932. The tenant farmer, Tom Wardlaw, fled and was the object of a massive man hunt led by National Guard units, including units from outside Abbeville County. He was found miles away in the Long Cane bottoms and taken into protective custody.

The lynching of Allen Pendleton in 1905 and of Mark Smith in 1919 were similar to the Crawford lynching in some respects. None of the three dealt with threats to women, and all three involved revenge for injuries inflicted by the victim on whites.

Pendleton was involved in a quarrel with two white men, Sam and Jim Moore, about three miles below Honea Path. In a fight, Pendleton inflicted a fatal cut upon Jim Moore, and he was captured by a crowd of Moore's relatives and friends. Despite attempts by some leading men of the area to get the prisoner turned over to the police, he was taken down into Abbeville County and lynched. The coroner's jury later came to a verdict that "Allen Pendleton came to his death by the hands of parties unknown to the Jury." A controversy ensued between Anderson and Abbeville county officials over who was responsible for his burial.

In the case of Mark Smith in 1919, Lester Cann, along with two others representing the Abbeville Sheriff's office, went to Smith's home to search for illegal liquor reputed to be there. Smith exchanged fire with them, and both Cann and Smith were wounded. Smith escaped and fled to Washington, D. C., but he was caught and returned for trial. In the ensuing trial, Smith's attorneys successfully maintained that Mr. Cann and his associates were not properly armed with a warrant, and Smith was found "not guilty." James S. Stark was the foreman of the jury and Hon. Frank B. Gary presided at the trial.

A few months later, Smith and his family were in his Overland automobile heading out to his home, when a party of armed men took him from the car and when he tried to run away, he was shot down. Days later, the body surfaced in the Savannah River. The coroner's jury found that he came his death by "parties unknown."

T. Lester Cann's own life ended two years later in an equally violent conclusion. Cann became a deputy sheriff in January, 1921 under Sheriff F. B. McLane. He was present at the Opera House in Abbeville the night of November 10th for a musical showing of the Lassies White, and according to many witnesses he was drinking heavily. He and several friends had to be quieted by the Abbeville police during the show, and after it was over at the request of the manager two policemen went upstairs to get them to leave. His friends did leave, but Lester Cann would not and an exchange of gun fire resulted in the death on one policeman, H. B. Cannon and the serious wounding of another police, Clarence Crawford and Cann himself. Cann died a few days later, and Crawford survived with a wound in his mouth which would be with him for the rest of his life

Two black ministers of the county suffered violent beatings in 1939 and 1948, respectively, over attempts to exercise their voting rights. The first, B. J. Glover, became the pastor of the Mt. Lebanon church in Due West in the late 1930s. Glover was a native of Promised Land, a black community just south of Greenwood. His family had sent him to Ohio to live with his aunt while he completed his high school education and his college and seminary training at Wilberforce University. His father was a minister in the AME church. In 1936, young Glover went to the Abbeville Courthouse to register to vote. When he was rejected despite the fact that he was obviously able to pass the literacy tests, he told his congregation about "the unfairness" of what had happened to him at the courthouse.

This incident and a number of other activities which brought some notice to him as a potential "troublemaker" and led the Klan in the area to mark him for an attack. That attack came in September, 1939 after he had taken a bus from Due West to Greenwood to renew his driver's license and to visit his parents. He later found out that the Klan "knew I was leaving Due West and coming to Greenwood. I had gotten off the bus and was walking down the street. A group of white men stopped me at that time and asked me my name." They seized him and took him out and beat him unmercifully. Rev. Glover later told this writer that when he was in bed for a month in Due West and could not preach at Mt. Lebanon, "Dr. Jamie" Pressly, pastor of the ARP Church, preached at his church and "would drop in" and give him the collection before he went to preach at the morning service at his own church. Although he recovered from his beating, it caused him to return to Ohio to recover spiritually. He did return to the Mt. Lebanon church by 1941.

The second black minister, Rev. Archie Ware of the Springfield Baptist Church near Calhoun Falls in August, 1948 went to the school gymnasium to vote in the Democratic primary. A court decision in 1947 had ruled that Negroes were guaranteed the right to vote in local elections.

Harold Lawrence in his poem, "Trouble At the Primary" in his book, *Southland*, described what happened with these lines:

Abbeville Lynchings

The volunteers who ran the polls
 signed him in with everybody else
 but whispered conversations dropped
like stones thrown in a well
and splashed in quick succession
when he pulled the curtain back
and fed the ballot into the box
with those lean black fingers
as white as theirs on the underside
changing the world of a few who watched
 idle and slack jawed
as it rearranged itself
right there in the school gymnasium
forever deliberate and irrevocable.

Once outside the ordered lines
of smiles and decorated tables
the summer glare was not as harsh
as the men who ringed him
throwing punches timed by words and slurs
and buffeting him like children
in a friendly game of shove
the Chief's son taking out his wind
in a hail of pounding blows
so fierce and biting in the ribs
he never saw the knife
that sliced his stomach open
melting the surly faces to lumps
of nauseous and dispersing gray.

No one was left to cast aspersions
as he walked those solitary blocks
laced with aging oaks and box woods
bearing a faint brown and yellow tinge
and the first of autumn's ragged butterflies
to the door of the doctor's house
where he was refused and sent away
both hands clutched to his stomach
like one bent on dying

Abbeville Lynchings

who could already see beyond the veil
and made to stand in the puddle
of his own helplessness
until someone driving by took pity
all the way to the county hospital.

The paper played it down
but word surged like electric current
through analogs of conversation
and federal agents came for weeks
to drift around and ask their questions
like the one he asked the Chief
when he had the first occasion
putting the query to him straight
about why he let his son
beat and reduce a man to helplessness
to which the Chief made quick reply
that Negroes had no business at the polls
and that anyone who came on ahead
got what was coming to him

Before he left the Chief he said
that something bad would come of it
leaving the pronouncement to hang there
like a rancid joint of meat
by the main street store fronts
and he moved away to New York
while the Chief's son went off to war
to do distinguished service
and so the dark moment slept
long and deep and dreamless
in the psyche of the town
and on the bottom of page two
of the Abbeville Press & Banner
and it did not awaken.

Some things just have to lie and wait
like rabbits in a burrow
who want night to fall

or the scent on the air to change
and some things when picked up again
like old cold trails and blood trails
are never what they were
and thoughts of retribution have to scatter
as leaves do in a wind
before some things go full term
as this one did one April
when the Chief's son took his bride
of fifteen minutes over a blind hill
and straight on into the everlasting arms.

Rev Ware recovered from his wounds, but he moved away from the community and never lived there again.

In sharp contrast to its brief note on Rev. Ware's beating in 1948, the *Press and Banner* of April 17, 1952 carried a front page story with a picture from the *Anderson Independent* with captions, "Car in Which Honeymoon Couple died" and "Lieut. Powell and his bride of some fifteen minutes, the former Faye Lee Ayers, both of Calhoun Falls, died as a result of the three car collision on Sunday. . . Four persons, including the honeymoon-bound Calhoun couple married only 20 minutes, were fatally injured and eleven others were hurt Easter Sunday afternoon in Abbeville's worst highway accident. . . Lieut Fred Powell, 24, recently returned from Korean combat and the son of Police Chief W. L. Powell."

What was perhaps the last attempted lynching involving Abbevillians occurred less than two years earlier, December, 1950, on a dirt road about eight miles below the town of just off the road to Saluda. The Greenwood *Index-Journal*, Dec. 12, 1950 reported that "Six Greenwood, Eight Abbeville man were named after almost a week long investigation by the Sheriff and SLED. The story as told by John Moore. Father of Clayton Moore, was as follows: "On the night of December 6, several white men attempted to take Clayton Moore, a black, away from his home. The men came to Moore's home and asked for water for their car. . . When Moore started to the well with them he was covered with a pistol and told he was going to be taken with them. When Moore struggled, he was seized by them, and he called for his wife and son to bring him his shotgun. Then one of the men who had a pistol disengaged himself from Moore's arm and headed to stop his 14-year old son who was bringing the shotgun, the young boy shot one of them. The visitors then scattered, leaving one of their number, Geo. S. Ferguson, who had been killed. The Moores barricaded the outside door. They heard the white men start up the car, go down the dirt road and turn around and go back to the main highway.

Greenwood Sheriff J. Cal White had reported to the *Index-Journal*, Dec. 7, that the case had "some bad angles." Geo. Ferguson's funeral was held at Warrenton Presbyterian Church near Abbeville. He was survived by his wife and six children.

One of the Abbeville men, Adrin Davis, cooperated in the investigation. When the case came to trial in Greenwood, thirteen white men plead guilty of the charge of Conspiracy to Abduct. Whip and Commit Assault and Battery with Intent to kill Clayton Moore. The men whom defense lawyer J. Moore Mars (Abbeville's state senator) called "good boys, " ranged in age from 48 to 26. Mars said they came from good families. They were sentenced to serve 1 year or pay $600 fine with the provision that when they paid $200 or served 2 months in jail, the sentences would be suspended. Davis for his cooperation was given a suspended sentence.

Only two causes were advanced for the planned attack on Clayton Moore. One was that Clayton Moore, who had been a janitor at Matthews Mill for thirteen years, had not been sufficiently deferential to some of the white workers. One of the incidents cited dealt with his action in moving some boxes which some of the white workers had told him not to move. The investigators found that he followed his supervisor's orders and was well thought of by the Mill managers. The other charge which appeared to have been more decisive was that he carried a picture of a nude white woman in his pocket. The Greenwood deputy sheriff who investigated these charges said he could find no evidence of this.

Following this settlement the court moved to try Clayton Moore, Jr. for murder of G. S. Ferguson and a jury had been chosen when Solicitor Hugh Beasley moved for a directed verdict of not guilty. Both Beasley and the veteran presiding judge, T. B. Greneker, agreed that it was not wrong to defend his family in the face of illegal action. Greneker said that in his career he had never experienced any case like this.

Since the writer wrote about the lynching of Anthony Crawford in *Old Abbeville* in 1992, he has continued to search for new information. After examining the tax records for the county in 1916, he found that only about 170 taxpayers were paying a larger tax bill than Anthony Crawford. .

The writer also examined the reports in the papers of Gov. Richard I Manning at the S. C. Archives. Manning hired a private investigator, John B. Ernst, usually styled JBE in his correspondence. JBE secured an affidavit before magistrate J. S. Hammond that on October 23, 1916 Jess Cann, J. O.

Abbeville Lynchings

Cann, Lester Cann, Will Cann, Sing Findley, Bert Ferguson, Ervin Ferguson, Sam Adams, Joe Elgin, J. A. Brock, W. A. Brock, W. Bell, Walker Clamp, Joe Wright, Mack Williams and S. Aiken were charged with forcing the black operators from their local stores. .

Sheriff R. M. Burts wrote Manning, Nov. 7, 1916 that the persons who first whipped Anthony Crawford were J. O. Cann, Will Cann, Sam Cann, Eugene Nance, J. E. Cheatham, J. S. Banks and Sam Adams. Among the lynching crowd he listed Lester Cann, Sam Adams, J. O. Cann, Joe Elgin, Geo. White, R. B. Ferguson and Jno. Dawson. On Nov. 1, State Senator J. Howard Moore reported to Gov. Manning that at the inquest which was conducted by Coroner F. W. R. Nance, "no witnesses could be found who knew the cause of the death of the negro Crawford."

In Nov. 19, JBE said that he talked with son of Jailer McLane who said his father took the key with him but was overtaken by the crowd who seized the jail key. He said the town police kept their distance, especially Chief Johnson. He heard it reported that Crawford had taunted the merchant W. D. Barksdale, by saying that he had as much money as he did and he did not get his through marriage. . . others said that Crawford was insolent and got what he deserved. On Nov. 24th he reported that Miss Kate Marshall says it took place on their property. She and Mrs. Judge Gary and daughter were very much distressed. Miss Kate sent word to Joe Elgin by Jim Cochran that "he was to take the next lynching he had charge of to some other place.' She received no reply.

At the end of the first week of his investigation, he reported that be believed "that a number of the crowd was from around Abbeville Mill and most of them were drunk." He found "that the stores around the mill district likely sold whiskey, especially the Dixie Café where the lower strata hung out." He found "that whiskey could be gotten at the drug store, the pool parlor, the Greek Café and from "most any niggers."

On the other hand, JBE found that some of the 'very best people gave the most trouble. The other evening while passing City Hall I saw a light in a window and after quietly getting to the door I opened it and saw a five hand crap game in full bloom, the players all being young men all well connected. Got another line on the morals of this community and find that it is very low. The whites cohabit with the niggers."

Twenty years after the lynching apparently an opportunist in New York was using the Anthony Crawford story for her own benefit. The following letter addressed to "Capt Jack" Perrin was discovered in the Clerk of Court office long after his death. Miss Parks was the daughter of the Abbeville County Auditor in 1916, and in a long and distinguished career as a teacher, she

Abbeville Lynchings

sometimes spent her summers at Teacher's College at Columbia University:

"519 W. 121st Street N. Y. C.
July 25, 1936

Dear Mr. Perrin,

Is it not strange how events which happened long ago in Abbeville have culminated in New York City? Do you remember a negro [sic], Anthony Crawford, whom you tried to help by taking him from a mob of angry factory men and putting him safely in jail? Claude Gambrell gave him first aid ,but, I think that he died that night from the injuries which had received. His wife and daughter sold his farm in the country and came up here to live in Harlem. The students at Columbia College [Teachers' College of Columbia University] go on trips to Harlem and there see how the negroes ((sic) live and listen to their Red and Communistic speeches. One of the speakers is Angy Crawford, a daughter of Anthon. She tells the story of life in Abbeville and gives it as a reason for being a communist. As I remember the events of her father's death, she has embellished them very much, although they are bad enough when the truth is told.

These are the facts as I can recall them. Crawford brought some cotton to town to sell but was not offered the price which he thought he should have received. He made his displeasure known and stated that he would take it home before he would let it go at that price. Some factory men who were standing near him resented his speech and attitude and gave him a severe beating before the townspeople knew what was happening. The negro [sic] in some way got off the square and hid in Richard Roman's blacksmith's shop. From there he sent word to you to please come and help him. You and a few other men took him the back way to the jail, set a guard there, and then called Claude to dress his wounds. That night Anthony Crawford died, his body was given to his friends, and, think the matter ended.

This is my recollection of this unfortunate episode, but Angy tells it quite differently. She says the white people were made angry just because her father said he would rather take his cotton home than sell it at the low price offered him for it. A rope was then tied around his body and he was dragged to a place where he was lynched. When his wife came to get his body, it was so riddled with bullets that she had to pick up the pieces of it and wrap them up in a sheet to carry them home. After this happened her mother was so terrified, that she sold their home and came here to live.

Another one of Angy's grievances is that although she went through school and college with white people here, she has never been able to get into the office of any one as a secretary or in any large department store as a clerk. As soon as the fact of her being a negro (sic] is known, no one will give her work of this kind. The only things which she is permitted to do are to teach negro [sic] children in Harlem and to make Communistic speeches there and in various parts of the country.

Mr. Perrin, I have written you this long story because I think the conductor of student groups at Columbia should know how much of Angy' speech is true and how much of it is her own imagination. If he wants to continue to exploit Angy, why that is up to him, of course, as it is quite thrilling to hear her tell her story. I did not go to Harlem myself, but a friend did, and immediately wanted to know if we did things of this kind at Abbeville.

Please return my letter with your comments if you think as I do that the truth should be known.

With kindest regards to you and your family, I am.

Yours sincerely,
A. Winton Parks"

Obviously Mr. Perrin was unable to return her letter with comments that would be of use for her purpose. As for "Angy Crawford," her own account seems mostly, if not entirely, a work of fiction. W. C. (Walter) Crawford, wrote Gov. Manning, Nov. 25, 1916 that he was the oldest of Anthony Crawford's thirteen children who survived him. He said his mother died in 1910 and his father "never married any more." He wrote, " there are twelve children at home with about fifteen grand children, six of the twelve are married and they all live there. I have been in the ministry for 16 years and have held pastoral charges in the AME church for 13." He was in his second year at Due West (Mt. Lebanon church), and he gave references in Due West of the banker, two leading merchants, the pastor of the A RP church and president of Erskine College. Four of Anthony Crawford's children were daughters. By 1918, Florence was married to a Dawson and was still in the area when her next oldest sister, Minnie died. The other two were twins, Bessie and Jessie and they were at the Crawford estate when they were given the carriage (along with sister Minnie) and their shares of the livestock. A few years later Jessie had married a Smith and was living in Philadelphia.

Abbeville Newspapers & Special Emphasis upon Three Publishers/Editors

For a local historian, newspapers are a prime source. This is particularly true in the case of Abbeville, because a series of fires in the1870s destroyed most of its public records. For its first half century, the county had to rely upon newspapers from Edgefield, Pendleton and Anderson for publication for public sales, especially estate notices and sales. Earlier, public notices had to be read from the pulpits of churches. The first upcountry newspaper, Miller's *Messenger* was published in Pendleton, but it carried very few notices from Abbeville District. The Edgefield *Carolinian* in 1831 carried some news from Abbeville.

In October, 1831, John Taggart, an Abbeville printer, published a prospectus for a weekly paper to be issued. He declared in his notice that "Subscribers may be assured that this shall not add another to the failures, which, by some strange fatality, have occurred in the attempt to establish a newspaper in this wealthy and populous District." His paper was to begin in October , 1831, a weekly devoted to the issues of free trade and States rights.

Despite Taggart's assurance, the Abbeville *Republican* never appeared. A year later Samuel A. Townes launched the first newspaper at Abbeville, *The Abbeville Whig and Southern Nullifier*. It did not survive the Nullification controversy, but in 1833 it carried the first printed town ordinances of Abbeville. Only a few copies are now known to have survived, and they are at the Cooper Library at Clemson University.

Charles H. Allen, then only 23 years old, began the Abbeville *Banner* in 1844. Mrs. Fannie Marshall in Feb., 1925 at the time when Fred West, Sr. had acquired the *Medium* (its press, subscription lists and good will) wrote an article about the experience she had at the age of 12 when the first issue of the *Banner* was printed in 1844. She wrote that "it was published by Mr. Henry Allen in a small wooden building, formerly a servant's house, facing on the street about where Mr. A. M. Smith's warehouse now stands. In the morning the citizens were invited to come and see the wonders of the printing press and each time a person would call, a paper would be printed to show the curious how it was done. In the afternoon the school children were invited. The press looked like a small cooking range of today, about 3 by 4 feet in size. It printed only one sheet, then printed this sheet on both sides."

No issues from 1844 and 1845 have survived, but, although *the Banner* continued its run until the Civil War, its existing files are very sparse. Allen was also a poet and later a druggist and merchant. C. H. Allen used a masthead motto in 1844 of "Liberty and my native soil." By 1850, the masthead motto had changed to "The Union of the South, for the sake of the Union." C. H. Allen, who was called Henry Allen in the 1860 census, was also the father of

Abbeville Newspapers

James Clark Allen, perhaps the first casualty in the Civil War. On Feb. 13, 1861, he was with the Minute Men of Capt. Perrin's company stationed at Moultrie House on Sullivan's Island when he was killed accidentally.

In April, 1853 Frederick W. Selleck succeeded C. H. Allen as editor of the *Banner*. In 1841, Selleck had moved to Abbeville from Augusta to work in R. H. Wardlaw's store. He remained there until he entered the Palmetto Regiment in the Mexican War. He was wounded, became a Lieutenant, and was awarded a medal (thought by some Abbevillians to be the Congressional Medal of Honor) for raising the first American flag on the walls of Mexico City. Later he was elected as the Ordinary for the District.

While Selleck returned to Abbeville as the hero of the Palmetto Regiment, another member of the Abbeville company, Ben Lane Posey, who would become his rival in Abbeville, had gained a reputation for lack of courage in the mind of some of the company.

In my *Old Abbeville*, I summarized the Selleck-Posey feud as follows: "Posey was a Mexican War veteran who seemed to love controversy. Apparently he had gained the dislike of Frederick Selleck, the acknowledged hero of the Palmetto Regiment, and the Colonel of the regiment, J. Foster Marshall, and this enmity continued even after their return to Abbeville.

"Bad feelings reached a climax when some of Selleck's friends blackballed Posey from a formal dance in Abbeville to which other eligible young men were invited. Posey's family was quite respectable. His father had been sheriff of Laurens District and later a prosperous hotel keeper in the village of Abbeville, and young Benjamin Lane Posey studied at the South Carolina College. It was rumored, however, that Posey had lately been seen with a young slave girl in his carriage.

"Posey considered the matter a calculated insult, and he challenged the chairman of the invitations committee, Dr. Warren Lomax, to a duel. The latter accepted and chose Selleck as his second, Posey secured a young friend from Edgefield to attend him."

While Selleck was editing the *Banner*, Posey founded *The Independent Press.*, May 12, 1853. The motto of his paper was "Willing to praise, but not afraid to blame." Hugh Wilson later wrote, "When Ben Lane Posey started the publication of *The Independent Press*, he inaugurated a system of fault finding with everybody and everything, exposing all the errors, sins, and crimes with which people who held up their heads had ever been suspected. He proclaimed time and again his readiness to fight anybody who might choose to resent his insults. He, of course, vested all manner of spleen against his local competitor the *Abbeville Banner*, and no effort was spared to injure its reputation and what the brilliant editor had to say. He was a scholar and used perfect English. Because of the low price of the paper and the sensation it created, the subscription list in a short time had run up to fifteen hundred copies. But the people tired of Mr. Posey's methods and began to stop their subscriptions, and in order to save the paper from wreckage, he sold the office at the end of the first year.'

Unfortunately, there are no extant copies of *The Independent Press* during his tenure as editor, but I can testify to Posey's talent as a writer, because in 1855, he sent back very interesting accounts of his new home in Montgomery, Alabama.where he was admitted to the practice of law. He was also engaged as the political writer for the *Montgomery Mail*. For the next few years he edited newspapers at Prattville and Marion, AL. In 1858, moved to Mobile where he practiced law until the outbreak of the Civil War.

He organized a company called "The Red Eagles" which was one of the first companies organized in Alabama for Confederate service. Later he rose to the command of the 1st Ala. CSA regiment. Captured at Missionary Ridge, he escaped by jumping from the train and he made his way back into Confederate lines.. After the war, he resumed his law practice in Mobile. Later he moved to Bay St. Louis, Miss. where he died in 1888. Here he became known as "the leading lawyer of the Mississippi seacoast."

In 1854, *The Independent Press* was purchased by Coleman C. Puckett who had several partners until 1859 when he sold the paper to W. A. Lee and Hugh Wilson The paper continued publication during the Civil War until the end of 1863. *The Banner* had suspended two years earlier when its last pre-war editor, William C. Davis, went into the Confederate service. Davis was killed during the war, but both W. A. Lee and Hugh Wilson survived their Confederate service. Hugh Wilson was wounded at the battle of Chickamauga.

In July and August of 1865, Hugh Wilson published a two page sheet called the *Abbeville Bulletin*. In October, 1865, Lee & Wilson resumed the publication of their paper, now known as *The Abbeville Press*. In 1866, the *Banner* resumed publication, and in 1869 its owner, James S. Cothran, sold it to W. A. Lee and Hugh Wilson who combined the papers.

In 1876, Lee sold his share to Hugh Wilson. Wilson had a partner in W. C. Benet from 1877 to 1880, and Benet was replaced as partner by H. T. Wardlaw from 1880 to 1883. For the next quarter century, he ran the paper as the only editor.

Hugh Wilson was born in Laurens District, the son of Hugh Wilson who had emigrated from Scotland. The older Hugh Wilson was a millwright who moved to the Abbeville District at a mill which was at the head waters of Turkey Creek (now the site of the American Legion Lake southeast of Honea Path).

Young Hugh was apprenticed to J. I. Bonner at the *Due West Telescope* in 1851, at the age of 13. Robert A. Thompson, later the long time editor of the *Keowee Courier* of Pickens, came to work there shortly afterwards, and he remembered that when he asked Dr. Bonner who was there to get the paper printed, he replied "a colored man" to help with the press and the forms, and then pointed to a corner of the building where a small boy stood. The boy had the reddest hair and the most of it I ever saw on any boy's head, and this hair was standing straight up. 'That boy,' said Dr. Bonner, 'helps about, too, and he is mighty handy." Thompson added in his memoir of 1910, "That little boy was Hugh Wilson, who grew up to be one of the best and most successful newspaper men South Carolina has produced. I always liked Wilson, we have been friends every since and that's saying no little for Hugh Wilson is one of the 'kicking' kind of folks, if he don't like you."

The Abbeville *Medium* was founded in 1871 by R. R. (Robert Reid) Hemphill and his younger brother, J. C. (James Calvin) Hemphill, joined him the next year. J. C. Hemphill joined the staff of the Charleston *News and Courier* in 1880 and soon was in charge of that paper's Columbia bureau. Three years later he returned to Charleston to become managing editor of the *News and Courier*, and on the death of Francis Dawson, he became the editor-in-chief. Later he was editor of newspapers in Richmond, Charlotte, and Spartanburg.

. R. R. Hemphill was its editor until his death in 1908, but for much of his last years the paper was largely run by his daughters. R. R. Hemphill was a dedicated advocate of women's rights, including the suffrage, and his daughters were his helpers. Grace R. Hemphill (after 1910 Grace H. Rogers) was its editor for two years after his death.

When the *Medium* was sold to a stock company of Abbeville business men in 1911, Grace Rogers wrote, "Since my father started the *Medium* nearly 40 years ago, it has been the custom for each of my sisters as they grew old enough to assist with the office work . I was the youngest, and my turn came in 1907. .During the last two years, the *Medium* was run only by women, Miss Hannah Cochran, Miss Carrie Cochran & Miss Nellie Hughes. Andrew Bradley – our janitor and pressman, was the only man about the house."

The *Medium* was bought by The Medium Publishing Co. in 1911 and in the 1920's was titled *The Evening Medium* . It was published as a semi-weekly, as a tri- weekly, and by 1924, it was a daily paper except on Sundays. It was edited by E. C. Horton and cost $6 a year or 50 cts. for 4 weeks."

Abbeville Newspapers

Surely the most important person in the history of Abbeville newspapers was Hugh Wilson, at least from 1859 until his death in December, 1917. His successors at the *Press and Banner*, W. W. and W. R. Bradley (who purchased the paper in 1908) declared in an editorial tribute, Dec. 21, 1917: "As an editor, Mr. Wilson was an independent thinker. His views were expressed with clearness, and opposition did not deter him from making known his views. He never sought popularity. He made a modest fortune, all from his paper. He was a patriotic citizen and a friend of the town in which he lived. He subscribed to the capital stock of most of the enterprises which have been inaugurated in Abbeville.

"He never married. At one time he was connected with the Associate Reformed Presbyterian Church at Due West and later with the Episcopal church in Abbeville, but at his death he did not hold membership in any church."

In January, 1918, W. Christie Benet wrote the paper his memories of Wilson as follows: " The friendship between Hugh Wilson and me began in 1868 and continued unbroken until ended by death. Forty years ago I was his partner in the *Press and Banner* office. Our work together for several years brought us very close . He was a wonderful worker. He had his own way of working, which he could not alter. The paper was a weekly and came out each Wednesday morning. Other weekly papers might be ready for the press on the evening before publication; but that was not Hugh Wilson's way. The work was nearly all performed on Monday and Tuesday – the most of it on Tuesday and on Tuesday night, and on until two or three or even four o'clock Wednesday morning. Not once during our partnership was the paper printed before midnight. Until the last copy was printed he worked at high pressure. I can see him now – in his shirt sleeves, his beaver on, setting type in hot haste, his faithful henchmen by his side, James Martin, the most accurate typesetter I have ever met with. About midnight the negro boy would bring in the late supper for all in the office, which was soon disposed of. All I could do was to read proof. But he would stay until the last paper was off the press, and various bundles made ready for the morning mail."

Benet added, "Hugh Wilson thought he was handicapped by the lack of school and college education, and by the lack of familiarity with the habits of "good society ," but in Benet's opinion "his printing experiences gave him a better education than many college educated."

Benet continued, "You said he was never married. No man was ever more anxious to marry. What prevented him? Just the same diffidence and undervaluing of himself. He lacked confidence in himself. He had several love affairs, some of them not very serious; one of them profoundly serious, affecting his long life to the end. He made me the confidant of his affairs of the heart; and I will not lift the veil. His life would have been a happier one if he had been fortunate in the one great passion that dominated him for years."

Some years ago while I was discussing Hugh Wilson with a lady from Donalds whose late husband was his great-nephew, I said "But, of course, he left no descendants." We were in Plaxco's Drug Store in Due West. She paused and then she came over and whispered in my ear "he did." She said that it almost broke the heart of her father-in-law that Hugh Wilson had a long time affair and children by a Negro woman. She said he told his family that he would marry her except for the conventions of society, and my informant said that Wilson took care of her and her children.

I tried to check that story out, but I never found any evidence of its truth, even though I could not imagine why she would have told it unless she thought it was true. In any case, it may have explained his sympathy for the black people which he displayed to an unusual degree. I can cite only a few of the numerous examples in his editorials.

In 1876 when the white Democrats regained control of the local town government, he wrote "the election of a town marshal takes place next Monday. We think justice and our best interest as a town demand that a colored man get the place. " A week later, he reported that Alfred Ellison was re-elected. In April, 1878, he wrote that "It is alleged by some that it is a great shame that a Negro policeman should be allowed to carry a white man to the guard house while others contend that it is a greater shame that a white man should conduct himself so as to put the Negro under the necessity of carrying him to the lock up."

Similarly, in April, 1896 he wrote of a series of services at a colored Baptist church in Abbeville where a 10 year old girl preacher was drawing crowded audiences which included whites who were particularly attracted by the singing. At one point some of the whites were noisy, and the girl's mother, Mrs. Avery, reprimanded the white persons by saying, "We look to you white folks to set an example for us to follow, and we think you ought to behave yourselves when you come to our meetings". Wilson commented, "It is a reproach to white people, if they must be taught good manners in a negro church."

He often cited examples where negroes did not receive fair treatment in the Abbeville courts and else where. In Nov., 1883, he said that in a recent Abbeville Court a negro and white man were convicted of the same offense. The former was sentenced to the penitentiary for 6 months, the latter to the county jail for 3 months, or to pay a fine. In Feb., 1885 he noted that in the case of Sam Jefferson, colored, the defendant was accused of stealing $3.25 and convicted of petit larceny and given a year in the penitentiary. He said the jury convicted Jefferson with the expectation of a sentence of 30 or 60 days, but the judge sentenced him to one year. Wilson commented that judges "forget that a black man has a family that is entitled to his services." In Dec., 1886, in an editorial entitled "A Word About Stealing," Wilson warned colored people not to attempt to steal more than a chicken or turkey."

In June, 1888, he wrote of a white man who was convicted of stealing a mule and selling it in Anderson county for $125 who was sentenced to serve 18 months in state penitentiary while earlier a negro was tried in Anderson for stealing a mule and selling it for $20 in Abbeville county. The latter was sentenced to 3 years. in the penitentiary. In the same issue, he carried an account in the *Augusta Chronicle* in which an Abbeville correspondent wrote that "Hugh Wilson's strictures are unjust to the people of Abbeville on the administration of justice to white criminals."

In July, 1889, Wilson paid tribute to W. C. Benet's defense of poor negroes, specifically the case of Jeff David . He said that for Benet "the very weaknesses of these poor ignorant and penniless creatures in defending themselves against the great state of South Carolina, not only awakens his deepest sympathies, but calls for the exercise of the great power of a fearless and independent lawyer. Last year Benet received the largest vote ever made in this county despite the fact that he has saved more negroes from gallows than any lawyer in the state."

In Aug., 1889, Wilson wrote of a white woman, a tenant of Mr. James Haddon, who was whipped by the white caps (vigilantes) for telling fortunes for negroes., and she was given notice to leave the neighborhood. Wilson said that "they" (the white caps) should be made known and punished."

Sometimes he was sarcastic in his comments on the lack of justice for colored victims. On Sales Day in November, 1890, a negro man was shot down for cursing in an act which Wilson said "would be a disgrace on an Indian reservation." No one was convicted for the homicide, and Wilson commented, "While nobody expects to see a white man punished for the simple act of riding up behind a negro and shooting him, perhaps he could be prosecuted for violating the law against concealed weapons."

In Sept., 1891, Wilson wrote that in Abbeville county 10 negroes were under the sentence of hanging for the murder of negroes, but he said it was very unlikely that the courts would ever sentence 10 white men to hang for any crime. In March, 1893, he wrote that "in view of the fact that no white man, as far as we now remember, has ever been punished for killing a negro, we suggest that the statute against killing negroes be repealed, as far as white men are concerned."

In Nov., 1895, Wilson in an editorial entitled "A Word to Colored People," he warned "them as a friend to their race to avoid crimes of violence as they are almost certain to be caught and they lack the money to get the best legal talent."

In Feb., 1897, in an editorial he said, "At Abbeville, we believe it is a rule to acquit a white man who is charged with murder. In the few rare cases in which verdicts have been obtained against white men charged with murder, the Supreme Court has generally given the necessary number of new trials to secure acquital."

More rarely, Wilson found occasion to compliment juries for fair treatment of black defendants. In Nov., 1884, he said of the juries in a recent court, "They exercised their manhood in deciding cases strictly according to the law and the evidence, without reference to the color of the accused. The monotony of convicting every negro that was charged with a crime was changed and many of them were acquitted."

In the same issue, Wilson gave another testimony to his sympathy for the colored people in a story about the burning of the Rock Hill school building. This colored school house was near Mr. T. P. Milford's five miles northeast of Abbeville. The story reported that it was burned through the carelessness of several white men who were drunk and stopped there on the way home from "the big meeting" at Abbeville. Wilson commented that although the building was of small money value, "it was a useful house to the colored people, who had bought the land and built the house by their own exertions."

It was through Hugh Wilson's colored helpers that there was published a newspaper for the colored people in Abbeville in 1883. It was printed at his press, and was published by Rev. S. H. Jefferson & Sons. Jefferson was pastor of St. James A. M. E. Church in Abbeville, and his boys learned the printing trade by working at the *Press and Banner*. It was called *The Journal of Enterprise*, and it was published in 1883. There are apparently no copies extant

Perhaps the most unusual paper ever published in Abbeville was the Abbeville *Scimitar* which was launched in July, 1914 by William P. Beard In January, 1894 Beard, who, according to the wedding story, had come only a year or two ago to Abbeville, was married to Miss Kate Strickle who was originally from Kentucky, but had lived in Abbeville for several years with her sister Mrs. John Knox who was a widow. In his little paper, Beard later said that he knew both Charley Lyons and Charley Bruce, the Federal Marshal and Assistant Marshal, since they were boys. Beard was a director of the newly chartered ' Tugaloo Iron Works' of Abbeville, and the paper said he "was proficient in the iron business."

W. P. Beard became better known for his political activities. He became a supporter and for some time a bodyguard for "Cole " Blease. In 1911 he edited a pro-Blease newspaper in Greenwood entitled the *News-Scimitar.* until it was suspended in 1913. In July, 1914 when he began his *Abbeville Scimitar* , his paper carried a motto, "Eternal Vigilance is the Price of Liberty. "The next year he added " The Scimitar is a Free Lance. It Wears no Man's Collar. "'All Coons Look Alike to Me.' Among the persons he sent a copy of his first issue was Federal District Attorney J. William Thurmond, and Thurmond became a subscriber. Beard's little paper was solely devoted to politics, and he claimed in 1915 that he had written during the last four years "several thousand articles and letters" dealing with politics." Beard printed his paper at first in the *Press and Banner* office until W. P. Greene bought the paper and he refused to print it. At W. W. Bradley's instructions he turned "a considerable amount of type to W. P. Beard which Bradley said Beard would pay for."

He was an inventive writer and often wrote satires on "King Richard" [Governor]Manning, President Wilson , "Great Fizzler," and such persons as J. William Thurmond who he referred to as "Pussy-foot Bill." In September, 1915, he ran several articles on what he called "Peonage" at the Calhoun Falls Cotton Mill. The mill fired a number of workers who had attended union meetings, and forced them out of the mill village. When Beard specially targeted Jas. P. Gossett, the mill president, Gossett charged him with "malicious slander," but the case was *nolle prossed* by the solictor in October. At about that time Beard claimed that he received 27 requests to cancel subscriptions and 39 new subscriptions. In June of that year he said he printed 2,000 copies of his paper and none were left over.

He strongly opposed American entrance into World War I because from the outbreak of the war in Europe he favored the Germans and opposed the British, French and Russians. Beard was a strong advocate of white supremacy, and he claimed that the Allies were using non-whites in their armies. He argued versus the Espionage Act and especially the Conscript Act which he considered unconstitutional. At first he proceeded cautiously. In April, 1917, he sent a copy of his paper to J. W. Thurmond who advised him that it was in violation of "the law," and Beard did not send it out. A short time later when he accused the Federal Office in Greenville of "graft," Thurmond sent that copy back with "Refused" written on it. Beard wrote the U. S. Attorney General and even President Wilson for clarification of the laws , but got no response until in July when District Attorney Thurmond wrote him that "as you are regarded an enemy to the government, it [this office] declines to advise you on the matter mentioned." Beard wrote in his paper that the government sent agents to gather evidence of his illegal activities, and his defiant response was "Pull in your claws, J. William, pussy cats don't look bad to bull dogs."

On May 14, 1918 –the *Press and Banner* reported that "Beard was arrested Sunday by Deputy Marshal C. J. Bruce and taken to Greenville where he was given a preliminary examination before a U. S. Commissioner on a federal warrant issued Saturday charging him with disloyal utterances against the government and with attempting to obstruct the operation of the Selective Draft Law. Beard it will be remembered was convicted at Greenwood some months ago of violation of the Espionage Act. . . . He has been out on bond since his conviction pending an appeal to the Circuit Court of Appeals."

Some observers accused Beard's old friend Cole Blease of deserting him, but Blease told *The State* newspaper, "I think it only necessary for me to say that I warned Beard frequently about articles that he was writing, and told him if he was not careful he was going to get into serious trouble. It is unnecessary for me to say what his reply was, for he is now serving a sentence for the charge which was preferred against him."

Beard later wrote, "In the trial I plead not guilty, and when Judge Johnstone in sentencing, asked me what I had to say why I should not be sentenced, I told him 'because the charge is a damned lie. I am not guilty.' I told President Coolidge the same thing in my application here," he wrote in 1927.

He contended that " had I been willing to make public retraction and apology, I need never to have served the sentence. Blood is thicker than water, and Woodrow Wilson's first wife and children as well as his brother-in-law are my close blood relatives, and also two influential cousins, one a brigadier general in the army and one a rear admiral in the navy. That was sufficient influence to keep me out of federal prison had I been willing to pay the price.

In 1920 on the League of Nations issue I voted for Harding. After the inauguration, northern Republican officials offered me a conditional pardon such as Debs' received, as a political favor and that was declined. In 1924, I supported LaFollette and therefore had no political claim on President Coolidge. Last summer I filed formal application with the Department of Justice with the required number of affidavits and certificates of character and many private letters of endorsement attached, including three letters from Judge Johnstone himself.

Anyway on Christmas Eve, I received notice that a full and unconditional pardon was granted and on New Year's Eve the pardon itself was received.

. . . I stand today where I stood in 1917, and look upon all war as a exploitation of human passions, to the end that opportunists should accrue to the powers of greed to plunder their fellow men, friend and foe alike."

Beard never resumed his paper. In the election of 1924 while he was still in the Atlanta federal prison, he was an elector on the LaFollette Progressive Party ticket which got 16 votes in Abbeville, twice as many as the Republican ticket polled. In 1928, he was an elector for the Socialist Party in South Carolina. He wrote the *Press and Banner* in late October that he was backing the Socialist ticket of Norman Thomas. He was apparently the only voter for the Socialist candidate in Abbeville.

The Coming of the S. A. L. (Railroad) and Abbeville Cotton Mill

The "preface" of Old Abbeville indicated that the author chose not to deal "with such important subjects as the coming of the railroad and the cotton mill to the town in the 1890's. These two events brought unprecedented growth in the population of the town in the decade from 1890 to 1900 from about 1300 to almost 3800." They also mark the beginnings of the modern period of Abbeville's history.

The *Press and Banner*, December 5, 1921. Published under the title of "The Man Responsible for the Coming of the S. A. L.."

"Editor *Press and Banner*:

During my very pleasant visit to Abbeville last May, I several times put the question to my friends – 'Do you know who deserves the credit of having brought the Seaboard Air Line Rail Road to Abbeville? 'To my surprise I found that not one of them knew. Since it happens that I know all about the movement – it would now be called 'the drive' – which succeeded in bringing the S A L from Monroe, N. C. to Abbeville and on to Atlanta. I feel that I owe it to the memory of a good man who now sleeps in Long Cane church yard to tell the people of Abbeville who it was to whom the credit is chiefly due. That man was Lewis W. Perrin. His characteristic modesty kept him from saying much about it himself; but the late William Henry Parker and I were witnesses to the fact that it was Lewis Perrin who first suggested the enterprise, and that the information he furnished was the egg from which was hatched the extension of the great railroad from Monroe to Atlanta.

It will interest – perhaps it will amuse – your leaders to learn how the thing was done. I doubt if any other great railroad enterprise ever had a beginning so strange and so small. . . . This how it happened. One evening Mr. Parker, Mr. Perrin and I were sitting just outside my office door – the old Law Range, which you, Mr. Editor, remember well, just behind the old Court House. We three, deeply interested in the welfare of our town and county, were wondering what could be done about the construction of a great trunk railroad that would run through Abbeville. We were quite despondent. Several schemes had been tried, and efforts made, and money spent; but all in vain. It looked as if Abbeville would have to content itself with being the terminus of the branch line from Hodges depot.

'Suppose we try to induce the Seaboard Air Line to come this way ' said Mr. Perrin. Where he got his information I never knew but he told us that the S A L had reached Monroe, N. C.. that the aim was to carry it on to Atlanta; that the danger was that it would run through our state by way of Columbia, and on to Augusta; but that legislative authority had not yet been asked for. He said he believed that if we could get the other towns along the route to join with us and

The Coming of the S A L Railroad and the Abbeville Cotton Mill

agree to issue bonds in and of the railroad through the upper part of the state, passing thought Greenwood and Abbeville and on to Athens and Atlanta; that, besides, this was much the shortest route, and free from competing lines. It was evident that Mr. Perrin had carefully considered the situation.

We discussed the matter a long time. We then took a bold step. We formed ourselves into an Executive Committee – self elected – Mr. Parker, chairman Mr. Perrin, Treasurer and Mr. Benet, secretary. On a printed postal card we issued a call for a convention of delegates from the towns along the proposed route from Monroe to Athens to a convention to meet in Columbia on a day named to consider the advisability of issuing municipal bonds in aid of the S. A. L. Railroad. As secretary I mailed the postal cards to the mayors of all the towns. I can with 'the inward eye' see that postal card now, with our three names subscribed as a 'executive committee.'

In a few days I began to receive favorable replies. No one seemed to question our authority, nor to ask whom we represented, or who elected us. The day came for the convention we had summoned. We three went to Columbia. We found the Columbia Hotel swarming with delegates. The newspaper reporters were at their wit's end to know what was up. They had heard nothing of a convention. They were puzzled. The 'Executive Committee' had to answer many questions.

The convention met after supper, was duly organized. The purpose of the call was explained. Resolutions in favor of the scheme were adopted, great enthusiasm was manifested. Best of all General Hope of North Carolina was there. He was the general counsel of the S. A. L. and had come to assure us of the favorable attitude of the railroad. This, too, was due to M. Perrin. It was he that asked me as secretary to invite him. The meeting was a great success. On my motion it was agreed that the convention would meet next time in Greenwood. At that meeting in Greenwood the important business was finally settled; and the S A L was soon being constructed from Monroe towards Abbeville and Atlanta.   W. C. Benet."

(*Press and Banner*, May 26, 1922), "The Coming of the Abbeville Cotton Mill."

In May, 1922, at the dedication of the S. M. Milliken Community Building at the Abbeville Cotton Mill, W.P. Greene in an address recounted something of the coming of the mill to Abbeville and specifically the role of S. M. Milliken in the story.

"The mill was incorporated in 1896, with a capital stock of $65,000. The incorporators were G. A. Visanska, W. C. McGowan, W. A. Templeton, Frank B. Gary, J. Fuller Lyon, R. M. Haddon, J. R. Blake, Jr., ,J. Hayne McDill and J.

The Coming of the S A L Railroad and the Abbeville Cotton Mill

C. Klugh. All these but three have gone to a better country. On their application, the charter was granted Feb. 24, 1896,with the following directors: J. C. Klugh, who was made the first president of the Mill. W. H. Parker who was secretary. G. A. Visanka, P. L. Grier, W. A. Templeton , Hugh Wilson, B. F. Bailey, G. A. Neuffer, and C. P. Hammond

Almost from the beginning the corporation experience financial difficulties. A contract was let for the building when there was not enough money to complete even it. In June of the same year, 1896. it became necessary to increase the capital stock, the amount of authorized capital being made $200,000. On the certificate of increase, the name of Benjamin S. Barnwell, who became one o f the staunchest friends and supporters of the enterprise,, occurs as a director for the first time.

Mr. B. R. Busby, who had during the summer made a considerable investment in the stock of the company and on account of being at that time the largest stockholder of the corporation, succeeded J. C. Klugh as president, the latter soon after being elected a Judge of the Circuit Court of the State. But the money contributed to t he corporation the issue of new stock was soon exhausted and there was no visible means of carrying forward the project to completion. The corporation had borrowed largely on its notes, endorsed by the directors. I recall vividly the declaration of my old law partner, Hon. Wm. H. Parker, who always declared when asked to endorse another note, that he had already endorsed to such an extent for the mill that he felt free and easy to make any other endorsed of him.

The point had been reached at length where somebody else must come to the rescue, or the Abbeville Cotton Mill faced an inevitable receivership. It was at this time that Mr. Stephen Greene of Boston, one of the architects of the building. Discovered for the directors a man capable of leading the mill out of the wilderness of its financial troubles. This man was S. M. Milliken, the real builder of the Abbeville Cotton Mill and the developer of this mill village.

This was 1897. Mr. Milliken was then sixty one years of age."

Index

Index

Index

Barksdale, Fanney, 73
  Henry, 78
  Hickerson, 73
  John, 73
  Joseph, 78
  Richard, 73
  S., 101
  Sherard, 111
  W. D., 191
  William, 73
Barmore, E., 101
  Enoch, 111
  James, Est., 92
  James, 70, 73, 78
  Larkin, 54, 92, 101,
    111,122, 135
  Lucy, 92
  Nancy, 122
  Peter, 85
  Sarah, 122
  William, 78, 101
Barnes, C. V., 122, 146
  Christian V., , 111
  James, 146
  Jane T., 122
Barnet,John J., 111
Barnett, H., 122
  J. J., 101
Barns, Mercer, 92
Barnwell, Benjamin, 33, 207
Barr, Elizabeth, 70
  Rebecca, 122, 142
  W. H., 101
  William H., 85, 92
Barron, Eriah, 85
Bartee, Thomas, 74
Bartin, James Y., 92
Barton, John A., 92
Baskin, Capt. Wm., 70
  F. Y., 101
  Hugh, 70
  J. H., 101
  James H., 85, 92, 111
  James T., 111, 122, 138

  Jane, 111
  Jas. S., 101
  John, 78, 85, 92, 102, 111
  John A., , 92
  Prudence, 70, 74
  Sarah, 74
  Stewart, 122, 140
  Thomas, 78
  William S., 111
Bass, William, 78
Bastee, Thos., 74
Bates, Fleming, 70, 74
  Margaret, 78
Beachum, Daniel, 111
  David, 122
  David S., 143
Beard, C. F., 102
  Henry, 102, 111, 138
  James, 78
  Jno. Bat, 70
  Mary, 78
  Samuel, 102, 111
  William P., 200-204
Bearden, 92
Beaseley, Edmond, 70
  Hugh, 191
  Jesse, 92
  Nancy, 111
  W. F., 122
  William, 92
  William B., 102
Beckley, Francis, 92
Belcher, R. E., 102
  Robert E., 111
  W.W., 50, 56, 58, 102, 122
  Washington, 85, 92, 102
  William N., 111, 137
Bell, Abraham, 78, 85, 92
  Allen J., 146
  Duke, 74, 76
  Elizabeth, 85, 122, 142
  J. E., 102
  J. F., 102
  James E. G., 111 122, 145

- 210

Index

Index

Edna, 112
Edney, 102
Elizh., 85
G. R., 123
George, 93(2), 138
Harriet, 102
J. G., 102
James, 70, 74, 86, 92
Jas., 102
Jno., 70
Jno., sr., 70
John., 102
John G., 93
Norwood, 102
Robert, 102
Samuel, 85, 93
Thos., 102
W. H., 102
William, 137
William H., 93,102, 112
Wm. C., 123
Wm. H., 102, 112, 123
Calhoun, Agnes, 102, 112
Alex, 78, 86
Cuddie (2), 43
Downs, 102,112
E. B., 42, 43
E. R., 102, 123
Edward, 102, 112,123
Edward Boisseau. 42
Edwin, 135
Eliza W., 112, 123
Ephraim, 93, 150-151, 152,
   156-157
Ephraim R., 112, 136
Ezekiel, 78, 86, 158
Ezehiel, jr., 78
F. A., 123
Fanny, 123
Floride Bonneau, 158-160, 161
Francis, 3, 102, 112
George M., 112
J. W., 123
James, 78, 86, 93, 133

James Edward, 43 (2), 69 (2),112,
   123, 158, 165 174, 175. 176.
James C., 123
Jas,, 102
Jas. C., 142
John, 78
John A., 41, 69, 102, 112,
   123, 133
John C., 43, 46 (2), 49, 93, 158-
   160, 162
John Ewen, 93
John F., 145
John J., 112
Joseph, 46, 48, 74, 78, 81, 93
Joseph, jr., 78
Martha, 74, 86, 93
Nancy, 172
Nathan, 93, 102, 112, 123, 133
Nathaniel, 86
P., 102
Patrick, 46, 48, 67, 78, 82, 93, 158
S. A., 102
Saidee,, 43
Sallie, 42
Sarah, 112
Susan, 123
Thomas P., 93
W. H., 102
William, 78,(3), , 93 (2)
William D., 112
William H., 86
William, jr., 74, 78
Wm.., 102
Wm (Saluda), 78
Wm. B., 102
Callaham, B., 102
Basil, 112, 123, , 140
Elihu,112
J., 102
John, 102
Nancy, 123
S.W., 123
William, 74
Calvert, Hugh A., 93

214 -

Index

Index

Index

Index

Index

R. H., 137
Sarah, 113, 124
Thomas, 113, 124, 136
Eaves, Daniel, 79
Eddings, Benjm, 70
Elizabeth, 70
William, 94
Wm., 70
Eddins, William, 103
Edmonds, James A., 113
Samuel C., 113
Edmunds, F. H., 124
J. A., 124
John, 124
S., 103
Edwards, Ambrose, 70, 74,87
Amus, 103
Andrew, 71, 113, 124
Elizabeth. 74, 94
James, 74
James M., 124
Joseph, 74
Mary E., 103
Matthew, 74
Thomas, 74, 79
Egnew [Agnew]. James, 74
Elgin, Ann, 70
Hezekiah, 124
Joe, 191
Robert, 74
Elins, Jack, jr., 124
John, 144
Ellice, Joseph, 70
Ellington Dice, 79
Fanney, 74
John, 79, 87
Ellinton, Enoch, 70
Elliott, Alexr.,70
Ellis, Christopner, 124,141
James, 139
James A., 124, 146
Jams C., 103, 113, 124
James L., 142
Jesse, 124

John E., 94, 104, 113
John Eli, 54
John L., 94, 114, 124, 135
Joseph, 124
Mrs. Wm., 124
Robert, 79, 87,104, 114,
124, 134
Robert, junr., 94
Robert N., 94
Thomas, 124, 143
William, 144
Ellison, Alfred, 199
Elmore, Ann E., 124
Stephen, 124, 143
Emerson, Thomas, 74
English, Daniel, 94, 114
Danl., 104
Ernst, John B.,100, 191
Eskridge, Richard, 75
Richd., 79
Etheridge,D, 124
Evans, Gov. John Gry, 172
William, 94
Everts, William M., 176

Fair, Archible, 95
Jas., 95, 104, 114, 124
Robert A., 66
S., 124
Faulkner, John, 116
Farret, Barret, 71
John, 71
Ferguson, A. J., 2, 124, 185
Andrew J., 2
Bert, 192
Ervin, 192
Geo., 189, 190
James, 2
Joseph, 2
Owen J., 147
Thomas E., 104
Fewer, Henry, 95, 104
Fife, Samuel, 104
Figgs, Jessiah, 71

Index

Index

Index

Joseph, 95
Robert, 70, 125-
Robt., H., 114
William, 95
Hammond, C. P.,206
J. S., 200
W. J., 125, 144
Hampton, E., 104
Gov. 7, 16, 17, 20.
34, 41
Handon, Isabella, 125
Ralph, 125
Handy, Isham, 87
Hnvey, Matilda 114
Harden, Isabella, 144
J. G., 104
Hardy M., 104
Mike, Est, 114
Harkann, James, 80
Harkness, Robert C., 114, 146
Robert E., 104
Harmon, John, 144
Mrs. M., 125
Robt. C., 125
Thomas, 95
Harper, H. H., 135
James C., 114
L., 104
Lindsay /Est,, 95, 114
Harris, E., 104
Eleven, 95
Elizabeth, 104, 114,
125, 134
Handy, 70, 75
Hearn, 70
Jeperich , 125
Jno. P., 125
John, 75, 80, 95,147
John L., 95
M., 104
Mary, 70, 95
Milly, 125, 144
N., 104
Nathaniel, 95, 114

Richard, 75, 80, 95
Richmond, 75, 80, 95, 104
Samuel, 80
T. A., 145
T. L., 104
T. W., 104
Thomas, 70, 75, 95, 142
W. M., 125
William, 70, 80, 95, 115
William H., 115
William S., 145
Wm. S., 125
Harr, Francis, 104
Harriman, Thos., 104
Hart, Brantley G., 125, 143
Haskell, Charles R., 105
Charles T., 69, 114,., 133
William E., 115
Haslett, Nancy, 95
Hatton, Benjamin, 80
Wm. R., 125
Hawthorn A. C., 66, 67
Andrew C., 148
David O., 104, 115, 124, 133
James, 79
John, 004
John M., 115, 125
Laney, 95
Mrs. Mary, 125
Thomas, 115, 125
Thos., 104, 142
Hatward, Virginia, 145
Hay, John C., 126, 143
Hill, R. E., 177

Ingram, Kiett, 35-36
Madison S., 36, 37
Mrs., 36
Nathan, 126
Irvin, E. S., 115
John, 115
Irving, Jno.., 7
Joseph, 70, 75
Isham, John W., 126

Index

Index

228–

Index

Index

Index

Munday, John, 118
Murphy, Mary, 118
Murray, Benjamin, 89
Murry, James, 98

Nance, Eugene, 192
  F. W. R., 192
Nash, Abner, 82
  Ezekiel, 82
  Nimrod, 82
  Polly H., 76, 82
  Reuben, 76, 82, 89
Nealy,John, 82
Neel, W. G., 129, 138
Neely, Charles, 98
Nelson, Enoch, 107, 118, 129, 134
  Henry, 98
  Henry H., 118 -
Neuffer, G. A., 205
New, Daniel, 63, 118, 129, 136
Newby, John N., 82
  James, 129
  Wiley, 146
Nibs, Wm., Esq., 82
Nibbs, William, 89
Nichols, Eliz. B., 147
  John, 89
  Julius, 76
  Mrs. E. B., ,125
  William, 76, 82
Nicholls, Thomas, 118
Nickles, Bob, 9, 10, 13, 2, 27, 29
  George, 118, 129, 136
  Henry B., 144
Nickery, William, 76
Noble, Alex, 72, 76, 82
  Andrew A., 107, 118
  E. P., 107
  Edward, 63, 118, 138
  Ezekiel, 82, 89, 98
  James, 72, 82
  Mary, 98, 107
  Mary H., 98
  Pstrick, 89, 98

  William, 82, 89
  William P., , 98, 118, 139
  Wm. P., 107
Norrell, Joseph, 107
  Tom, 184
  Watson, 184
Norris, Andrew,89
  Eli, 98
  Elizabeth, 76
  Jno., 72
  John, 82, 89
  Joseph, 89
  Park, 72
  Wilson, 82
North , Jane, 107, 118
  Jane G., , 60, 129
Northcutt, Benjamin, 89, 98
Norwood, Capt John, 72
  Daniel, 98
  Isham, 82
  James A., , 40, 41, 69,
    111, 129,133
  Jas., 107
  John, 98, 107
  Mary, 118
  Nathaniel, 82
  Sarah (Sallie),42, 43
  W., 107
  Williamson, 59, 82, 89, 98
  Willie, , 42

Oliver, A., 107
  Alexander, 98, 107, 118, 129, 137
  J., 107
  James, 72, 76, 82
  John, 89, 118
  John C., 89
O'Neal, G. P., 129
  J. B., 129
O,'Neill, Gideon, 6, 7, 8, 9, 12
  23, 24, 25, 27, 29
Orr, Solicitor, 23, 31
Orsburn, John, 98
Osborne, Thomas, 89

Index

Index

Index

Index

Index

Index

Sheppard G., 120
Thomas, 120, 130
Stokes, Joseph, 120
Stone, William, 77
Strauss, Maurice, 139
Street, William, 176
Strickle, Kate, 200
Stuart, Dr. Alex, 83
   Dr. James A., 135
   John A., 120, 130
   Larkin, 91
   Nimrod, 136
Studard, Saml., 108
Sturkey, M. B., 130
Suber, John W., 120
Sullivan, D., 100
   Elizabeth, 100
   Mr., 17
   Seaborn, 100
   W. P.,130
   William F., 139
Sumner, Benjamin, 100
Swain, Ann, 108
   Anna, 100, 120
   Jane A., 131
   John, 83, 91
   Robert, 76, 83, 91.
     100, 108
   Wm. R., 108
Swansey, Dr. Saml., 83
   Rosannah, 76
Swarubgum, Ansel, 120.
   131, 136
Swift, Jonathan, 91
Swilling, John, 83,109, 120
Swindle, George, 76
   Thomas, 76

Taber, Mr., 148, 154, 155
Tabot,B., ,109
Tagard, David, 84
Taggart, Capt., J., 131
   Dr. Mc., 131
   James, 52, 91, 100

James, jr., 131
James, sr., 109
Moses, 91, 96, 100, 109
Oliver, 109
W. H., 131, 138
Talbert, B ., 131
   Benjam., 131
   Danl., 109
   James, 120
   Jas., 109
   John, 91, 100
   Joseph, 91
   Robert R., 109
   Robert, sr., 109
Talbot, B., 131
   Benjm., 120
Tallman, T. W., 109
Talloon, Charles, 84
   Sarah, 84
Talmon, Bailey, 10
   M. O., 131
   Morison, 131
   Moses O., 120
Tarborough, ., 109
Tarrant, J. R., 131
   J. R., 131
   Jno., 134
   John R., 109, 190
   Robert, 100
Tatom, C. S., 109
   Thomas, 120
   William, 77, 120
   William T., 138
Tawnehill, Jas., 73
Taylor, Andw., 73
   C. J., 131
   Elizabeth, 131, 145
   James, 131
   Jane, 135
Templeton, W. A. 205
   William L., 120
Tennent, Eliza, 131
   Martha, 91, 100
   Patrick, 131

Index

Index

Index

Index